A BEGINNER'S GUIDE TO
Airsports

A BEGINNER'S GUIDE TO
Airsports

Keith Carey

A & C Black · London

First published 1994
by A & C Black (Publishers) Limited
35 Bedford Row, London WC1R 4JH

© 1994 Keith Carey

ISBN 0 7136 3834 6

A CIP catalogue record for this book
is available from the British Library

Cover photographs courtesy of Sporting Pictures UK Ltd.
Illustrations by the author.
Typeset in Monophoto Photina by August Filmsetting, St Helens

Printed and bound in Scotland
by Bell and Bain Limited, Thornliebank, Glasgow

Contents

Acknowledgements

The writing of this book was made possible by the kind assistance of many air-minded people. I would like to thank the following individuals and organisations for their considerable help and cooperation: Gary Savage of Alan Mann Helicopters Ltd; Alan Noble of Cameron Balloons Ltd; Wyndham-Leigh Ltd; Brian Godden of Meridian Ultralights Ltd; Sarah Fenwick of Airwave Gliders Ltd; Alison Phillips of Air Touring Services Ltd; Headcorn Parachute Club; Val Whiting of Sport Air UK Ltd; Rosemary Waterkeyn of Sloane Helicopters Ltd; The Cabair Group Ltd; The British Parachute Association; The British Hang Gliding Association; The British Gliding Association; The Helicopter Club of Great Britain; The British Association of Paragliding Clubs; Julie Wells of Southern Air Ltd; Peter Battern of Westland Helicopters; and finally Pilatus Britten-Norman Ltd.

Note Throughout the book instructors, administrators and potential pilots are referred to individually as 'he'. This should, of course, be taken to mean 'he or she' where appropriate.

Prices quoted in the following text are correct at the time of writing. However, neither the author nor the publishers accept responsibility for their accuracy subsequent to publication. Readers wishing to check current prices are advised to refer to the most recent copy of *Pilot* magazine.

Introduction

This book is a guide for the newcomer to the exciting world of aviation. It is not an authoritative manual of airborne training; it is intended rather to whet the appetite of the interested reader who wishes to take up one of the airsports described in its pages. Whether you wish to try your hand at flying a traditional light aircraft, hover a helicopter, soar in a glider, float in a balloon, or demonstrate your intrepidity in a free-fall parachute jump, this book will explain exactly what is involved. It discusses the principles behind each airsport, and describes the requisite training. Finally, it shows the reader how he may set about obtaining the relevant qualifications.

Each chapter illustrates a different aspect of civil aeronautical activity, and shows that anyone can learn to take to the air for no more than it costs the average person to buy a cheap second-hand car. Of course, if you want to pilot a helicopter or a multi-engined aircraft, it does come a bit steeper! However, where there's a will, there's a way.

To the person interested in getting airborne at the weekend, the airspace above the United Kingdom may seem hopelessly crowded. Commercial airliners, military jets, airlanes, control zones and low-level routes seem to fill the sky. Luckily, however, the sort of flying we are interested in usually takes place well away from these diversions and obstructions in what is called 'uncontrolled' airspace. In most parts of the country the amateur aviator is left to pursue his chosen sport without concerning himself too much with these technical complications.

The sheer joy of flight on a summer's day is something that must be experienced; it cannot be described. When viewed from a height the earth unfolds into a new and beautiful panorama. The shadow of your racing aircraft seems to dart over the woods and fields, and cars meander like toys along the streets and lanes far below. Before you can experience these delights for yourself, however, you must undergo a strict training course in your chosen airsport.

It is essential that you learn correctly and safely to avoid endangering yourself or others. Some of the training programmes you will come across may seem quite strict and regimented, but we have an excellent safety record for airsports in this country, and the various individual controlling bodies and organisations are determined to keep it that way.

To assist the reader further, a complete list of clubs and schools, useful addresses, and a selection of books, magazines, videos and training tapes for continued study can be found in the appendices at the end of the book. This should enable the would-be aviator to gain an understanding of his chosen airsport without needing to question a busy club instructor on every item. Moreover, a good way to find out what will be required of you in your new activity is to take a short trial lesson. This applies especially to potential light aircraft, helicopter, glider, microlight and balloon pilots.

Chapter 1

THE LIGHT AIRCRAFT

This chapter will take a detailed look at the training that a potential private pilot can expect to undergo, and at the further avenues of flying that will become open to him once he is qualified. Unfortunately, no book or series of magazine articles can actually teach you to fly: only a qualified flying instructor imparting his knowledge to you in the aircraft cockpit can turn you into a pilot. The great majority of private flying in the United Kingdom is carried out in small, single-engined light monoplane aircraft like the American Cessna 152 or Piper Warrior trainers. Both of these types of aircraft are ideal for the beginner (or *ab-inito* student, as he is sometimes known) to master the basics of airmanship. The Cessna 152 in particular is universally popular among our flying schools and clubs; it is easy to fly, safe, responsive, and has no unpleasant handling characteristics.

People with no knowledge of flying often express surprise at the fact that pilots of small light aircraft do not wear parachutes. A parachute is no doubt an extremely useful item if your aircraft is being shot at by another aeroplane and is in imminent danger of plunging earthwards. Otherwise, even a lightweight backpack is rather bulky in the small cockpit of a modern light aircraft, and the chances of your Cessna being 'bounced' by a marauding Messerschmitt are nowadays rather remote.

The layman who takes a quick glance into the cockpit of a modern light aircraft may at first be bewildered by its seemingly complex array of dials, switches and instruments. A closer study, however, reveals that really they are not a lot different from those to be found in his own car. Apart from flying-specific instruments such as an altimeter, magnetic compass, directional gyro and artificial horizon, he will find a fuel gauge, a rev. counter, a speedometer, a battery-level indicator, and oil pressure and temperature gauges. As you can see, we are a long way from the complex instrument panels of the large, multi-engined commercial jets.

The easy-to-fly Cessna 152 is one of the most popular training aeroplanes in use in our many flying clubs and schools (Photo: Keith Carey)

FIRST LESSONS

After reading everything on flying you can lay your hands on, and after much careful thought and consideration (not to mention repeated checking of your bank statements), you should make contact with the appropriate person at a school or a club. They will make you an appointment for your first 'trial' lesson. The idea of this is to introduce you gently to your new learning environment without putting you under any undue pressure actually to commit yourself. It is merely intended to expose you to the air and to the aeroplane: flying in a light aircraft is a very different sensation from flying in the cramped economy section of a jet taking you off to your summer holidays.

You can wear your normal clothes – the days of open cockpits and bracing wires humming in the wind are sadly gone, so sheepskin flying jackets and goggles will not be needed (though once you have got your licence you can still learn on pre-war biplanes such as the celebrated Tiger Moth). If you have not flown in a small aircraft before, this 'trial' lesson will serve as your 'air experience' flight, and will either greatly increase or quench your desire to fly. In the latter case you will have saved much wasted time and money. In the former, you will have had a chance to become familiarised with the type of aircraft on which you will subsequently train for your Private Pilot's Licence.

Before the flight you should receive a briefing on what you are going to be doing once you are in the air. Your instructor will then show you around the aircraft in what is called the *pre-flight inspection*. If you subsequently decide to take regular flying lessons you will have to carry out all sorts of different checks on the aircraft, both inside and out, for the various phases of flight and pre-flight. Don't worry, however; you will not be expected to remember everything on this 'trial' flight and you will notice that most of it is common sense anyway. The tyres will be checked for the correct pressure; the oil level checked and topped up as necessary; the fuel level checked as sufficient for the flight, and fuel filler cap securely fastened; the flying surfaces as clean and undamaged. You may wonder why these items need to be checked at the start of every flight, but as the pilot before you may have done something amiss it is only sensible to satisfy yourself that all is well before taking to the air.

You will then get into the cockpit – you, the student, taking the left-hand or 'command' seat, and your instructor the right-hand one. After carrying out the internal pre-flight checks he will start the engine and perform an instrument check, pointing out to you some of the more important items. Via the

A thorough pre-flight briefing by the instructor will ensure that you are fully prepared for your lesson
(Photo: Kent Messenger Group Newspapers)

11

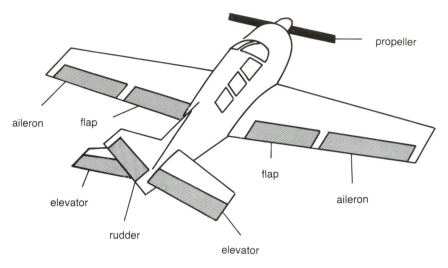

Figure 1 *The control surfaces of a light aircraft*

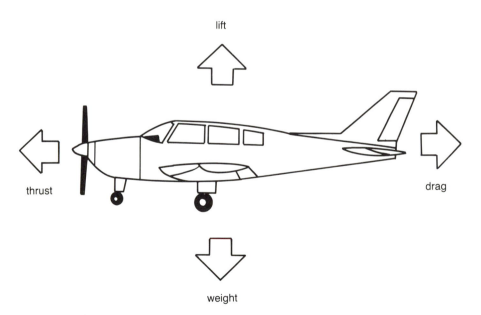

Figure 2 *The four forces acting on an aircraft in flight*

control columns he will then check the flying controls for free movement and give you a brief idea of what each one does. Finally, checking some vital actions and carrying out an engine run-up check, he will obtain radio clearance, taxi the aircraft from its parking space around the perimeter track to the active runway, and take off.

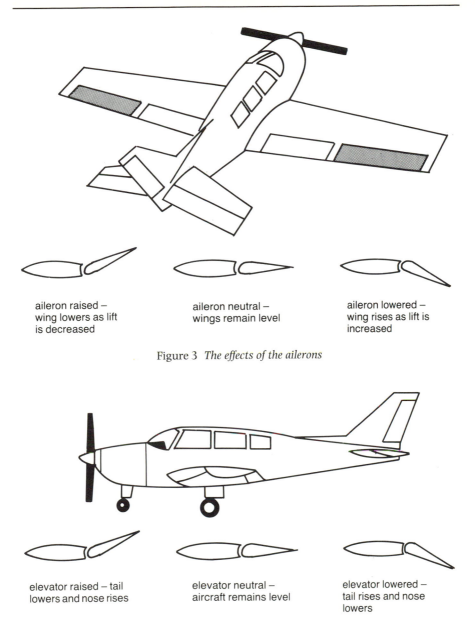

aileron raised –
wing lowers as lift
is decreased

aileron neutral –
wings remain level

aileron lowered –
wing rises as lift is
increased

Figure 3 *The effects of the ailerons*

elevator raised – tail
lowers and nose rises

elevator neutral –
aircraft remains level

elevator lowered –
tail rises and nose
lowers

Figure 4 *The effects of the elevators*

Once you are well away from the other air traffic around the airfield the instructor will level off the aircraft and demonstrate to you the effects of the various controls – all the while keeping a sharp lookout for other aeroplanes, a habit you will be expected to adopt after your first few lessons. You will be asked to hold your control column gently and look at the horizon ahead of

13

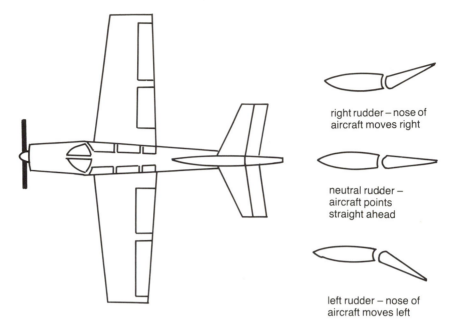

right rudder – nose of
aircraft moves right

neutral rudder –
aircraft points
straight ahead

left rudder – nose of
aircraft moves left

Figure 5 *The effects of the rudder*

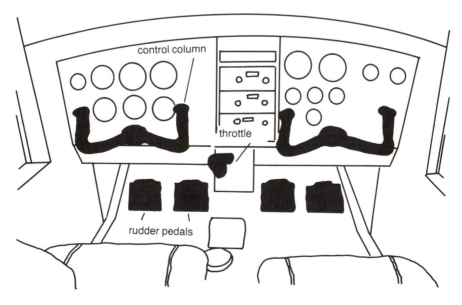

Figure 6 *The typical arrangement of a light aircraft's controls*

A 30-minute 'trial' lesson at your local flying club could be the start of an exciting new hobby (Photo: Kent Messenger Group Newspapers)

you; he will then ease *his* controls forwards so that the nose of the aircraft goes down. When he eases his control column gently back to its starting position the nose of the aircraft will come up. Notice the small control movements amount to little more than gentle pressures – all that is required.

Next you will turn to the sideward movement of the control column. Look out at each wing tip in turn and note that the aircraft is flying level. Then move the control column slightly to the left; you will see that the left wing goes down and the right wing rises up. Now ease the control column over to the right; the right wing will move downwards and the left wing will rise up. Return the control column to its central or neutral position and once again the aircraft will resume a level flying attitude.

Finally, you will try out the rudder control. This control, mounted at the rear of the vertical fin, produces the effect of yaw. Place your feet lightly on the pedals mounted under the instrument panel. As the instructor applies a firm but gentle pressure to the left pedal you will see that the nose of the aircraft swings to the left. When the right pedal is depressed it will swing to the right. Once again, when the pedals are centralised the nose will point straight ahead. These movements are known as the *primary effects of control* and they form the basis on which the skill of learning to fly is built.

The instructor will demonstrate all these exercises for you and then invite you to have a go for yourself. As this is your first lesson, and as you have probably been feeling more than a little apprehensive, it will be a short one – 30 to 40 minutes being the norm. The instructor will fly the aircraft back to the airfield, possibly pointing out one or two landmarks of local interest, before rejoining the circuit and landing.

If you should feel a little sick during or after this first flight, please tell your instructor. There is absolutely nothing to be ashamed of. In no way does this mean that you are unsuitable to train as a pilot. It should be stressed that it is not unknown for a pupil to feel slightly queasy during a first flight; the sensation is usually overcome as the next few lessons progress. Many pilots never feel a qualm in the air but would not dream of boarding a cross-channel ferry.

LEARNING TO FLY

Now that you have completed your 'trial' flight and have decided that you want to learn to fly, you will be required to join the club or school. The flying club will take some personal details from you for its records, such as your name, address and age, and give you a copy of the club rules. You will then be a 'flying' as opposed to a 'social' member. This will allow you to fly the club's aircraft under instruction until you have your own licence, and ensures that you are covered under the club's insurance scheme – a very necessary precaution considering the valuable machinery you will be operating, and a legal requirement.

In your next lesson, the first proper of your course, you will be given your own check-list and will start to learn the basics of aircraft handling. For the first five hours or so of your course this will cover the following: control functions; climbing, descending and turning; maintaining straight and level flight; take-offs and landings; and general manoeuvring on the airfield. You will also be taught what happens to a wing when it *stalls* – when the smooth airflow over its upper surface is broken down, so that the wing is unable to continue providing lift – and how to recover safely and easily to level flight. When your flying instructor is happy that you have mastered the basic manoeuvres satisfactorily and can operate the aircraft in a smooth and coordinated manner, you will be introduced to the discipline of the circuit.

The *circuit* is an imaginary oblong shape over an active runway. It comprises the following: a take-off and a climb through 90° to whatever circuit height is in use at your airfield (different airfields use different heights, though 1,000 feet is probably the most common); a 'downwind' leg flown parallel to the runway from which you have just taken off; another 90° turn on to what is called the 'base' leg; and another, final, 90° turn on to 'finals'. This will have positioned the aircraft pointing back at the same runway from which you took off, at a height and speed conducive to a safe final approach and landing.

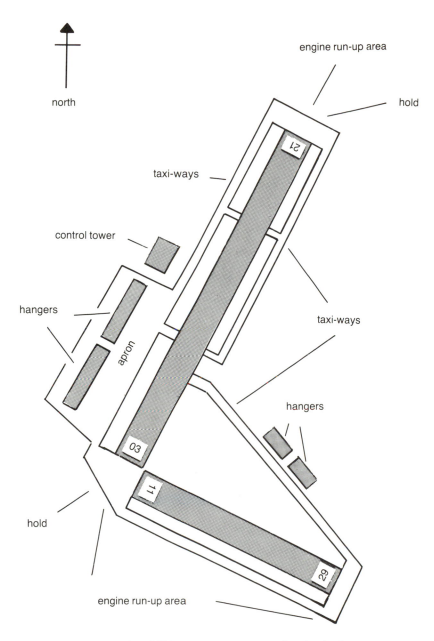

Figure 7 *A typical airfield layout. Runways are referred to by their compass bearing in the direction of usage*

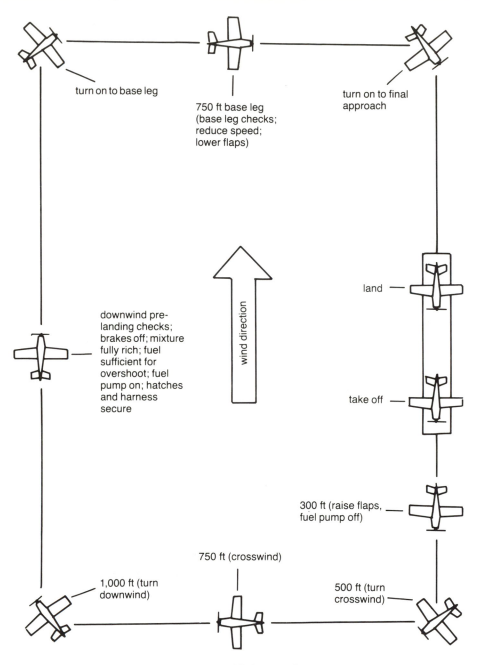

turn on to base leg

750 ft base leg
(base leg checks;
reduce speed;
lower flaps)

turn on to final
approach

land

wind direction

downwind pre-
landing checks;
brakes off; mixture
fully rich; fuel
sufficient for
overshoot; fuel
pump on; hatches
and harness
secure

take off

300 ft (raise flaps,
fuel pump off)

750 ft (crosswind)

1,000 ft (turn
downwind)

500 ft (turn
crosswind)

Figure 8 *A typical light aircraft circuit*

Flying the circuit should not present a student of average ability with too much difficulty: it is only a matter of flying accurate headings, though drift caused by the wind can sometimes complicate things a little. It is what comes at the end of every circuit that causes the most frustration among student pilots – and sometimes even among qualified ones – the landing.

It has often been said that learning to fly comprises little more than learning to land. Whilst it is a little more complicated than that, this is essentially true. The landing is the one exercise that is truly difficult for the instructor to teach, involving frustrating repetition until the student develops sufficient confidence and coordination. Do not be too disheartened; every pilot before you has been through it and eventually succeeded.

Once your lessons are progressing, you should not make the mistake of thinking that learning starts and finishes in the aircraft cockpit. It *is* possible to learn in this way, but it will cost you far more in time and money in the long run. You should familiarise yourself with the aircraft and the ground activities on your airfield, so that later in your training you will find that you already possess a basic understanding of what is going on around you. Become familiar with the flight record sheet at your club or school, so that you can see which aeroplane you will be flying and with which instructor as soon as you arrive. If your club or school has a flight briefing room, acquaint yourself with the various charts and information notices on the walls. Furthermore, now that you are training to be a pilot you will need a personal flying log-book in which to enter details of your flights. This is a legal requirement: you can obtain one fairly cheaply from the office of your club or school. Take care when filling in the various columns, as you will find it very satisfying to look back through the pages at a later date and recall the various flights that you have made.

The term 'airmanship' will frequently be used during your pilot training, and indeed throughout the rest of your flying life. It covers all those parts of flying not directly concerned with the pure handling of the aircraft, such as not smoking in a hanger or in the vicinity of an aeroplane, ensuring that you can reach all the controls in the cockpit comfortably, and adjusting the seat and rudder pedals if necessary.

The basic course of flying instruction for the Private Pilot's Licence is 40 hours in duration. The course is divided between *dual* (i.e. flying under instruction) and *solo* flying. The Civil Aviation Authority specifies that of these 40 flying hours, 10 must have been flown solo – in other words on your own without an instructor. During the first part of your flying training – up to the first 10 or 11 hours – the instructor will continually assess the pupil pilot in readiness for his first solo flight. The timing of this event is of prime importance. If the student is allowed to fly solo before he is ready, the resulting flight could be an unnerving and dangerous affair for all concerned. If it is left too late, though, the student might lose interest in flying, with a resulting deterioration in his personal flying standard.

The student who progresses satisfactorily will be permitted to fly solo after perhaps 10 hours. This flight will consitute the most important 15 minutes of his flying training, if not of his airborne career. Many people think that the moment when the instructor leaves the aircraft and the pupil pilot is on his own must be distinctly unpleasant. This is most definitely not the case. Most students actively look forward to it, and think themselves ready to fly solo long before their instructor considers them sufficiently safe and competent. A student being dispatched on his first solo is sent off quickly, the instructor telling him to go through his checks and then leaving the cockpit with some nonchalant remark like: 'You know what to do, so off you go.' He is allowed little time to worry.

The first solo is unique, and when it is completed you will have experienced something that can never happen again in your flying life. You will be expected to perform a normal take-off, fly a circuit of the airfield, and land. You will also be required to cope with any emergency that may arise during the flight, for which remote possibility you will have been given adequate training. It should be said that while there may have been the occasional rough landing, there have been almost no serious accidents during first solos. In any case, the first solo does not signal the end of dual flying training with your instructor. There is plenty more of that to come during the next few hours of your course, which will include consolidation exercises, circuit flying and approach and landing, as well as some further hours of solo flying at the discretion of your flying instructor.

The internal and pre-start check-list for the Cessna 152 is as follows.

Internal checks
- Seat – adjusted
- Hatches, harnesses – closed, secure
- Parking brake – on
- Controls – working fully and freely
- Trimmer – set neutral
- Flight instruments – set correctly
- Radio/Navaids – off
- Engine instruments – glass unbroken
- Master switch – on
- Lights – as required
- Carb heat – set cold
- Throttle – closed
- Mixture – rich
- Circuit breakers – in and secure

Start checks
- Fuel – on
- Brakes – on
- Beacon – on
- Prime – as required

- Throttle – $\frac{1}{2}$-inch open
- Check – clear
- Magnetos – on (both)
- Starter – operate
- RPM – 1200
- Starter light – out
- Oil pressure – rising

After start
- Low voltage light – out/charging
- Suction – indicating
- Radio – on/test
- Navaids – as required
- Flight instruments – set correctly
- Magnetos – dead cut
- Flaps – up
- Radio – taxi call

Taxi checks
- Brakes – check
- Rudder freedom – check
- Flight instruments – check

During the remaining hours of the course you will perform some advanced exercises away from the airfield, in what is called *upper air* flying. You will learn how to execute turns at a higher than normal angle of bank, and some manoeuvres that are more ambitious than those covered in the pre-solo stage. These exercises will help to improve your coordination and confidence in handling the aircraft.

Also included in this period of advanced training will be stalling the aircraft and instruction on how to cope should the engine fail. You may wonder why this is necessary, especially if you are only interested in flying straight and level. The answer is that stalling, in all its many forms, is the result of a mishandling of the aircraft's controls, so it is vitally important for you to learn the following:

- how to recognise an approaching stall (i.e. low airspeed, lack of control and effectiveness);
- how to recover quickly and efficiently with the minimum loss of height;
- that a spin can develop as a direct result of bad control handling at or near the stall.

With regard to engine failure, forced landings with and without power will also be covered, giving the student some experience in selecting emergency landing grounds such as stubble fields, heathland and beaches. Although engine failure in today's modern light aircraft is very rare, it does occasionally happen, and so you can expect to spend a good deal of time perfecting this exercise, practising how to adopt the best gliding speed for your aircraft, and positioning yourself to arrive safely on your selected field.

After all this consolidation work comes perhaps the most interesting part of the course – the *navigation phase*. Thus far your training as a student pilot has concentrated on teaching you how to handle the aircraft itself. The navigation phase will now teach you the 'bread-and-butter' work of flying – how to pilot the craft accurately from one destination to another. Many students approach the subject of navigation apprehensively but, while it can be a complex and difficult subject in its higher forms, your instructor will ensure that you enter the subject progressively from the shallow end. You will start by flying a number of short dual cross-country flights, often in the form of a triangle, before going on to fly them yourself as a solo exercise. This period of training will also include a navigation test carried out by an examiner, often the Chief Flying Instructor of your club or school. At the end of this phase you will complete a long solo cross-country flight, around a triangular course which will include one leg of at least 50 miles in length and landings at two other airfields before returning to your own. The satisfactory completion of this flight forms part of the qualification required for the issue of your Private Pilot's Licence.

Also included in your training will be four hours of *instrument appreciation work* intended to give you an insight into instrument flying skills and problems. The purpose of this is not to teach you how to fly in poor weather conditions (something you will not be allowed to practise until you have more flying experience and hold an IMC licence), but to show how to get safely out of bad weather if you are inadvertantly caught out. The reason behind this safety training is the following: the human body is not really designed for flight, but rather is adapted for life on the ground. Sight, and a sense of balance provided by the inner ear, help us to move smoothly around. When an aircraft enters cloud, external visual references are denied. Similarly, the aircraft is a moving platform: this, coupled with a lack of outside vision, will quickly produce all sorts of nasty and misleading sensations which can rapidly become extremely hazardous.

Figure 9 *A simplified light aircraft landing sequence*

1 Aircraft on approach to runway, lined up on the centre line
2 Descent checked, power reduced. Allow aircraft to sink towards runway
3 As aircraft descends, maintain gentle back pressure on control column
4 As main wheels touch down, continue to hold back the control column to keep the weight of the aircraft off the nose wheel and to allow aerodynamic braking to help slow the aircraft
5 Allow speed to decay before applying brakes

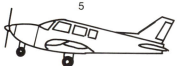

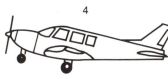

PREPARATION FOR THE LICENCE

At this advanced stage in your pilot's training you will have a period in the air with your instructor in which you will go over all the exercises that you have learnt so far. You will probably go through each sequence of the syllabus once or twice to check that you have it absolutely taped. Then, if both you and your instructor are satisfied that you are ready to have a crack at the General Flying Test for the Private Pilot's Licence, you will find yourself with an appointment with an authorised examiner.

Your examiner is likely to be the Chief Flying Instructor of your own flying club or school, and the test will take approximately one hour to complete.

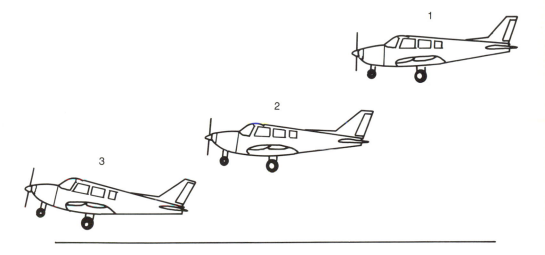

Figure 10 *A simplified light aircraft take-off sequence*

1 Aircraft lined up on runway, brakes on. Apply full power
2 Release brakes, keep aircraft running straight with use of rudder. Keep weight off nose wheel with gentle backward pressure on control column
3 At recommended take-off speed, pull back on the control column and rotate the aircraft off the ground
4 Adjust power for best climbing speed and trim the aircraft
5 At recommended safe height, retract the flaps (if used on take-off) and continue climb to desired cruising height

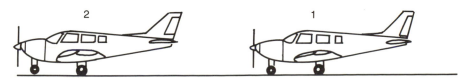

A Piper Warrior aircraft getting airborne at Manston Airport
(Photo: Kent Messenger Group Newspapers)

The examiner is not there to fail you or to trip you up; his aim is simply to assess whether or not you are ready to exercise the privileges that go with the granting of the Private Pilot's Licence. In making this decision he carries a certain heavy responsibility, because once you have qualified for your licence you may then carry passengers and fly a British registered aeroplane – as long as it only has one engine and weighs under 12,500 lb – anywhere in the world. During the flying test itself the applicant will be required to demonstrate competence in the full sequence of flying manoeuvres, and a correct observation of the relevant ground procedures.

The rules of the flying test require that the student pilot under examination occupies the left-hand cockpit seat of the aircraft and the examiner the right-hand seat. The test will follow the Civil Aviation Authority approved aircraft syllabus. The student pilot will be assessed on airmanship, including circuit procedure, airfield discipline, the setting and use of the flight instruments fitted to the test aircraft, pre-flight inspection, engine start and run-up procedure, cockpit checks, and vital actions.

The PPL General Flying Test may include some or all of the following:

- taxiing and take-off, including assessment of the cross-wind component;
- simulated engine failure after take-off;
- action in the event of a fire;

- straight and level flight;
- short-field landing;
- assessment of landing with a cross-wind component;
- landing the aircraft without power from a position and height selected by the flying test examiner;
- overshoot procedure from a powered approach;
- turns with various degrees of bank, with and without power;
- climbing and descending turns;
- recognition of the approach to the stall;
- stalling and recovery.

The examiner will also ask specific questions about the aircraft in which you are being tested, and he will expect a good deal more polish in your flying than your instructor did when sending you off on your first solo. He will be looking for competence in your airmanship and general handling, and you will almost certainly be asked to attend a re-test if you taxi carelessly, fail to carry out your checks, disobey ATC instructions or indulge in any other malpractice. An applicant who fails any part of the test may be requested to undertake further dual flying instruction before being accepted for re-test, but don't worry too much about it: the examiner is human, and will excuse a slightly untidy approach and landing, for example, as long as you know what you did wrong.

If all goes well, your club or school will post off to the CAA the results of your written ground examinations, together with your log-book and formal licence application form duly signed and stamped. Only a few weeks will elapse before you hold your coveted PPL.

THE GROUND EXAMINATIONS

The mere mention of the word examination is enough to send shockwaves of horror through some potential students. If truth be known, there is little to be afraid of. The written examinations for the Private Pilot's Licence are nothing like those dreaded 'O' or 'A' levels many of us suffered at school; they are simply multiple-choice papers. You are presented with three possible answers to each question, two of which will be plausible enough but wrong, leaving one correct answer for you to identify with your tick. The usual pass-mark is 70%. Some clubs and schools have their own preference as to when you sit the individual examinations; for example, they require you to have passed the air law examination before going solo, or the navigation examination before the navigation phase of the course. Other clubs simply require you to sit all the examinations in one batch at the end of your flying course – before you undergo your General Flying Test. Some leave the choice of when to take the examinations to the individual student. Whatever the case, all the tests must be passed successfully before you can be granted your pilot's licence by the Civil Aviation Authority.

The subjects for the ground examinations themselves are: navigation; meteorology; aviation law; aircraft technical; and, newly introduced in 1992, human performance and limitations. Although this list sounds quite daunting, the textbooks you will have been reading since beginning your flying lessons, plus lots of tips from your instructor along the way, will have prepared you more than adequately to achieve good pass-marks. However, a commitment to some homework and hard study will still be required.

Navigation

This is a very important paper, as you will wish to fly across country and visit other airfields once you have your own licence. The ability to navigate accurately and safely is of prime importance. The Civil Aviation Authority views with absolutely no enthusiasm light aircraft whose pilots stray into controlled airspace through faulty navigation.

The practical side of the navigation phase of your flying course will cover a lot of what you need to know to pass this paper. Questions may include the following: locating and plotting positions; dead reckoning; compass variation and deviation; the 'one in 60' rule; and the calculation of fuel consumption, ground speed and time *en-route*.

Meteorology

This is not the most interesting of subjects, but nevertheless a knowledge of the atmosphere and its weather systems is as important to a pilot as a knowledge of the sea is to a sailor. Questions you can expect to encounter include: types of cloud; frontal systems; different types of fog and the conditions required for their formation; dew point spread; and aircraft icing.

Aviation law

This examination is based upon a student's knowledge of the United Kingdom Air Pilot. The Air Pilot is a large, thick book that can be found at most flying clubs or schools, and is the flyer's equivalent to the driver's Highway Code (though much more comprehensive). It contains everything you need to know about flight regulations and flying in the United Kingdom. Radio frequencies, navigation aids, airfields and airspace regulations are just some of the topics to be found within its pages. The student pilot, however, is not expected to purchase his own copy of this very expensive book. A much smaller publication, Civil Air Publication (CAP 85), available from the office of your club or school or from a shop such as *Transair Pilot Supplies* (for around £3.50 at the time of writing) will suffice for the student's needs, as it is based on extracts from the weighty Air Pilot. The paper may include questions on the following: types of airspace, airways and control zones; customs procedures; quadrantal flight rules; ground signals; and aircraft lighting.

Aircraft technical

This examination requires the student to demonstrate his knowledge of aerodynamics and aircraft systems and a general understanding of the group of aircraft he wishes to fly. You don't have to be an aircraft engineer to pass this; the questions are all of a general nature, concerning engine performance and handling, oil quantities and levels, and tyre pressures and sizes. It may also refer to the various requirements of the certificate of airworthiness. A good deal of the information required for this paper may be obtained from the aircraft's operating handbook, and by the end of your flying course questions such as these should pose no particular problems.

Human performance and limitations

This sounds like quite a mouthful! It is a relatively new subject, introduced into the syllabus in 1992 by the Civil Aviation Authority in an attempt to increase flying safety among all new private pilots. Its implementation followed studies that showed the actions, reactions and decisions of pilots, particularly inexperienced ones, to be the cause of around 80% of the accidents in general aviation. The topics covered include: the factors affecting human capabilities and limitations; the physiological aspects of aviation medicine; and aviation psychology. Despite the long words, the paper is nowhere near as complex as it sounds: it is simply about human beings in the cockpit and the factors that affect their ability to fly safely.

MEDICAL REQUIREMENTS

Private pilots are not supermen or women, and need only a Class 3 medical certificate issued by a Civil Aviation Authority authorised medical examiner. The typical charge for this examination is around £40 at the time of writing, and the standard of fitness is about the same as that required for a life-insurance medical. Your own local GP cannot issue the certificate; your flying club or school will supply you with a list of approved local doctors authorised to carry out the examination. You do not necessarily need to obtain a medical certificate before you start taking flying lessons, but you must have one before you will be allowed to fly solo.

The examination itself is not unduly rigorous. It will include a general questionnaire on your health record and checks on your hearing, reflexes, eyesight (eyesight defects pose no problem if you normally wear glasses or contact lenses, provided they can be corrected to acceptable limits, and if you are colour blind you may fly only in daylight hours), respiratory system and blood pressure. Students over 40 years of age must also undergo an *electrocardiograph test* (ECG) and an *audiogram*. The medical certificate is valid for five years if you are aged under 40; for two years if you are aged between 40 and 50; for one year if you are between 50 and 70; and for six months if you are aged 70 years or over. There are some medical conditions which may exclude you from being granted a certificate. These include cardiac problems, diabetes (if it requires constant medication) and epilepsy. It is probably wise to complete your medical examination before starting any flying lessons, thus saving both time and money if you should fail the examination for any reason.

LICENCE RENEWALS

Now that you have completed your course of flying instruction, passed your General Flying Test and written examinations, and at last hold the coveted PPL, how do you keep it valid? As a private pilot you must always maintain a current medical certificate. Every 13 months you will be required to present your flying log-book to an instructor/examiner for stamping, to show that you have met the experience-level requirement within that period. In effect, this means that you must fly at least five hours within the 13 months in order that a 'Certificate of Experience' may be entered in your log-book; this re-validates it for another 13 months. Of the five hours, two may be under dual instruction, leaving only three hours of solo to be completed. In practice, however, you should aim to fly as often as time and money will allow. The legal minimum as laid down by the CAA is nowhere near sufficient to keep you sharp and competent, and many clubs and schools will insist that you fly every six to eight weeks or else be required to undergo a dual safety check with an instructor. Failure to complete the required amount of flying within the specified time will not automatically invalidate your pilot's licence, but you will be required to take another General Flying Test to renew its privileges.

PRIVATE PILOT RATINGS

As his knowledge and flying experience increases, the private pilot may wish to add one or all of the following ratings to his licence.

Night rating
A night rating will enable the holder of a Private Pilot's Licence to fly as pilot-in-command of an aircraft at night. It can be obtained after completing a short night-flying course of approximately five hours duration.

IMC rating
An IMC or Instrument Meteorological Conditions rating will allow you to fly in weather conditions below the basic PPL minima. It is a useful rating from both a practical and a safety point of view, removing some of the restrictions placed on the holder of a basic licence. It can be obtained after completing a course of approximately 15 flying hours, during which you will be taught

some of the basics of instrument flying and radio navigation. It is a very popular post-PPL qualification.

Twin rating

If you later aspire to step up from a simple single-engined aircraft to a complex multi-engined type, you will need to obtain a twin rating. This involves a short course usually spread over two days and is of approximately seven flying hours duration. It culminates in a multi-engined General Flying Test.

Instrument rating

At this stage of your flying career this qualification is perhaps a little ambitious. The instrument rating permits the holder to fly in controlled airspace and in bad weather. There is a tough written examination and a stringent flying test conducted with an examiner from the Civil Aviation Authority Flying Unit. The instrument rating is much more comprehensive than the IMC rating, although having said that it is not beyond the reach of a competent and experienced private pilot. It is by no means cheap, often costing as much as if not more than the price of the basic PPL course.

HOW MUCH WILL IT COST?

Learning to fly never has been, nor ever will be, cheap. However, for around the cost of a good long-haul holiday or a reasonable second-hand car you can become the holder of a Private Pilot's Licence. The prices at flying clubs and schools vary a great deal, and although if at all possible you should aim to learn at the nearest airfield to your home, it does pay to shop around. Make a list of clubs and schools in your area and visit them in turn before parting with any money. When you arrive at the club or school of your choice, does anyone bother to ask if they can help you? If your reception is offhand then try somewhere else. You will be spending the best part of £3,000 on gaining your Private Pilot's Licence: if that particular flying club or school does not seem to value your business there are plenty more elsewhere that will.

Other good pointers to an efficient and friendly club or school are: how many aircraft of the same type they have available for training; whether or not these are kept clean; whether they assign one flying instructor to you throughout your course; whether there are separate briefing rooms available for your ground instruction; whether there is a pre- and post-flight briefing before and after every instructional flight; whether the premises are clean and tidy; whether the staff are attentive; and how many instructors they have.

There is often no difference between a flying club and a school. At some of the smaller clubs, however, the atmosphere is decidedly more 'clubby' and you may find yourself being roped in to help with tasks such as answering the telephone, making coffee and getting aircraft out of the hangers. In reality, this is no bad thing: by helping with such tasks and talking to the members you can pick up useful knowledge that will benefit you directly. After all, you will be spending a great deal more time on the ground at the airfield than you will actually up in the air.

At the time of writing, the average hourly rate for dual instruction at flying clubs and schools is between £75 and £100. It would be wise, therefore, to budget for between £3,000 and £3,800 for your Private Pilot's Licence course. When you are selecting a club or school at which to take lessons, remember to check if VAT, textbooks and landing fees are included in the price or are extras. Also, don't forget to ask if there is a discount. Many clubs and schools will offer a discount for blocks of flying hours if you book and pay in advance. However, if you are offered a discount for paying for the complete course in advance, think carefully. A small number of operators have collapsed in recent years, leaving students who have paid in advance with little hope of recovering their money. Although the above prices are an average of what you can expect to find across the country, it is possible to fly for less than the figures quoted. Some clubs and schools have rates starting as low as £55 per hour for dual instruction, though you will have to hunt to find them. One of the best ways of doing this is to buy yourself a copy of *Pilot* magazine, the leading general aviation magazine for the private pilot. *Pilot* publishes a comprehensive 'Where To Fly' guide every April; this gives details of courses, membersip fees and hourly flying rates at almost every flying club and school in the United Kingdom.

Another factor affecting the eventual cost of your licence is how often you fly. With finances usually being the governing factor, the great majority of potential private pilots spend a year or two flying one hour every weekend until they qualify. Other pilots, with greater available funds, get their licences in a few months or even weeks. Without doubt, the best way to get your PPL (if you can afford it and can get two or three weeks off work) is to take a full-time course. This can be done at your local club or school if they can arrange it; at one of the many clubs and schools offering this facility elsewhere in the country; or even overseas with a company such as 'Flight Training International' which specialises in training students for their British PPL on intensive package courses on the French Cote d'Azur. The great advantage of a full-time course is that it offers a concentrated learning period. Flying two or three times a day you will quickly make rapid progress; flying once a fortnight you will have to spend a proportion of every lesson reminding yourself of what you learnt the last time. This inevitably means that you will end up flying between 60 and 70 hours in order to achieve your licence, as opposed to a little over the legal minimum of 40 hours (depending of course on individual aptitude) on a full-time course. Thus, in real terms, someone who takes a year or two to gain their licence will pay almost a third more than the student who can afford to complete the course in a concentrated burst.

Should money for your training be a problem – and there is little doubt that the total sum involved is a serious financial commitment – a number of clubs and schools offer credit facilities negotiated with popular finance companies. A word of warning here, though: do please check the interest rates of any loan scheme offered by a club or school very carefully, as the annual percentage rate (APR) can be significantly higher than on a comparable personal loan offered by a high street bank or building society. Most clubs and schools also accept the popular credit cards such as Access and Barclaycard, other visa and mastercards and American Express and Diners Club. Again, a word of warning: some clubs and schools, in common with certain high street retailers, have begun to add surcharges to bills paid with credit cards. Typically, this surcharge is around 3%; assuming the hourly rate at your club is £80, paying by plastic will therefore cost you an extra £2.40. Over the duration of your PPL course this can easily add up to the cost of an extra hour of flying, so do watch out.

AFTER OBTAINING YOUR PPL

You will obviously be proud of yourself and of your shiny new licence, and quite rightly so. It is an extremely worthwhile qualification to have, and there are only around 40,000 holders in the United Kingdom's population of over 56 million. Now that you are a pilot, by all means spread your wings a little and make the most of it; but remember, regardless of whether you fly on private business or for pleasure, you have only 45-60 hours of flying experience behind you and are still very much a learner. The issue of a Private Pilot's Licence, just like that of a driving licence, represents nothing more than a licence to learn. No matter how adept a pilot you are, or think you are, stay within the limits laid down while you were training until you have built up more practical experience. There is a lovely saying in aviation: 'Flying itself is not inherently dangerous, but the air, to an even greater extent than the sea, is terribly unforgiving of any carelessness, foolishness, incapacity or neglect.'

The most obvious obstacle to smooth, safe flying in this country is our weather. Even the most experienced professional pilots can be caught out by Mother Nature, and they will generally be operating far more sophisticated, weather-tolerant aircraft than your club aeroplanes. If you plan to go off on a cross-country flight, watch the television weather forecasts, call one of the many 'phone-in' weather lines, and get a proper meteorological briefing at your club or school. If, during the subsequent flight, you encounter any conditions beyond your experience (such as strong turbulence or heavy rain), *turn back.*

Failure to turn back in deteriorating weather conditions is one of the main causes of General Aviation accidents. It is sometimes nicknamed 'press-on-itis', and it can kill you. There is no shame whatsoever in turning an aircraft around because of strong winds or poor visibility. It comes under the heading of good airmanship, which we outlined earlier; it is also called common sense.

'Dos and don'ts' for the private pilot

- A private pilot may not fly for what is called 'Hire or Reward'. This means that the pilot may not receive any remuneration for his services. To fly for reward, one must qualify for one of the professional licences, such as a BCPL, CPL or ATPL. However, if you set off on a cross-country flight, say from Surrey to the Isle of Wight, you can take a friend along who shares the cost of hiring the aircraft with you. What you cannot do is hire an aircraft from your club or school and then charter yourself out for payment.
- If you fly over your local football team on a Saturday afternoon to cheer them on from the air, you will be breaking civil air law. This states that *an aircraft must not fly over or within 915 m (3,000 ft) of any open-air assembly of more than 1,000 people*. The rule may however be waived if written permission from the event organisers and the Civil Aviation Authority has been obtained in advance.

Private flying is one of the safest ways in which to travel. If you fly only in reasonable weather – and most adverse weather is predictable – thoroughly prepare your flight plan, make sure that you have enough fuel plus reserves for the intended journey, and apply plenty of common sense, you will not go far wrong. Always remember, flight in cloud or in bad weather requires instrument flying skills; despite the four hours of instrument appreciation included in your course, as a newly qualified pilot you do not possess them.

This modern four-seater SOCATA TB10 Tobago is used for flying training and self-fly hire at Air Touring Services, based at Biggin Hill
(Photo: Air Touring Services Ltd)

Now that you are a fully fledged pilot you may hire aircraft for touring purposes if you so wish. Besides the fleet at your own club or school there are a number of companies offering self-fly hire arrangements. Prices vary a great deal from company to company. Many pilots soon build up a list of favourite trips and places to visit, and destinations such as Paris and Amsterdam are within two hours' flying time of the South-East, Biarritz and Frankfurt within three. One of the most enduringly popular trips for the private pilot with a few hours of experience under his belt remains the short hop across the English Channel. A trip to Le Touquet for the afternoon (and some duty-free shopping) is enticing and presents few, if any, problems.

In this country there are over 240 airfields you can visit and almost 100 private strips. There are many different types of aircraft to fly; you can try your hand at aerobatics; or perhaps pull on that sheepskin flying jacket and goggles after all and get checked out in a vintage Tiger Moth.

Group flying

Now that you have your licence, another possibility is joining a flying group. Group operation can drastically reduce the cost of your flying, typically halving the rates you will have been paying whilst training for your Private Pilot's Licence. To find out more about group flying you should either join the 'Popular Flying Association', whose address can be found in Appendix 9, or, as mentioned earlier, get yourself a copy of *Pilot* magazine which carries advertisements each month of flying groups looking for new members.

With every good thing there is usually a catch, however, and group flying is no exception. The main drawback to this type of flying is that you usually have to buy a share in the aircraft (although this can easily be sold on if you decide to leave the group). You also have to agree to subscribe to a monthly payment on top of the hourly flying rate. Depending on the group you join, the share price can be anything from a few hundred to several thousand pounds. Similarly, the monthly subscription can range from £15 to £115. Generally, the rule is: the simpler the aircraft, the cheaper it will be; the more complex the aircraft, the more expensive it will be. Although (given the extremes of variation) it is not possible to quote an average price, joining a typical flying group that is operating an older type aircraft could be costed out as follows.

One-tenth share in an Auster aircraft	£1,200
Fixed monthly sum of £30 to cover fuel, oil, hangarage, maintenance, etc.	£360
Fixed sum of £25 per flying hour (and you fly 35 hours during the year)	£875
Total outlay discounting share purchase	£1,235
£1,235 divided by 35 flying hours equals	**£35.28 per hour**

Whatever you eventually decide to do with your new pilot's licence, you have taken up one of the most exciting and stimulating of recreations. At times it will be maddeningly frustrating, rain pouring on to the airfield and keeping you firmly inside the clubhouse when you want to fly. On other occasions your favourite aeroplane will have become unserviceable since you booked it, leaving disappointed friends denied their flight and you with little option but to re-book and try again another day. Yet after all the hard work and the learning of new skills – not to mention a significant financial outlay – you will have been rewarded with access to a vast arena, a vista denied to those who exist solely on the ground. You will see our countryside as it was meant to be seen, as it can only be seen, for you can fly.

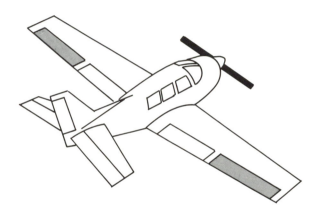

Chapter 2

FLYING A ROTARY WING

The helicopter is one of the most versatile forms of transport known to man. It can fly you to your destination relatively fast, and do so in a straight line; it can lift off and land almost anywhere – even in your own back garden if it is large enough, or from the car park at work – it can stop anywhere *en-route* and change direction in an instant. Inevitably, then, it is a complicated aircraft, but the challenge is stimulating and the sense of achievement when you master a helicopter is unparalleled in any other form of flying.

The world of aviation is sometimes guilty of surrounding itself with an aura of mystery which 'outsiders', or those who would like to find out more, can often find discouraging. Flying helicopters in particular may seem to many to be very specialised indeed, and perhaps beyond the capabilities of the hopeful amateur. This is simply not the case: if you can drive a car or ride a motorcycle you have the ability to learn to fly a helicopter.

Since the introduction of small and relatively inexpensive light helicopters, interest in rotary-wing flying in this country has increased tremendously, as supported by the steady rise in the number of Helicopter Pilot's Licences that have been granted by the Civil Aviation Authority. The great majority of private helicopter training carried out in the United Kingdom is conducted in the Robinson R-22 helicopter. This small American two-seater is modern, fast, reliable, economical to operate and easy to fly, and in recent years it has become the best-selling light helicopter in the world.

As with learning to operate a fixed-wing light aircraft, the best introduction to helicopter flight is to book a 'trial' lesson. Contact the club or school nearest to your home (the address can be found in the reference pages at the back of this book). The idea of a 'trial' lesson is to introduce you to the helicopter and to your new training environment without any undue pressure being put on you to commit yourself. Your instructor won't be able to tell you how good or bad a helicopter pilot you will be at the end of it, but at least you will have had

The easy-to-fly Robinson R22 is the most popular helicopter in use in training schools. This example is operated by Sloane Helicopters of Sywell, Northamptonshire (Photo: Sloane Helicopters)

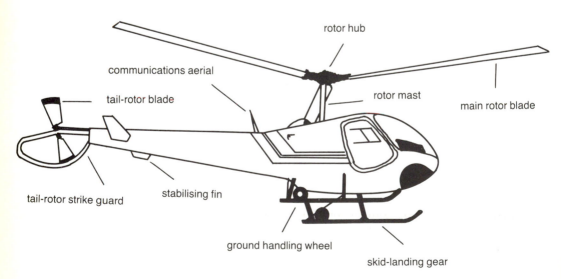

Figure 11 *Major component parts of a helicopter*

*All of your flying lessons will begin and end with a thorough briefing.
Here, an instructor is explaining to his student the basic effects of a
helicopter's controls in forward flight* (Photo: Sloane Helicopters)

a 20-30-minute flight, which should be enough to give you a good idea of
whether or not you want to start a course of lessons.

Like a fixed-wing 'trial' flight, the procedure will consist of a short briefing
on what you can expect to be shown in the air and a pre-flight inspection. You
will not be expected to take everything in on this first flight, but you will notice
that much of it is common sense. The rotor blades will be checked for any
damage; the oil level checked and topped-up as necessary; and the fuel filler
cap securely fastened. These items need to be checked at the start of every
flight because the pilot before you may have done something amiss. It is only
safe and sensible to satisfy yourself that all is well before taking to the air.

You will then climb into the cabin – you, the student, taking the right-hand
seat, and your instructor the left-hand seat. *This seating arrangement is the
complete reverse of most fixed-wing types, in which the command seat is always on
the left.* After the pre-start checks the instructor will start the engine and
conduct an instrument check, pointing out one or two of the more important
items. Then, via the control column (called a *cyclic stick* in a helicopter), he
will test the rotor disc for freedom of movement. Finally, after checking some
vital actions, he will obtain radio clearance, lift into a hover, hover-taxi to the
active runway, and lift off.

Once away from the other traffic around the airfield the instructor will level
the helicopter and demonstrate to you the effects of the controls – all the while

keeping a sharp lookout for other aircraft, a habit you will be expected to adopt after your first few lessons. The following brief explanation of how each of the four primary controls function will help the reader to understand a little better how a helicopter is flown.

Cyclic control (steering stick)

The equivalent to the aileron and elevator control column or 'joystick' in a fixed-wing aircraft. The cyclic gives pitch and roll control in all phases of flight, much like an aircraft's control column; however, it controls the rotor disc (wing) *directly*, not through ailerons or elevators. Bank-turns a helicopter in forward flight. Movement of the cyclic tilts the rotor disc in any desired direction, giving the pilot complete attitude control.

Anti-torque pedals

Equivalent to the rudder pedals in a fixed-wing aircraft. The anti-torque pedals control the angle of pitch in the tail-rotor blades. They are used to keep the helicopter on a heading parallel to the desired line of flight. They are also used for spot turns and precision work whilst the helicopter is in the hover. Any change in collective pitch or throttle (see below) will require a compensating change in pedal pressure.

Collective pitch (up-and-down stick)

This control has no real equivalent in a fixed-wing aircraft, but if anything it bears some similarity to propeller pitch control. It is so-named because it increases and decreases the pitch of the main rotor blades all at the same time, or 'collectively'. It controls lift, and therefore the lift-off, climb and descent of the helicopter.

Throttle

Equivalent to the fixed-wing aircraft's throttle, but requiring greater management and co-ordination. The twist-grip throttle of a helicopter is rather like that of a motorcycle, but rotates the opposite way, and it is mounted on and synchronised with the collective pitch lever. The throttle can be adjusted independent of the collective control, and is used independently in engine starting, warm-up and other rpm adjustments required in flight.

The instructor will ask you to look at the horizon ahead of you and, with you gently holding the cyclic control, ease his control forwards. You will see that the rotor disc dips down, as does the nose of the helicopter. He will then pull his cyclic control slowly back to its starting or neutral position: the disc will rise and the nose of the helicopter will come up. You will have noticed the very small control movements involved, amounting to little more than gentle pressures – all, in fact, that is required. Next will come the sideward movement of the cyclic. Look horizontally to the left, and then gently move the

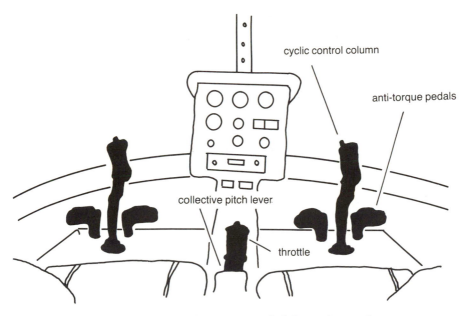

cyclic control column

anti-torque pedals

collective pitch lever

throttle

Figure 12 *The typical arrangement of a helicopter's controls*

cyclic in that direction. You will see the rotor disc dip slightly and the helicopter will start to bank left. Now ease the cyclic over to the right; the right-hand portion of the rotor disc will move downwards and the helicopter will start a bank to the right. Return the cyclic to its central or neutral position and once again the helicopter will resume a level flying attitude.

Next the instructor will demonstrate the *collective pitch lever*. This is normally used in conjunction with the cyclic control, but was omitted from the previous description of controls for reasons of simplicity. Your instructor may demonstrate a small climb. For this he will combine several control functions. He will add a little more power with the throttle (which you will recall is mounted on the end of the collective lever), raise the collective lever, and maintain heading with the anti-torque pedals (mounted on the floor).

Satisfied that you have understood the basic control movements, the instructor will return the helicopter to straight and level flight to demonstrate the last remaining primary controls. These are the *anti-torque* or *tail-rotor pedals* which create the effect of yaw. In the same way that a light aircraft will move its nose either to the left or right when the appropriate rudder pedal is pressed, so too will a helicopter. Push gently on the left pedal and the nose of the helicopter swings left. Push gently on the right pedal and it will swing right. Return the pedals to their central or neutral position and once again the nose of the helicopter will return to pointing straight ahead.

Although I have simplified somewhat the manner in which these controls are co-ordinated and operated, these are the primary effects of a helicopter's

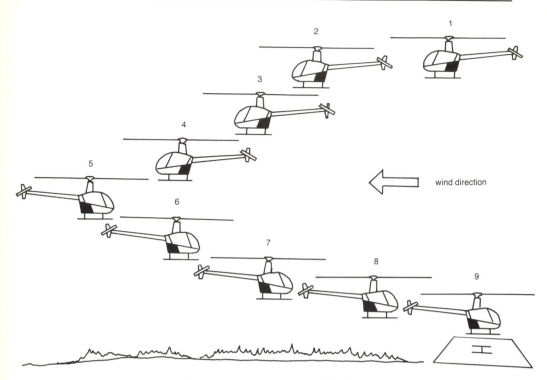

Figure 13 *Normal approach to the hover*

1&2 Abeam landing site. Reduce speed and start approach turn
3&4 Adjust turn into the wind
5&6 Adjust power as necessary
7 Passing 200 ft, level the helicopter
8 Passing 100 ft, begin the transition to the hover
9 Hover at 3 ft, ground speed zero

flight controls. The instructor will demonstrate all these exercises for you and then invite you to have a go for yourself. As this is only a short 'trial' flight he will then head back to the airfield, possibly pointing out one or two local landmarks of interest on the way. Prior to landing he may set up the helicopter in a hover over the airfield's practice area, so that you can see for yourself how easy it is – or appears to be – to remain motionless over a given position. He will then hover-taxi back to a parking spot and land the helicopter.

If you should feel a little sick during or after this flight, do please tell your instructor. There is absolutely nothing to be ashamed of. In no way whatsoever does this mean that you are unsuitable to train as a helicopter pilot. Most helicopters have a degree of noticeable vibration, and if you have not flown much before your 'trial' flight it is hardly surprising if you do feel queasy. Although most students never experience any form of discomfort and fly in complete comfort, for those who do it is usually overcome quite quickly as the lessons progress.

PILOTING THE HELICOPTER

Having completed a 'trial' flight you may decide that becoming a helicopter pilot is for you. You then have to learn to fly one of these marvellous machines, which have been described by both pilots and engineers alike as 'a collection of spare parts flying in loose formation'. Any initial difficulties are usually due to a lack of co-ordination when operating the various controls. Unlike a fixed-wing aircraft (in which, within reason, you can take your hand off the controls when you are in difficulty and allow the aircraft's inherent stability to sort things out), a helicopter is not inherently stable. Good co-ordination is a skill that can only be acquired through practice. For this reason, a student helicopter pilot may initially have more difficulty learning to fly his rotary-winged aircraft than one training to fly a light aeroplane. When the flying course has been completed, however, helicopter handling may arguably be easier: lift-off and landing techniques are simpler; there is a greater range of speed available; and cockpit visibility is superior.

The next time you come to the airfield, then, will be for the first proper lesson of your course. For the first four or five hours of your instruction you will follow more or less the same path as that of a fixed-wing pilot. You will cover the functions of the controls, climbing, descending, turning, and maintaining straight and level flight. When you have mastered these manoeuvres satisfactorily your instructor will begin to teach you the more specialised aspects of helicopter operation, such as hovering, transitions, spot turns and sideward and backward flight.

The exercise which seems to present most difficulty to student helicopter pilots is *hovering*. The ability to hover a helicopter motionless over a fixed spot is the single most important skill a potential rotary-wing pilot has to master: only in this way can the helicopter be landed smoothly. Any sideward movement could tip the machine over, and backward movement might cause the tail-rotor blades to strike the ground.

Vertical lift-off
The helicopter is raised vertically from a spot on the ground to the normal hovering altitude of around 1m (as measured from the bottom of the skids to the ground), with a minimum of lateral and/or fore-and-aft movement.

The helicopter should be faced into the wind before the engine is started. After the starting and run-up of the engine have been completed, using the throttle, set hover rpm keeping the collective pitch lever in its fully down position and the cyclic control stick in its central or neutral position. Apply a touch of anti-torque pedal, to compensate for the engine torque when the skids leave the ground, and smoothly raise the collective pitch lever, simultaneously adjusting the throttle to maintain the proper rpm. (Throttle adjustments should be made by means of a 'slow squeezing movement' – it is often said that if you just think of the adjustment it will be enough.)

1 Set correct rpm
2 Raise collective pitch, forwards with cyclic
3 Continue to climb the helicopter
4 Maintain maximum power without loss of rpm
5 Ease nose forwards and continue normal climb

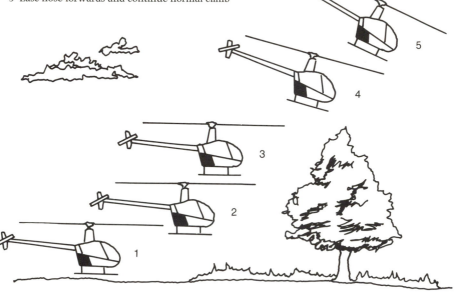

Figure 14 *Take-off from a confined area*

As the helicopter becomes light on its skids, make any necessary cyclic adjustments to ensure a level attitude on becoming airborne. When the skids have left the ground, smoothly adjust the collective pitch setting to effect a hover at approximately 1m of altitude. Whilst in the hover make a clearing turn to check for any other air traffic prior to departing from the lift-off area. Then smoothly and slowly ease the cyclic control forwards from its neutral position to build airspeed, and follow this action immediately by progressively raising the collective pitch lever to prevent settling when the helicopter departs from its ground effect. A lesser amount of anti-torque pedal will now be needed to maintain a straight flight path over the ground.

As forward speed is obtained, continue to increase the collective pitch control. Adjust the cyclic control as necessary to gain one foot of altitude per mile of airspeed. In the transition from the hover to a climbing forward flight the helicopter will be in a 'nose-down' attitude. As it continues to climb forwards, however, and as an optimal climbing speed is achieved, raise the nose of the aircraft to the normal climbing attitude. This is equivalent to its attitude as it stands on level ground. The helicopter will then fly in this attitude until the desired height is reached.

When flying a helicopter one is instructed never to do anything suddenly or violently; gentle manoeuvres are ideal. Hovering in ground effect will account for a good proportion of your training time as you learn to co-ordinate all four of the helicopter's controls. All sorts of little 'dance exercises' are devised, such as: moving the tips of the skids around the four sides of an imaginary square at a height of a metre or so; hovering in a circle whilst always facing the centre or always facing outwards; and flying a rectangle, halting the helicopter at each corner before performing a 90° turn. It's amazing how much fun you can have, and how much of a challenge flying within a metre of the ground, and within 30m (100 ft) of the lift-off spot, can be.

Once it is up in the air and flying along, a helicopter does not behave all that differently from a fixed-wing aircraft, with the exception of the use of anti-torque pedals in turning. Ease the stick forwards and the helicopter speeds up and descends; ease it back and it slows and climbs; ease it to the side and it will bank and turn. The major difference, of course, is the transition from hover to forward flight and back again. Landings are trickier than lift-offs at first, especially if you have some fixed-wing experience and are converting to heli-copter flying. Such pilots often find it difficult to accept the fact that they can terminate the approach by flaring all the way to a complete standstill without losing airspeed, stalling and crashing. An aeroplane-style circuit is flown (downwind, base and final legs), while the pilot picks out the intended landing place through the cockpit canopy, freezes it in position, and watches it grow in size as he approaches at a constant angle of descent. Ideally, as your airspeed decreases steadily and constantly, power must be increased (since the helicop-ter has until now been getting part of its lift from its forward speed through the air). Landing is a skill that is born of constant practice, and you may spend a number of fruitless hours repeatedly flying the same approach too slow, too far out, or speeding helplessly too fast past the intended touch-down point.

The basic course of flying instruction for the Private Helicopter Pilot's Licence comprises 40 flying hours. The course is divided into *dual* (flying with an instructor) and *solo* flying. The Civil Aviation Authority specifies that, of these 40 hours, 10 must have been flown solo. During the first part of your flying training – up to the first 10 or 11 hours, for example – the instructor continually assesses the pupil pilot in readiness for his first solo flight. The timing of this event is of prime importance. If the student is allowed to fly solo before he is ready, the resulting flight could be a dangerous and unnerving affair. If it is left too late, the student may lose interest in flying, with a result-ant deterioration in his personal flying standards. The student who progresses satisfactorily, however, will be permitted to fly solo after 10 or 11 hours of instruction, and it will be the most important 15-minute flight of his training, if not of his airborne career. Many non-flyers think this moment must be nerve-wracking, but this is not in fact the case. Most students actively look forward to going solo, and think themselves ready long before their instructor considers them sufficiently safe and competent.

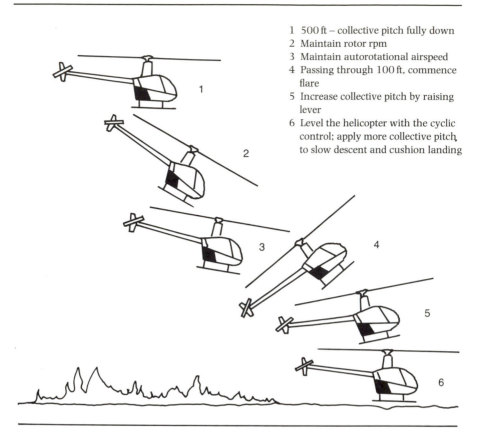

1 500 ft – collective pitch fully down
2 Maintain rotor rpm
3 Maintain autorotational airspeed
4 Passing through 100 ft, commence flare
5 Increase collective pitch by raising lever
6 Level the helicopter with the cyclic control; apply more collective pitch to slow descent and cushion landing

Figure 15 *Autorotation or 'gliding' flight in a helicopter*

The first solo flight is unique, no matter what type of aircraft you are learning to fly. The helicopter pilot will be expected to perform a normal lift-off into the hover and transition into forward flight; to fly a circuit of the airfield; and to return to the hover and land. He will also be expected to cope with any emergency that may arise during the flight – but don't worry about this! You will have been given adequate training to deal with such a remote possibility.

As is the case with fixed-wing aircraft, the first solo flight does not mean the end of dual flying with an instructor. The next few hours of the course involve consolidation exercises of the manoeuvres you have learnt so far, and will also go on to cover some of the more complex areas of helicopter flying such as 'out-of-wind' manoeuvres, sloping ground landings, limited power flight and confined area operations.

As a point of interest, the full Private Helicopter Pilot's Licence air exercise syllabus as used by Sloane Helicopters Ltd is as follows.

● Familiarisation with the helicopter.
● Preparation for flight – starting and stopping the engine and rotor.

- Air experience – an introduction to helicopter flight.
- Effects of controls – what the controls do in forward flight.
- Attitude and power changes.
- Level flight, climbing, descending and turning.
- Basic autorotation – 'gliding' a helicopter.
- Hovering.
- Lift-off and landing.
- Transitions – leaving the hover to achieve forward flight and returning to the hover from forward flight.
- Circuits – an exercise to practise accuracy within a circuit at an airfield.
- First solo – the first of 10 hours of pilot-in-command time; i.e. no flying instructor present.
- Sideward and backward manoeuvres.
- Turns on the spot – turning through 360° in the hover.
- Flight in the *vortex-ring* condition – the nearest event to a stall in a rotary wing.
- Engine-off landing – how to 'glide' a helicopter and land safely without the engine running.
- Advanced autorotations – 'advanced gliding'.
- Forced landings – making an autorotation to a selected landing area.
- Steep turns – turning the aircraft at more extreme angles of bank than are normal.
- Transitions from the hover to the hover at low altitude.
- Quick stops – coming to the hover rapidly but safely from cruise speed at low altitude.
- Pilot navigation – navigating a helicopter away from an airfield.
- Advanced lift-offs, landings and transitions.
- Lift-offs and landings on sloping ground (it's not always level).
- Limited power – operating a helicopter with limited power.
- Confined area – how to approach, enter, manoeuvre in and depart from a confined area safely, i.e. a woodland clearing or a small field.

These exercises will help to improve your co-ordination and confidence in handling a helicopter.

Also included in this period of advanced training will be the important subject of *advanced autorotations*. Although you will have been taught about autorotations prior to your first solo flight, a basic understanding of this flight manoeuvre will be of interest to the reader. If a helicopter were to suffer an engine failure, what do you think would happen? It doesn't have any wings to glide with, so it must surely simply stop flying and crash to the ground. In fact, the rotor blades of a helicopter *are* its wings, and autorotation is the term used to denote the gliding condition of flight when these blades are driven, rather like a windmill, by the action of the wind only. Autorotation therefore allows a helicopter to land safely after an engine failure or other in-flight emergency.

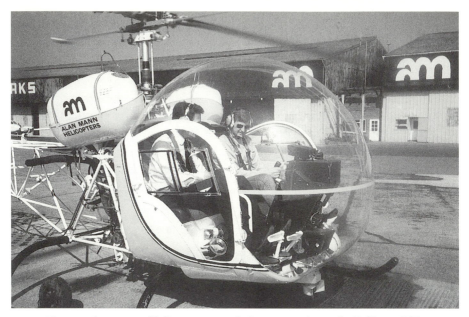

*There are four types of helicopter currently in use as trainers: the Robinson R22,
the Enstrom F28, the Hughes/Schweizer 300 and the Bell 47. Although the
majority of helicopter schools use the Robinson R22, Alan Mann Helicopters of
Fairoaks Airport near Woking in Surrey are one of two UK operators who still
use the venerable Bell 47 (as seen in M.A.S.H.) for basic training*
(Photo: Alan Mann Helicopters)

When engine power is driving the main rotor, the blades produce lift and pull
air down through the rotor system; this enables the helicopter to fly. Should
the engine fail for any reason, however, it can be disengaged from the main
rotor using a clutch, thus allowing the blades to continue turning freely. The
rotor blades will go on producing lift, but air will now flow upwards through
the rotor system as the helicopter descends or 'glides' down to make a per-
fectly safe, controlled landing.

Following all this consolidation training in advanced conditions of helicopter flight comes the navigation phase. Thus far your lessons will have been
teaching you how to handle the helicopter itself. The navigation phase will
now show you how to use it as a tool to get from one destination to another.
Many students approach the subject of navigation apprehensively, but,
although it can be a complex and difficult subject in its higher forms, your
instructor will ensure that you enter the subject from the shallow end. You
have a great advantage at this stage over your fixed-wing equivalent in that,
should you for any reason find yourself unsure of your position, you can
always slow the helicopter down to walking pace and read the road-signs.
However, to try and ensure that you never do get yourself lost, you will start

this phase by flying a number of short dual cross-country flights. These will often be in the form of a triangle. After a couple of such flights, you will go on to fly them yourself as a solo exercise.

During this period of training you will undergo a navigation flight test. Your examiner may well be the Chief Flying Instructor of your helicopter school. At the end of this you will complete a long solo cross-country flight around a triangular course, performing landings away at two other airfields. One of the qualifying legs for this exercise will be at least 50 miles long.

PREPARATION FOR THE LICENCE

By this stage you will be nearing the end of your course of lessons and you will start to revise, with the help of your instructor, all the exercises you have learnt so far. You will go over all the subjects in the syllabus two or three times to check that you are aware of and competent in all areas of private helicopter operation. Then, if both you and your instructor feel that you are ready, you will attempt the General Flying Test. Again, your examiner is likely to be the Chief Flying Instructor of your own school. The test itself will take approximately one hour to complete, and the examiner will simply assess whether or not you are ready to exercise the privileges that go with the Private Helicopter Pilot's Licence. In making this decision he carries a certain heavy responsibility; once you have qualified for your licence you may carry passengers and fly a British-registered helicopter anywhere in the world.

During the test you will be required to demonstrate competence in the full sequence of flying manoeuvres, and in the correct observation of relevant ground instructions and air traffic control procedures. The rules of the flying test require that the student under examination occupy the right-hand cockpit seat, the examiner the left-hand seat. The test will then follow the Civil Aviation Authority approved helicopter syllabus. The student will be assessed on airmanship, including circuit procedure, airfield discipline, the setting and use of the flight instruments fitted to the helicopter, pre-flight inspection, engine start and run-up procedure.

The PPL(H) General Flying Test may include some or all of the following.

- Pre-flight inspection.
- Engine starting procedure and 'running up'.
- Air taxiing.
- Lift-off, hovering and landing into wind.
- Lift-off, turn 360° each way in hovering flight.
- Cross-wind landing within the limitations of the helicopter type.
- Straight and level flight at pre-determined airspeeds and power settings.
- Climbing and descending turns.
- Steep turns at a constant altitude and airspeed.

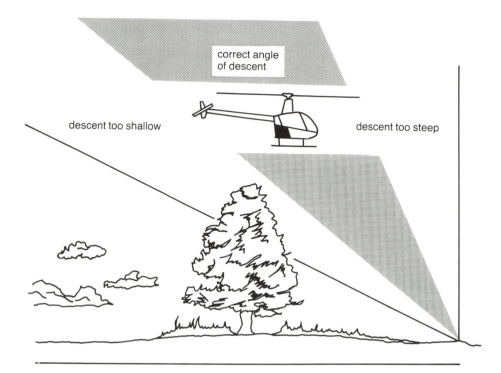

Figure 16 *Flying a steep approach*

- Entry into autorotation and overshoot procedure.
- Landing in simulated autorotation into a selected area.
- Recognition and correction of over-pitching.
- Limited power lift-off and landing.
- Action in the event of an in-flight fire.
- Flight into and out of a restricted landing area.
- Steep approach.
- Aircraft shut-down procedure.

The examiner will also ask you some specific questions about the helicopter on which you are being tested, and he will expect your flying to be a good deal more polished than your instructor did when he sent you off on your first solo. You will almost certainly be asked to attend a re-test if you hover-taxi carelessly, fail to carry out your checks, disobey radio instructions or indulge in any other malpractice. If all goes well, however, your school will post off the results of your written ground examinations, together with your log-book and formal licence application duly signed and stamped, and only a few weeks later you will receive your own PPL(H).

THE GROUND EXAMINATIONS

Your theoretical knowledge will be tested by way of a number of multiple choice examinations. These are quite straightforward and are nothing to get unduly worried about. The ground school lectures your instructor will have been giving you, plus the textbooks you will have been studying during your course, will amply have prepared you to sit them. The papers will present you

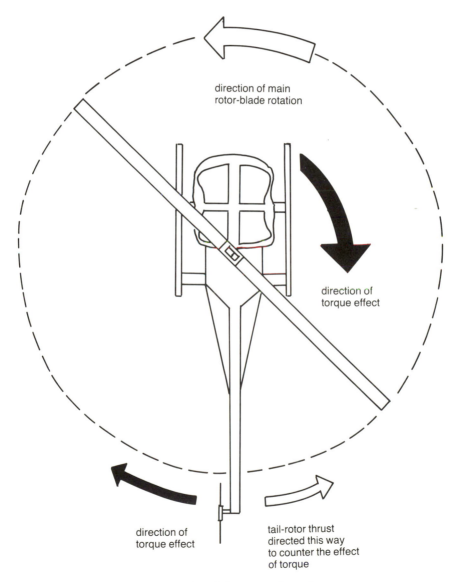

direction of main
rotor-blade rotation

direction of
torque effect

direction of
torque effect

tail-rotor thrust
directed this way
to counter the effect
of torque

Figure 17 *Why a helicopter needs a tail rotor*

with three possible answers to each question: all you have to do is to tick the right one. The usual pass-mark required is 70%. Some helicopter schools have their own preference as to when you take the individual examinations: for example, the air-law examination before your first solo; the navigation examination before the navigation phase of your course. Others simply require you to sit the examinations in one batch at the end of your flying course. Whatever the case, the whole series of examinations must be passed successfully before you can be granted your pilot's licence by the Civil Aviation Authority.

The subjects for the ground examinations themselves are: navigation; meteorology; aviation law; helicopter technical; and, newly introduced in 1992, human performance and limitations. The individual examination subjects are common to fixed-wing and helicopter students, and have therefore already been covered in some detail in Chapter 1. The only difference is in the helicopter technical examination. Although the subject matter of this examination is broadly similar to that of its fixed-wing equivalent, helicopter flight theory and aerodynamics are considerably more complex. A solid base of knowledge will be required, not only of the individual helicopter type being used for instruction, but also of subjects such as *disc loading, blade coning, gyroscopic precession, hunting, blade stall, advancing blade, translational lift, torque,* and *transverse flow effect.*

MEDICAL REQUIREMENTS

The medical requirements of the private helicopter pilot are identical to those of a light aircraft pilot. You will need to hold a Class 3 medical certificate issued by a Civil Aviation Authority authorised medical examiner. The typical charge for this examination at the time of writing is between £35 and £40, and the requisite standard of fitness approximately equates to that of a life insurance medical. Your local GP will not be able to issue you with the certificate, but your helicopter school will supply you with a list of approved local doctors who will. You need not obtain a medical certificate before you start taking helicopter instruction, but since it also serves the dual purpose of being a student pilot's licence it makes sense. You *must* have one before you fly solo.

The examination itself is not unduly rigorous. It will include a general questionnaire on your record of health and checks on your hearing, respiratory system and blood pressure. If you normally wear glasses or contact lenses there should be no problem provided that your eyesight defects can be corrected to acceptable limits – being colour blind will however restrict you to flying in daylight hours only. Applicants over 40 years of age must also undergo an electrocardiograph test (ECG) and an audiogram. The certificate itself is valid for five years if you are under 40, two years if you are between 40 and 50, one year if you are between 50 and 70 and six months if you are aged 70 years or over. There are some medical conditions which may prevent you from being granted a certificate: these include cardiac problems; diabetes that requires constant medication; and epilepsy. It is probably wise, then, to complete your medical before starting any helicopter lessons, thus saving both time and money if you should fail the examination for any reason.

LICENCE RENEWALS

You have completed your course of helicopter instruction, passed the General Flying Test and written examinations, and at last you hold the coveted PPL(H). But how do you keep it? Once obtained, the licence is permanent and valid for life, so earning it is a one-off expense. As a private pilot, however, you must always maintain a current medical certificate, and every 13 months you will be required to present your flying log-book to an instructor/examiner for stamping to show that you have met the experience level required within that period. In effect this means that you must spend at least five hours in flight within the 13 months in order that a 'Certificate of Experience' may be entered into your log-book, thus re-validating it for another 13 months. Of these five hours required by the Civil Aviation Authority, three at least must be completed solo. In practice, however, you should aim to fly as often as time and money will allow. The legal minimum of five hours is in truth nowhere near sufficient for you to remain sharp and competent, and many schools will insist that you fly at least once a month or else undergo a dual safety check with an instructor. Failure to complete the required amount of solo flying within the specified time will not automatically invalidate your licence, but you would have to take another General Flying Test to renew its privileges.

HELICOPTER RATINGS

As his knowledge and flying experience increases, the private helicopter pilot may wish to add one or all of the following ratings to his licence.

Night rating
A night rating enables the pilot to fly as pilot-in-command of a helicopter at night. It can be obtained after completing a short night-flying course of approximately five hours.

Turbine conversion
A turbine rating is necessary for a conversion from a piston-engined machine to a turbine-powered helicopter. A pilot undergoing conversion from the Robinson R-22 to the Bell Jetranger generally requires at least five hours of dual flying instruction. The Jetranger allows the pilot a greater freedom of operation because its gas turbine engine is controlled automatically, instead

of by the twist grip throttle. It offers superior speed, performance and pay-load in all aspects of the flight envelope.

Twin rating

If you and your wallet plan to step up from a single- to a twin-engined helicopter you will need to obtain a twin rating. The rating will involve a conversion course of approximately five to eight hours, as well as the completion of a twin-engined flight test. It is likely to cost around the same price – depending on the type of machine – as an entire course of basic helicopter instruction.

Mountain flying

Although this is not a rating course as such, many helicopter schools offer training in mountain flying. Given the extreme downdraughts and dangerous weather conditions that can be encountered in hilly and mountainous country, it is wise to take this course if you are going to be flying regularly in the more remote parts of Scotland or Wales.

HOW MUCH WILL IT COST?

Whilst flying a rotary-wing aircraft is one of the most exhilarating forms of powered flying available, it is also one of the most expensive. Only the

The Bell 206 Jetranger is a five-place turbine-engined helicopter used for charter work and advanced training (Photo: Alan Mann Helicopters)

relatively fortunate few can afford to fly them for fun, because the high operating costs are usually offset against business or commercial use. Its high cost can be attributed to the following four factors:

- higher and more frequent maintenance costs than are incurred for fixed-wing light aircraft;
- higher insurance premiums;
- a higher capital cost;
- higher salaries commanded by helicopter instructors (who are often ex-military pilots).

Prices at helicopter schools are reasonably consistent, but can vary by up to £60 an hour; so, although you should aim if at all possible to learn at the school nearest to you, it does pay to shop around. There are now increasing numbers of helicopter schools in operation, but still far fewer than there are fixed-wing clubs and schools, so you may have to be prepared to travel that little bit further for your training. Telephone those nearest to home by consulting the 'Where to Fly Helicopters' list on pp. 174–8, and then pay each one a visit before parting with any money. First impressions are important: you will be paying a lot of hard-earned money for your training, so make sure that you are going to get good value for it. Are the helicopters at your chosen school clean and well maintained? How many instructors does it have? Are there separate classrooms for ground-school briefings? Are the staff attentive?

When choosing a school, the potential helicopter student is perhaps more fortunate than his fixed-wing counterpart because helicopter schools tend to be very customer orientated – unlike some light aircraft operations which can offer a very poor 'take-it-or-leave-it' standard of service. Most can arrange to offer training on a full-time basis if you prefer to learn this way. In this case the necessary flying can usually be completed in a fortnight to three weeks, according to the student's aptitude (and, of course, the vagaries of the British weather). Alternatively, training can be on an *ad-hoc* basis to suit both the student and the school.

At the time of writing the average hourly rate for dual instruction at helicopter schools is between £160 and £220, so it would be wise to budget realistically for around £7–8,500 for the whole PPL(H) course. When you are selecting a school at which to take lessons remember to check if VAT and landing fees are included in the price. Also, don't forget to ask if there is a discount; most helicopter schools will offer a discount for blocks of flying hours – typically 10, bought and paid for in advance – and this can reduce the hourly flying rate by approximately £10. Consider very carefully, however, if you are offered a discount: a small number of operators – mostly fixed-wing schools – have collapsed in recent years, leaving students who have paid in advance with little hope of recovering their money. Most schools will accept the popular credit cards such as Access and Barclaycard, other mastercards and visa cards and American Express and Diners Club.

*The Westland/Aerospatiale Gazelle is available for advanced training and turbine
conversions, alongside Bell Jetrangers and Hughes 500s. It is easily identified, as
its tail rotor is totally enclosed inside a streamlined fin*
(Photo: Westland Helicopters)

Because of the high costs involved, most initial helicopter training is conducted in light piston-engined machines such as the Robinson R-22, Sch-
weizer 300C or Bell 47. Should the student wish, however, a gas-turbine-
powered helicopter such as a Bell Jetranger may be used from the outset for
basic flying training. If a helicopter student trains for his licence exclusively
on one of these, the overall cost of training will be more than twice the price of
the standard course. The average hourly rate of a more powerful helicopter
type like the Jetranger works out at approximately £450 per flying hour.

AFTER OBTAINING YOUR PPL(H)

Once the helicopter pilot has qualified for his licence the countryside becomes
a playground for his highly versatile machine. He does not need any runways
or airfields from which to lift off and land, and is free to operate from farmers'
fields and private property as long as it is done within safety limitations and
permission of the landowner has been obtained. Office to office, factory to
factory, construction site to construction site or any other combination you
care to think of, the helicopter is conveniently quick and flexible. The ease and

pleasure of speeding over the congestion and traffic delays below means arriving at your destination with a confident flourish. This is definitely what helicopters are all about. Using a helicopter saves valuable time that would otherwise be spent on the road enduring the weariness of long-distance car travel. Helicopters offer quick point-to-point commuting as shown by these typical journey timings.

From Southampton to:
Exeter – 55 minutes
Bristol – 35 minutes
Cardiff – 50 minutes
Birmingham – 60 minutes
London – 40 minutes

From East London to:
Dover – 35 minutes
Felixstowe – 40 minutes
Norwich – 50 minutes
Southampton – 45 minutes
Hull – 90 minutes

When operating a helicopter over towns, cities or other built-up areas, certain safety rules must be applied. Aviation law requires that the helicopter pilot must not fly below a height that would enable it to land safely without risk to persons or property in the event of an engine failure or other in-flight emergency and subsequent autorotation. Certain parts of the City of London are forbidden to helicopter traffic. There are, however, special airlanes set out for the use of helicopters and the River Thames forms the main thoroughfare for metropolitan helicopter traffic. The banks of the river and the adjoining land above the high-tide mark present a natural emergency landing ground in the event of a forced touch-down. Also on the river is the capital's one and only heliport, the Westland heliport set on the Thames' South Bank at Battersea.

'Dos and Don'ts' for the private helicopter pilot

● A private helicopter pilot must not fly for 'Hire or Reward'. This means that as a pilot you may not receive any remuneration for your flying. To fly for reward you would need to qualify for one of the professional qualifications such as a CPL(H) or ATPL(H). You may take a friend along for the ride and share the cost of the helicopter's hire between you; what you cannot do is hire a helicopter from your school and then charter yourself out, to your employer for instance, for payment.

● If you are caught out in bad weather conditions beyond your experience, slow the helicopter down to walking pace or set down in a farmer's field until the worst of it has passed you by. (In this respect you have a significant advantage over a fixed-wing pilot.) However, the vast majority of adverse weather is forecastable; if you are planning to fly, watch the television weather reports and call one of the phone-in weather lines to get a proper meteorological forecast before setting out. If during any flight you do encounter any conditions beyond your experience, such as strong turbulence or particularly heavy rain, *turn back*.

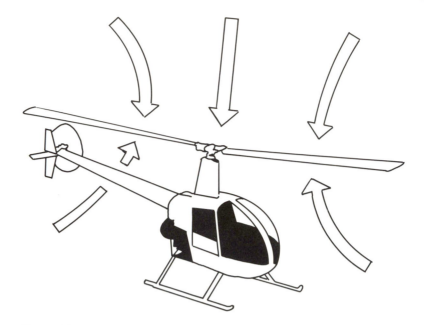

Figure 18 *Rotor airflow of a helicopter in autorotation or 'gliding flight'. When the engine is driving the main rotor, air is pulled downwards through the rotor system. When the engine is not providing power – i.e. when the helicopter is in autorotational or 'gliding' flight – air flows upwards through the rotor system. It is this upward airflow that keeps the rotor turning, allowing a safe, controlled landing to be made in the event of an engine failure*

Private helicopter travel is one of the safest ways in which to fly – statistically much safer than the family car. If you keep to flying in reasonable weather, thoroughly prepare your flight plan, make sure that you have enough fuel plus reserves for your intended journey (because of the slower cruising speed of a helicopter, wind has a much greater effect on helicopter range than it does on faster fixed-wing aircraft – it is a good idea, therefore, to allow a comfortable margin of fuel reserve on every trip), and apply plenty of common sense, you will not go far wrong.

Now that you are a fully fledged helicopter pilot you will be able to hire helicopters for pleasure flying, business or hour building. Most schools offer a hire facility to their former students, and there are also a number of private companies and individuals that hire helicopters by the hour, the half-day or the full day, or by leasing blocks or 'parcels' of flying hours. The hire rates can often be substantially lower than the sums you will have been paying during your training. Although rental is very popular, a large proportion of students do end up buying their own new or used helicopter at the end of their course. At the time of writing, prices for a small Robinson helicopter range from around £60,000 for a used machine to around £85,000 for a new model, depending on options and extra equipment fitted.

Chapter 3

THE MICROLIGHT

If you want to go flying for fun in a lightweight powered aircraft, but you don't have a fortune to spend, then the microlight could well be right for you. Purchase and running costs are easily within the range of the average pocket, and you could learn to fly at a microlight school near you.

Although you may think that the microlight owes its origins to 'those magnificent men in their flying machines', it in fact developed from earlier

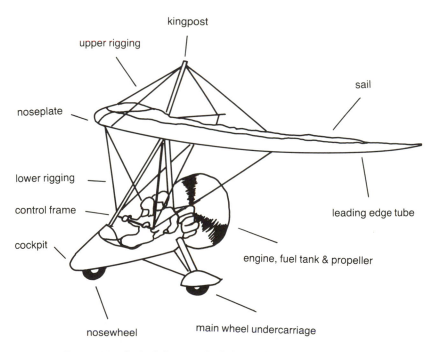

Figure 19 *The 'trike' or weightshift microlight and its components*

This flex-wing microlight is a Gemini Flash manufactured by Mainair Sports Ltd., a long-established builder of two-seat and single-seat trikes. It is taking off from a quiet landing strip (Photo: Eastern Daily Press)

types of powered hang glider and has grown in sophistication until today's standards of microlight construction can almost match those of a full production line General Aviation light aircraft. Microlight aircraft fall into two groups: *flexwing* or 'weight-shift'; and *fixed-wing* or 'three-axis'. The former is generally known as a 'trike'. With its distinctive delta-shape wing the trike is capable of doing most of the things a conventional aircraft can do; it is basically a powered hang glider controlled by a horizontal bar rigidly connected to the wing. The wing is free to pivot in the desired direction as the pilot pushes or pulls on the bar. The main drawback is that the microlight's control inputs are the reverse of those of the light aircraft and the rotary wing.

When the control bar on a trike is pushed forwards the aircraft will climb; when it is pulled back it will descend. To bank to the left the bar is swung over to the right, and to turn right the bar is moved to the left. Although it might sound rather basic and perhaps a little bit hit-and-miss, the pilot has adequate control and flying a trike is really quite easy. The take-off roll is very short – when the speed reaches about 20 mph the control bar is pushed forwards to its limit and the aircraft is rotated off the ground. Once airborne the pilot must pull the bar back immediately into the midway position. The aircraft will then gain speed and climb away at about 30 mph.

Once you are in the air you will find flying a trike simple and relaxing, requiring less concentration than other types of microlight machine. The approach and landing should be flown with plenty of speed: a burst of power just before landing will get the nose up and ensure a smooth touch-down. The main advantages of trikes over other types of aircraft are their simplicity and their portability. The design and development costs are a fraction of those of even the simplest three-axis type; for example, there are no control runs or control cables, and all are transportable on a small trailer towed behind the family car. The wing folds quickly and easily into a carrying rack on the trailer, allowing the aircraft to be taken home and stored in the average garage. This saves expensive hangarage costs.

The other main type of microlight is the fixed-wing or 'three-axis' machine. This is now available in a wide range of designs and is conventional in appearance, with a wing on either side of a fuselage, a tailplane with elevators, or an all-flying surface and a fin or rudder. Powered by either a pusher or puller propeller and fitted with one or two seats, flying this new generation of three-axis machine is almost identical to flying conventional light aircraft, the only real differences being a slower cruising speed and lighter weight.

LEARNING TO FLY A MICROLIGHT

Flying a microlight aircraft is exhilarating and fun, and once you have got your own PPL it is ridiculously cheap. Provided that you receive proper training from the start it is also very safe. Although the sport was initially

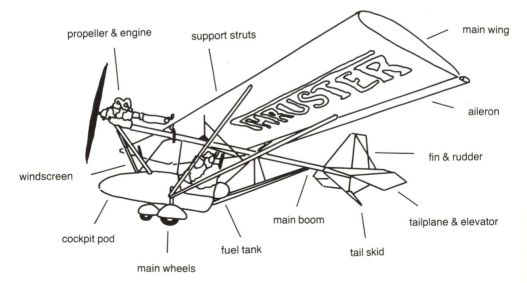

Figure 20 *The 'three-axis' or conventional microlight and its components*

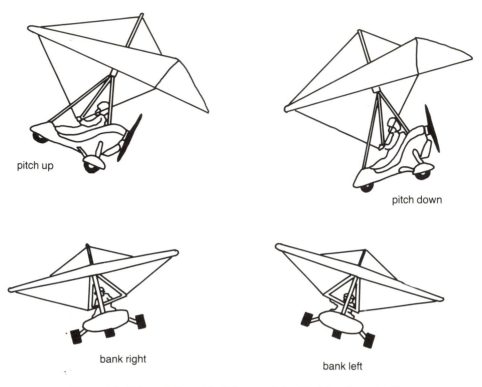

pitch up

pitch down

bank right

bank left

Figure 21 *Effects of the weightshift control bar. Pushing the control bar forwards makes the trike pitch up and the aircraft will climb. Pulling the control bar backwards makes the trike pitch down and the aircraft will descend. Swinging it left will bank the trike to the right; swinging it right will bank the trike to the left*

promoted on the basis that anyone could build and fly their own machine without any training – there were no rules and regulations to observe and no licence of any sort was needed – the resultant crashes and pilot injuries, some of them fatal, caused the Civil Aviation Authority to initiate sweeping safety controls. The introduction of microlight legislation in 1981 saw many of the earlier pioneers drift away from the sport, the new training requirements and safety rules perhaps biting too deeply into their idea of being free to do their own thing. Today, however, with the advent of British Microlight Aircraft Association control, greater numbers of people than ever are taking to the skies in a microlight.

So how safe are microlights now? As from January 1st 1984 it has been illegal for any microlight aircraft to have been constructed and flown unless:

- the manufacturer of the aircraft is approved by the Civil Aviation Authority, or the aircraft has been constructed under the supervision of the Popular Flying Association;

- the aircraft has a valid permit to fly and a noise certificate;
- the pilot has been trained by a rated flying instructor holding either a PPL (Group D) or a PPL (Group A).

Freedom to fly demands responsibility, so a pilot must have a licence or be under training with the aim of obtaining one. To fly a microlight aircraft solo, with or without a passenger, you must be in possession of a PPL (aeroplanes) Group D. To obtain this licence you must meet the following stipulations.

- You must be at least 17 years old.
- You must be in possession of a current medical certificate.
- All the flying instruction you receive must be under direct supervision of a Civil Aviation Authority authorised instructor.
- Within the 12 months preceding your application for a Private Pilot's Licence you must have passed a series of three simple, multiple choice written examinations plus an oral test on the particular type of microlight aircraft you wish to fly.

Most microlight clubs and schools offer a 'trial' flight facility; this is an excellent way to sample the sport before committing yourself to a course of flying lessons. For 15 minutes or so you will climb up to around 300 m (1,000 ft), then perform a gentle descent with the instructor demonstrating the effects of the controls. For the person who wants something a little more substantial there are one-day introductory courses which cover all aspects of the sport – usually through the use of videos and briefings. The highlight of the day is a familiarisation flight in a two-seat microlight aircraft.

There are two types of Private Pilot's Licence available to the student microlight pilot, the difference between them being the amount of training required and the privileges afforded after qualification.

RESTRICTED LICENCE

For this licence you will be required to undergo a minimum of 15 hours of flying instruction, of which at least seven must be solo. You must pass a General Flying Test conducted by an authorised instructor/examiner. The solo content must be completed within the nine-month period immediately prior to your application to the Civil Aviation Authority for a licence.

Flying on a restricted microlight pilot's licence means that you cannot fly when the surface wind exceeds 15 knots, when the cloud base is below 1,000 ft, or when the in-flight visibility is less than 4 miles. You will not be allowed to fly outside a radius of 6 miles from your point of take-off, or carry any passengers until you have flown for a further 25 hours, a minimum of 10 hours of which you must fly as pilot-in-command.

UNRESTRICTED LICENCE

A microlight student may work towards an unrestricted licence from the start of his training. In addition to the requirements already listed above for the restricted licence, the applicant must also complete a further 10 hours of flight instruction, of which at least five must be navigation training under the direct supervision of the student's instructor. During this navigation training the student must complete two solo cross-country flights, each of which is at least 40 nautical miles in length, and make a field-out landing during each at a site at least 15 nautical miles from his point of take-off.

THE GROUND EXAMINATIONS

Just as in the more conventional airsports of light and rotary-wing aviation, the microlight course demands that you pass a series of simple written examinations before your Private Pilot's Licence can be issued. The examinations themselves are straightforward multiple-choice papers which present you with three possible answers to each question: two of these answers will be plausible enough but wrong; you must identify the one correct answer and mark it with a tick. The usual pass-mark required is 70%. The subjects for the ground examinations themselves are: navigation; meteorology; air law; technical (principles of flight); and human performance and limitations.

Navigation
Given the vast improvement in the performance of microlight aircraft over recent years and their ability now to undertake impressive cross-country flights, knowing how to navigate accurately and safely is of prime importance. Your instructor will have covered much of what you need to know to pass this examination during the practical phase of your course. Questions that may be included in the paper are: locating and plotting positions; dead reckoning and the calculation of headings; ground speed; fuel consumption; and time *en-route*.

Meteorology
As microlights are significantly lighter and less weather tolerant than conventional light aircraft, an understanding of weather systems and the conditions required for their formation is vitally important. You can expect to be asked about cloud types; the different types of fog and the conditions required for their formation; the importance of temperature and humidity; and frontal systems and stability.

Air law
A thorough understanding of air law is important, since you will after all be sharing the same sky with a whole host of other users, from airline jets and

military fighters to hot-air balloons and hang gliders. The paper on this subject may include questions on types of airspace, quadrantal flight rules, ground signals, and operating rules and regulations.

Technical (principles of flight)
Given that microlights, particularly flexwing 'trikes', are simple aircraft, this examination is of a fairly basic nature. You will be expected to demonstrate a knowledge of the particular microlight type you fly, plus a general understanding of aerodynamics and the principles of flight.

Human performance and limitations
Since 1992, microlight pilots have been required to demonstrate a general understanding of the factors affecting our ability to fly safely. Although it covers the same subjects of aviation medicine and psychology, it is in fact a simplified version of the paper sat by PPL(A) and PPL(H) applicants.

MEDICAL REQUIREMENTS

Unlike the light aircraft or helicopter pilot, you do not need to undergo an aviation medical in order to fly a microlight. All that is required is a declaration of fitness made by you and countersigned by your own doctor. You do not necessarily have to have your declaration of fitness signed up before you start taking lessons, but, since it also serves the dual purpose of being a student pilot's licence, your doctor must sign it before you can fly solo. The certificate will ask you to declare to the best of your knowledge and belief that you arc in good health, that you are not receiving any medical care at the time the declaration is signed, and that as far as you are aware you have not suffered and are not suffering from any of the following conditions: epilepsy; fits; a recent severe head injury; recurrent fainting, giddiness or blackouts; high blood pressure; coronary artery disease; insulin-controlled diabetes; any psychiatric disorder; or any other disorder liable to cause incapacitation. The declaration is valid for five years if you are aged under 40, for two years if you are between 40 and 50, for one year if you are between 50 and 70, and for six months if you are aged 70 or over.

LICENCE RENEWALS

Having completed the relatively short course of flying instruction for the microlight licence, passed your written examinations, and taken your General Flying Test, you will now have your own PPL (Group D). In order to keep it you must always maintain a valid declaration of fitness, and every 13 months you must log at least five flying hours (at least three of which must be as pilot-in-command). At the end of each 13-month period your log-book must have a 'Certificate of Experience' stamped into it by an instructor/examiner which will re-validate it for another 13 months. Although the figure of five hours is the legal minimum laid down by the Civil Aviation Authority, in practice this is not enough time to keep your piloting skills current and you should aim to fly as often as time and money will allow. Failure to complete the required amount of flying within the specified period will not automatically invalidate your licence, but you will be required to take another General Flying Test to renew its privileges.

THE BRITISH MICROLIGHT AIRCRAFT ASSOCIATION

The British Microlight Aircraft Association represents in the widest sense those people interested in the operation of microlight aircraft in the United Kingdom. This organisation seeks the support of all those involved with microlights – pilots, constructors, commercial bodies, and all those still making up their minds about whether or not this is the type of airsport they want to take up.

First formed around 1979, known then as the British Minimum Aircraft Association, it served as a forum for the discussion and exchange of ideas on the potential capabilities and flying techniques associated with the ultralight aircraft. Soon changing its name to the British Microlight Aircraft Association, however, its role grew rapidly as the Civil Aviation Authority delegated to it the responsibility for:

- the issue and renewal of 'Permits to Fly';
- the issue and re-validation of 'Exemptions';
- the type acceptance of pre-January 1984 microlight aircraft;
- the issue of the Private Pilot's Licence (Group D);
- the issue and re-validation of flying instructor ratings.

Excluding overseas subscriptions there are currently four levels of membership, and at the time of writing these are costed as follows: single membership for one year £25.50; family membership for one year £35.75; single membership for three years £76.50; and family membership for three years £107.25. None of the above prices include the one-off joining fee of £3.00. Membership of the Association brings the member:

- a bi-monthly copy of the Association's magazine *Flight Line*;
- a bi-monthly newsletter in the months between the issues of the magazine;
- a bi-monthly technical newsletter;
- free advice on technical matters from a full-time technical officer;
- free advice on the legal status of any microlight aircraft that you may wish to buy;

● access to third-party legal liability insurance;
● access to other types of insurance at considerably reduced rates.

HOW MUCH WILL IT COST?

Bearing in mind that no form of private flying is or ever will be truly cheap, the cost of microlight aviation has been estimated at around a third of that of conventional light aviation. Training rates for dual microlight flying instruction are approximately half those charged at light aircraft clubs and schools and, considering that the minimum experience required for a restricted PPL (Group D) can be as low as 15 flying hours (against a minimum of 40 for a light aircraft licence), it is possible to become a microlight pilot for well under £1,000.

At the time of writing (1992), the average hourly rate for dual instruction at microlight flying clubs and schools is around £45, so it would be realistic to budget for around £1,000 for the restricted licence course and £1,500 for the 25-hour unrestricted course. These are all inclusive, but textbooks, examination fees and the issue of the licence itself are extra. If after taking a 'trial' flight you are sure that you have found the right airsport for you, and are confident enough to consider purchasing your own new or used microlight aircraft, you will find that most of the clubs and schools offer the facility of flying instruction on your own machine. Prices for this are typically between £30 and £35 per hour, so the cost of getting your licence in this way can be very economical indeed. Prices for new machines vary from about £6,000 to £20,000 depending on the degree of sophistication, while thoroughly airworthy older types and used aircraft can be bought for as little as £1,000. Maintenance of the machine can be carried out by the owner at home, subject only to a check by a British Microlight Aircraft Association inspector if you modify or carry out any repairs to your aircraft. Check-flights and periodic inspections cost from around £40, and annual renewal of the aircraft's 'Permit to Fly' or 'Exemption Certificate' is around £45. With no hangarage costs and very low fuel consumption figures, the direct operating costs of your own machine can be as low as around £10 per flying hour.

AFTER OBTAINING YOUR MICROLIGHT LICENCE

Now that you are a pilot, by all means spread your wings a little and make the most of your new licence. Remember, however, that you will only have between 20 and 30 hours of flying experience and are still very much a learner. Your PPL, whilst admirable, is nothing more than a licence to learn. No matter how adept a pilot you are, or think you are, stay within the limits laid down in training until you have built up more practical flying experience.

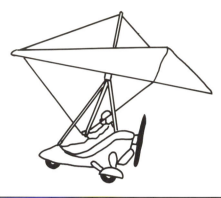

3 Once into the air, pull the control bar back
slowly to maintain a steady climbing
attitude

Figure 22 *A simplified weightshift microlight take-off sequence*

Figure 23 *A simplified weightshift microlight landing sequence*

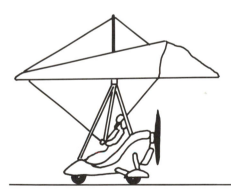 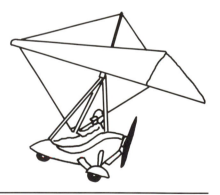

4 Hold the wing slightly nose-down, and
allow the speed to decay

3 With the ground only 2–3 ft below, flare
the trike for landing by pushing the control
bar forwards

There is a lovely saying in aviation: 'Flying itself is not inherently dangerous,
but the air, to an even greater extent than the sea, is terribly unforgiving of
any carelessness, foolishness, incapacity or neglect.'

The most obvious obstacle to smooth, safe flying in this country is our often
foul and dirty weather. Even the most experienced professional pilots can be
caught out by Mother Nature, and they will be operating far more sophisti-

2 As take-off speed is reached, push the control bar forwards to rotate the microlight

1 At full power begin take-off run holding wing steady

2 Nearing the ground, check the rate of descent by moving the control bar forwards

1 With the power reduced and the control bar pulled back the wing will be in a nose-down attitude and the 'trike' will descend

cated, weather-tolerant aircraft than your small microlight. If you plan to fly, even if it is only in the local area, watch the television weather forecasts, call one of the many phone-in weather lines, and get a proper meteorological briefing at your club or school. If during the subsequent flight you encounter any conditions beyond your experience, such as strong winds or heavy rain, *turn back*.

Figure 24 *A simplified three-axis microlight take-off sequence*

3 As take-off speed is reached, rotate the
   microlight off the ground and maintain a
   steady climbing attitude

Figure 25 *A simplified three-axis microlight landing sequence*

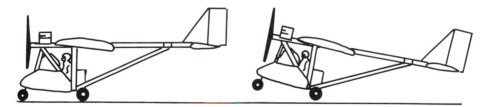

4 Allow speed to decay before braking

3 Maintain a gentle backward pressure on
   the control column until the main wheels
   touch down. Keep holding back the control
   column to keep weight off the nose wheel
   and allow aerodynamic braking to help
   slow the microlight

Failure to turn back in deteriorating weather conditions is one of the main causes of General Aviation accidents in the world. It is sometimes nicknamed *'press-on-itis'* and it is a killer. There is no shame whatsoever in turning your microlight around because of turbulent conditions or poor visibility. It comes under the heading of good airmanship, which we outlined earlier; it is also called common sense.

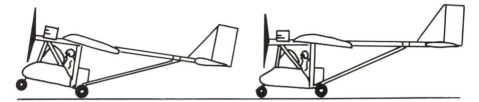

2 Keep the weight of the nose wheel off the ground during the take-off run with a slight backward pressure on the control column. Keep the aircraft straight by use of rudder

1 At full power, begin take-off run

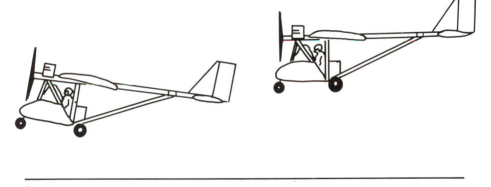

2 Descent checked, power reduced, allow the microlight to sink towards the runway

1 Microlight on approach to the runway, lined up on the centre line

'Dos and Don'ts' for the microlight pilot

● A private pilot may not fly for what is called 'Hire or Reward'. This means that the pilot may not receive any remuneration for his flying. To fly for reward one must qualify for one of the professional licences, such as a BCPL, CPL or ATPL. You may take along a friend to share the cost of hiring the aircraft; what you may not do is hire a microlight from your club or school and then charter yourself out for payment.

- If you fly over your local football team on a Saturday afternoon to cheer them on from the air, you are breaking civil air law. This states that an aircraft must not fly over or within 915 m (3,000 ft) of any open-air assembly of more than 1,000 people. This rule may be waived only if written permission from the event organisers and the Civil Aviation Authority has been obtained in advance.

MICROLIGHT AIRCRAFT

If any reader wishes to find out more about individual microlight aircraft, manufacturers and importers of the various types will be only too happy to supply further information. The British Microlight Aircraft Association will be able to provide you with their addresses and telephone numbers, although the following list contains details of most of the major contractors and some basic details of the microlight machines available. However, as the sport is rapidly growing and new models are always coming on to the market, contact with individual firms should always be made to obtain accurate information on price, specification and status of certification.

Flexwing or 'trike' aircraft

Pegasus XL
Many Pegasus XL flexwings have been manufactured, and they have a very well-deserved reputation for being safe and easy to fly. As they are very popular as a club training aircraft you will almost certainly find one or two in use at your local microlight club or school.

Available from: Solar Wings, 56 George Lane, Marlborough, Wiltshire (telephone (0672) 515066).

Flash 2 Alpha
From the long-established flexwing manufacturers Mainair Microlights, the Flash 2 Alpha comes in both single- and dual-seat models and has many impressive endurance flights to its credit, most notably Richard Meridith-Hardy's flight to South Africa in 1985.

Available from: Mainair Sports, Unit 2, Alma Industrial Estate, Rochdale, Lancashire (telephone (0706) 55134).

Puma and Raven
Both of these microlight types are two-seat designs with long, successful histories and a number of pioneering flights to their credit. Kent-based

The Pegasus Quasar is quite distinctive in that its cockpit and undercarriage are
fully contained within a streamlined carbon-fibre and fibre-glass pod
(Photo: Eastern Daily Press)

Medway Microlights, the manufacturers, are well known for turning out rugged, high-performance aircraft.

Available from: Medway Microlights, Burrows Lane, Rochester, Kent (telephone (0634) 270780).

Fixed-wing 'three axis' aircraft

Shadow
With the appearance of a conventional light aircraft, this high-winged two-seat pusher aircraft is available ready-to-fly or in kit form. Many holders of the PPL (Group A) have switched to flying the Shadow thanks to its low operating costs and the fact that it is very safe to fly, particularly at low speeds as it has no stall in the usual sense of the word.

Available from: CFM Metal-Fax, Unit 20, Eastlands Industrial Estate, Leiston, Suffolk (telephone (0798) 832353).

Renegade Sprit
Even more conventional in appearance than the Shadow, the Sprit emanates the halcyon flying days of the 1930s. A two-seat bi-plane, this Canadian aircraft is reminiscent of the Stampe and the Tiger Moth and its speed and

71

The high-performance CFM Shadow is a two-seat tandem pusher microlight that is safe and easy to fly, owing to the fact that it does not stall in the usual sense when at minimum flying speed. Shadows have won many flying competitions and have set long-distance records during flights to India and Australia
(Photo: CFM Metal-Fax Ltd)

The Renegade Sprit originates from Canada, and its appearance and performance are quite exceptional among microlights. These handsome two-seat aircraft evoke memories of the wonderful pre-war bi-planes from the golden age of flying
(Photo: Meridian Ultralights)

The RANS S4 Coyote is a strutted, high-wing, three-axis design with a fully enclosed cockpit. Originating from the USA, it can be purchased as a complete self-assembly kit for construction in your own garage (under the supervision of a qualified PFA – Popular Flying Association – aircraft inspector)
(Photo: Sport Air UK Ltd)

performance are far superior to that of most other microlight aircraft.

Available from: Meridian Ultralights, 51 Wold Road, Pocklington, East Yorkshire (telephone (0709) 304337).

MW6

An increasingly popular design available in two-seat tandem or side-by-side configuration. The aircraft is high winged with a pod-like cockpit and high boom to the tail unit. Many of these aircraft are under construction from prefabricated kits by members of the Popular Flying Association.

Available from: Skysports, The Vestry Hall, High Street, Glastonbury, Somerset (telephone (0458) 834754).

Minimax

A super little aircraft from the USA, the Minimax is of wood, plywood and fabric construction and is designed to be assembled from a comprehensive kit. A single-seat aircraft whose removable wings allow easy transportation and storage in a home garage to save on hangarage costs.

Available from: Ultralight Flying Machines, 19 Kingshill Road, Dursley, Gloucestershire (telephone (0453) 860755).

Rans Coyote

Another American microlight. The Rans Coyote is available as a single-seat or a side-by-side two seater. Both types are of strutted, high-winged appearance and have fully enclosed cockpits. The aircraft are approved for home construction from a kit under the supervision of the Popular Flying Association.

Available from: Sport Air UK, The Airfield, Felixkirk, Thirsk, North Yorkshire (telephone (0845) 537465).

Thruster

Originating from Australia, the Thruster is now manufactured and available in the United Kingdom and is of a high-wing design with a two-seat side-by-side cockpit pod. A very popular aircraft in service at a number of microlight clubs and schools for three-axis conversion or training.

Available from: Superavian, Greengate House, Pickwick Road, Corsham, Wiltshire (telephone (0249) 716241).

Chapter 4

GLIDING

All gliding in this country, and indeed in most other countries, takes place at local club level. A glider, unlike a powered light aircraft or microlight, cannot be launched without assistance from others. This is why a gliding club is a good place to make new friends – new members are always welcome. There is always plenty of work to be done on the ground at a gliding field: driving the tow car; operating the winch; getting gliders out of their trailers and rigging them for launch; and acting as a signal man. At this level, club gliding is one of the least expensive and most enjoyable, if time-consuming, ways of becoming involved in sporting aviation.

The first man-carrying glider in this country was built by an Englishman, Sir George Cayley, and flown by his reluctant coachman across a small valley on his estate at Brampton, near Scarborough in Yorkshire, in 1853. This tri-plane-type craft had all the ingredients of a flying aircraft; all that was needed was a powerful yet lightweight engine to make possible the progression from gliding to sustained powered flight. Unfortunately, the only practical man-made powerplant available throughout most of the nineteenth century was the weighty and unsuitable steam engine. Another, later aviation pioneer was one Percy Pilcher, a marine engineer by trade, who made many successful gliding flights between 1896 and 1899 near Glasgow in Scotland and later at Eynsford in Kent. But these were simple gliding flights on a descending course: the present popularity of gliding has its origins in the discovery that gliders can stay airborne for long periods, cover large distances, and reach great heights solely by exploiting the currents of the air. This manner of flight is called *soaring* and gliders that soar are sometimes called *sailplanes*.

In order to cut loose from the hills and soar across country it is necessary to use a different kind of up-current from the localised one caused by wind blowing up a hill. Thermal currents or *thermals* consist of warmed air rising

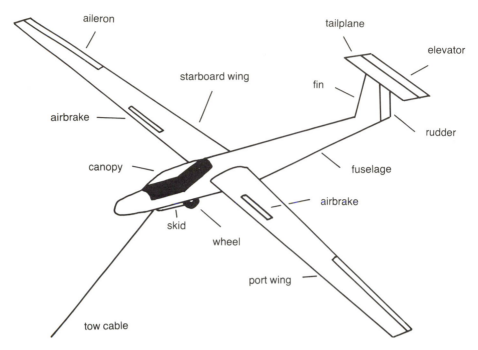

Figure 26 *The glider and its components*

The Junior is a wonderfully streamlined modern single-seat glass-fibre glider
(Photo: Keith Carey)

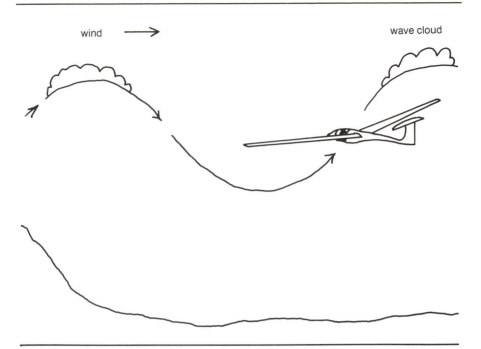

Figure 27 *Under certain meteorological conditions, air that has gone over the top of a hill or mountain can cascade down and then bounce up again in the form of a wave for a considerable distance. By flying in the upgoing parts of this wave system, the glider pilot can climb to great heights and travel long distances along the wave system*

from the sun-heated ground; as the air ascends in a relatively narrow stream, gliders (and birds) have to fly around in a tightish circle to keep within its boundaries and get carried up by the rising current. When a thermal has risen a few thousand feet and reached a level of cooler air it often condenses and a cumulus cloud may form at its top. In certain weather conditions these clouds may grow to enormous size, showers or even thunderstorms forming within them, with strong up-currents which can lift a glider tens of thousands of feet into the sky.

A glider flies or achieves upward motion in exactly the same way as a powered light aircraft, the flow of air over and under the wings providing lift. In a light aircraft, speed is provided by the engine pulling it through the air. The glider or sailplane, having no engine, obtains its speed by gliding down-hill using gravity as motive power. If the glider pilot cannot find up-currents of air (or thermals), he will only be able to glide steadily downwards until he has reached the ground and has to land. If he *can* find a thermal of rising air, ascending faster than he is descending, the glider will climb and thus gain height. This is known as *soaring flight*. A glider pilot soars across country by circling around in these thermals and gaining height. He then flies in a straight line, often quite fast, in the direction he wants to go. During this high-speed run the pilot will be losing precious height, so he will be constantly on the look-out for another thermal with which to repeat the whole process and continue on his way.

Most cross-country flights such as these are intended to finish at other gliding sites or airfields. Sometimes, though, the pilot runs out of lift. When this happens he has to select a suitable field or other landing area in which to put the glider down. Although some gliders are fitted with a radio, and some pilots carry hand-held transceivers, in most cases the pilot will have to find a nearby telephone to call his base and then wait patiently with his aircraft until collected by the club's retrieve crew. They bring the glider home by road in its trailer.

LICENCES AND CERTIFICATES

No formal pilot's licence is required to fly a glider. Instead, progression is via a series of certificates and badges which designate a certain level of achievement and acknowledge the completion of certain tasks. As far as a newcomer to the sport is concerned, his first aim will be to achieve his 'A' or 'solo' certificate. This will be awarded after the student has been allowed to fly solo, which requires on average 50 take-offs and landings. He will then be allowed to wear a badge with a single white bird in silhouette on a blue disc. The 'B' certificate requires the completion of three solo flights, with turns in both directions. Successfully completing this adds another white bird to the badge, making two in the silhouette. To attempt the 'C' or soaring badge, the applicant must already hold both the 'A' and 'B' certificates. The test for this badge requires the pilot to carry out a soaring flight of at least five minutes – although the instructor will tell his student to try and stay up for at least 15 minutes if possible – followed by a normal landing.

MEDICAL REQUIREMENTS

No medical examination of any kind is required to pilot a glider under British Gliding Association rules. Instead, aspiring students are asked to submit a formal statement of health, rather like that included in a driving licence application form. It will ask whether the student suffers from faintness or giddiness and whether he has adequate vision (i.e. is able to read a car number plate at 23 metres (25 yds)). Disqualification from flying is not automatic if you are not able to sign the declaration, but the individual gliding club may require further medical information before you will be allowed to fly.

LEARNING TO GLIDE

Anyone aged 16 or over may learn to fly a glider provided he is able to sign the required declaration of physical fitness. There are various ways in which you can then learn to glide, and it will not take you very long if you are already a qualified power pilot with experience of flying light aircraft, helicopters or microlights. In any case, whatever your previous experience, it is a good idea to visit a gliding club and have a trial flight – or perhaps go along for an (increasingly popular) one-day introductory course to the sport before committing yourself to joining a club as a full flying member. Learning to fly gliders is probably best accomplished by taking a one- or two-week holiday course. This is the quickest way to reach solo standard, but it is only by flying regularly that you will become a really proficient glider pilot.

If your flying lessons are separated by more than a week, learning to fly a glider can be a slow and time-consuming process. However, having joined the nearest gliding club the new pilot will soon discover that the more willing he is to help with rigging the gliders for flying, positioning aircraft at the launch point, keeping the flight log sheet, running at the wingtips to steady the glider during launch, and retrieving the gliders after landing, the more flying he will get. If you want to book an aircraft and have it ready and waiting for you to step into, you should forget about gliding and take up powered flying instead.

For your first few flights you do need good weather conditions to make quick progress. Any dry day without low cloud and with a light wind will be suitable for the beginner. If for some reason the weather is too bad to fly when you arrive at the gliding club, do not give up and return home; you can learn a great deal just by talking to the instructors and other more advanced students. The more knowledge you can acquire about gliding, the quicker you will learn and the more time and money you will save.

Your early flights will be made with the instructor explaining what the glider is doing and how the controls are operated. As with other aircraft, you will notice that as the control column is moved forwards the nose of the glider goes down, the airspeed increases, and the glider descends. When the column is eased back the nose of the glider comes up and the airspeed decreases. If the control column is moved to the left the left wing will drop, the right wing will rise up and the glider will bank to the left. Conversely, by moving the control column to the right the pilot causes the right wing to drop, the left wing to rise and the glider to bank to the right. Return the control column to its central or neutral position and the glider will resume straight and level descending flight. Your instructor will also demonstrate the use of the *rudder pedals*. These provide 'yaw'. You will see that by pressing the left pedal he causes the nose of the glider to swing left; by pressing the right pedal he brings the nose over to the right. Centralise the pedals and the nose of the glider will again be facing straight ahead. The rudder pedals are chiefly used to help balance the glider in turning flight, although they can also be used in conjunction with the control column if the pilot wishes to lose height rapidly or to 'sideslip'.

These movements are known as the *primary effects of control* and are common to almost every type of fixed-wing aircraft, large or small. On these early flights you may experience occasional 'vivid' sensations. The air is rarely still, and while you are flying you will often be tipped slightly this way and that by the currents in the air. While you are getting used to the glider and its controls these upsets can be rather disconcerting, but you will eventually correct them with the controls smoothly and automatically, rather as you react to traffic when driving your car. We all have an inborn fear of falling but, contrary perhaps to your expectations, when flying gliders you will not experience the same sense of vertigo that you sometimes get when standing close to the edge of a tall building or on a cliff.

A standard pre-flight check-list for gliders can be memorised by the initials CBSIFTCB.

- C = Controls: do the control column and rudder pedals move correctly, fully and freely, not obstructed by cushions or maps?
- B = Ballast: is the weight correct? A glider will only fly safely if the weight is within the limits stated on the flight limitations label. This must be checked and ballast added if the individual pilot does not weigh enough.
- S = Straps: are the seat harness straps of both student pilot and instructor fastened correctly?
- I = Instruments: instruments must be undamaged and the altimeter set correctly.
- F = Flaps: if flaps are fitted to the aircraft, is the setting correct? They should be set for take-off.
- T = Trim: does the trim lever move fully and freely? It should be set for take-off.
- C = Canopy: is the canopy closed and locked?
- B = Brakes: are the airbrakes closed? In a stiff wind it may be prudent to leave the airbrakes open while on the ground, but they should be closed and locked before the launch.

THE TAKE-OFF

As soon as the student glider pilot is able to handle the aircraft in the air, he can start learning the take-off drill. There are basically three ways of launching gliders: aerotowing, car launching and winch launching. *Aerotowing* is a method whereby a powered light aircraft tows the glider up to a height of 610 metres (2,000 ft) by means of a steel cable. Although the aerotow method gives a glider more height in which to practise turns, stalls and other manoeuvres, the tow itself requires more skill on behalf of the pilot than a car or winch launch. The important thing is to keep the wings level, maintain position behind the towing aircraft, and react to any small changes of attitude smoothly, correctly and immediately. You should also make sure that you know the aerotowing emergency signals. If at the end of the tow you cannot release the tow cable, pull over to the left-hand side behind the tug plane and tell the pilot by rocking the wings of your glider. The tug pilot, who can see the glider in a rearward-facing mirror, will then release the cable from the light aircraft and you will have to make an emergency landing with the cable still attached to the nose of the glider. If the tug aircraft rocks its wings during the tow the glider must release the towing cable at once.

Car and winch launching provide very simple and economical ways of launching gliders up to a height of around 300 metres (1,000 ft). As a student pilot you will find that these launches are ideal for training purposes; at this early stage in your gliding you will require lots of practice in circuit flying and take-off and landing procedure, rather than attempts at soaring flight. It should be noted, however, that with these methods of launching there is the remote possibility of mechanical failure. Should the steel towing cable break during the launch, the pilot should lower the nose of the glider immediately, drop the remains of the cable, and decide quickly if there is sufficient room to

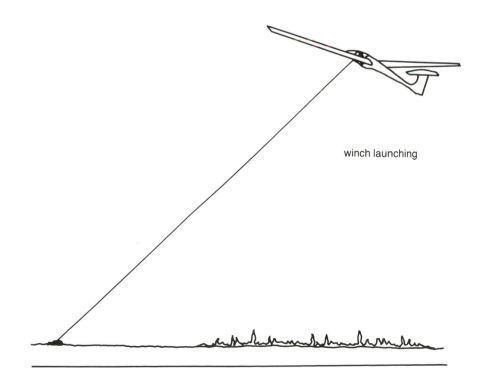

winch launching

Figure 28 *Winch launching*

land ahead or whether a turn will have to be made before the glider can be put down in the nearest convenient open space. The following are some points to bear in mind when you come to practise launches and landings for yourself.

Aerotow launches

- Use gentle movements of the controls.
- Keep your wings level with those of the tug aircraft.
- Check that the tow cable has released properly before turning away.

Figure 29 *Aero towing*

Car and winch launches

- Lower the nose of the glider before pulling the cable release.
- Think before you take off: what will you do if the cable breaks?
- In the event of a poor launch, always check your airbrakes to make sure that they are closed and locked.

THE LANDING

A good glider landing is made from a high, straight approach at the correct speed. The idea is gradually to reduce the path of the aircraft from a steep glide, so that when it arrives over the landing point it will be in the correct attitude for landing at or near its stalling speed. If the resultant flare is then made too high the glider will sink heavily on to the ground. If it is made too

Ready for a winch launch. A ground helper holds the glider wing steady whilst another member brings the cable over to be hooked under the glider's nose
(Photo: Keith Carey)

This two-seat training glider is on final approach to land. Note the open airbrakes on its wings (Photo: Keith Carey)

low the aircraft will strike its landing wheel and bounce, perhaps several times, resulting in a much longer landing run. As the glider approaches the ground the pilot should look well ahead, judging his height by what he can see from the corner of his eyes (peripheral vision) and adjusting with the flying controls as necessary. To achieve a good landing the glider should touch down on its mainwheel and tailskid at the same time. It must then be kept running straight, with the wings level, until the speed decreases and the glider comes to a halt. One wing will then gently drop to the ground.

By this stage in his training the gliding student will have flown a straightforward circuit, describing the shape of an oblong, with a launch, crosswind turn, downwind leg, base leg, final turn and landing. If all is going well the instructor will then make preparations for his pupil's first solo flight.

THE FIRST SOLO

Like their contemporaries in the light aircraft and helicopter world, most student glider pilots probably consider themselves ready to fly solo long before their instructor deems them sufficiently safe and competent. When the time does come, and the instructor actually steps out of the cockpit and casually tells you to take it around the circuit by yourself, you will almost certainly be caught by surprise. As the launching cable is hooked on under the nose and you go through your pre-flight cockpit checks, a distant voice that you realise is your own calls out: 'Ready for launch.' The cable becomes taut and the glider starts to move forwards, speed building; the man supporting the wingtip is quickly left running far behind. The speed settles at around 50–55 knots and the nose of the glider comes up and begins to climb. The control column is pulled further and further back as the glide angle steepens and the altimeter winds up towards the 300-metres marker. As the aircraft nears the desired height, the nose of the glider is lowered and with an audible click the tow cable is released.

At this point you realise, perhaps really for the first time, that you do not have your instructor with you – that you are flying the aircraft entirely on your own. Remember that the circuit is no place for day-dreaming so busy yourself with the pre-landing checks. Turn the glider downwind, then on to base leg and on to your final approach. The airbrakes come open with a bang and a roar, holding the speed at around 55 knots in the descent. Suddenly you recall that in a glider you are committed on the first approach and, unlike in a powered aircraft, you cannot go around again! The landing field is now floating up to meet you, however, so the control column is eased gently back, rounding out the glider a foot or two above the ground. The grass flashes past the canopy and with a bump you are down. There is what seems a horrendous bumping and crashing on the uneven surface as the glider runs to a stop: then, with a gentle sigh, a wingtip dips to the ground and all is quiet again.

An enormous grin of self-congratulation spreads over your face as fellow club members cluster around to ask you what it was like. You'll find the experience difficult to describe. Later you will consolidate your flight with a couple more solo circuits, just to prove to your instructor and to yourself that you can do it again – but the magic of your first solo can never be repeated.

THE BRONZE 'C'

The next stage in the glider pilot's training comes when he is judged ready to tackle the examination for the Bronze 'C'. This gives the pilot the right to leave

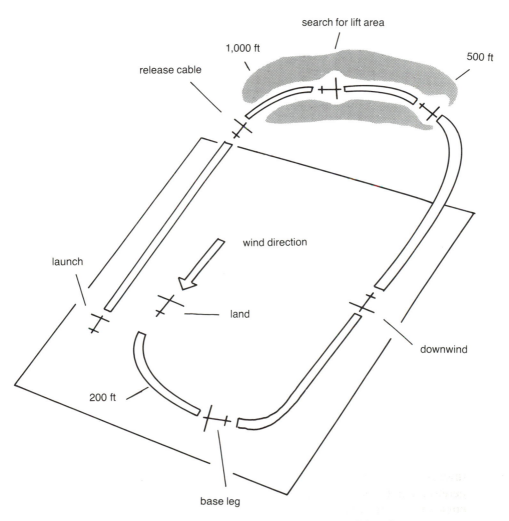

Figure 30 *A typical glider 'circuit' following a winch launch*

85

the circuit and embark on cross-country flights, and is in effect a full gliding licence. The examination syllabus for the Bronze 'C' laid down by the British Gliding Association is split into five sections.

Principles of flight
Demonstrate an elementary understanding of the following: aerofoils; lift and drag; forces acting on an aircraft during flight; turning, stalling and loading (placard speeds); effects of controls (axes); further effects of controls; stability.

Meteorology
Demonstrate an elementary understanding of the following: frontal systems (recognition of approach, associated pressure changes, order of stability); convection; cloud formation (lapse rates, condensation levels); weather maps (show a basic understanding of signs and symbols); gliding aspects (hill lift, wave lift and thermal soaring); and weather forecasts.

Navigation
Demonstrate an elementary understanding of the following: map reading; cross-country flying; the effect of wind on track and groundspeed; field landings; the magnetic compass (variation and deviation, turning and acceleration errors); and vector triangles and geographical appreciation (true and magnetic north, lines of longitude and latitude, the distribution of pressure in the northern and southern hemispheres).

Instruments
Demonstrate an elementary understanding of the construction, defects and uses of an ASI (Airspeed Indicator), an altimeter and a variometer.

Airmanship and general knowledge
Demonstrate a full knowledge of air law and ground handling signals.

THE AIR TEST

The candidate must have made at least two soaring flights, each of more than 30 minutes duration when launched by winch or tow car, or of 60 minutes duration after launch from an aerotow not exceeding a height of 600 metres (2,000 ft). Both of these flights must then have been followed by normal landings into designated landing areas. The student will also be required to complete a minimum of two dual flights, satisfactorily demonstrating an understanding of stalling and the correct recovery procedures, accurate general flying, and a further two field landings or landings into a marked-off enclosure on the gliding field without reference to his altimeter.

On achieving the Bronze 'C' the newly qualified pilot can add a small bronze filigree to his badge. Then, if he so wishes, he can go on to gain further badges and distinctions. The next of these is the Silver 'C', which roughly a quarter of this country's glider pilots are entitled to wear. The main tasks demanded of a pilot aspiring to this level are a height gain of at least 1,000 metres (3,281 ft) after launch and a cross-country flight of 50 kilometres (32 miles).

Having achieved the Silver 'C', the really ambitious pilot can then go on to aim for the Gold 'C'. Success at this level shows you to be up among the elite of the gliding world. To gain this qualification you must gain a height after launch of at least 3,000 metres (9,850 ft) and perform a cross-country flight of 300 kilometres (186 miles). A sealed instrument called a *barograph* is carried in the glider and this confirms, by way of a paper recording, that the glider has indeed reached the requisite height. As regards the distance requirement, the pilot may elect to fly a triangular route instead of a straight-line flight if he so chooses; in this case a camera is carried, enabling the pilot to provide photographic evidence of pre-set turning points to prove that he has completed the intended course. Gold 'C' pilots may gain further additions to their badge by means of 'diamond' ratings – rare distinctions indeed – which place their holders among the world's best glider pilots.

HOLIDAY COURSES

A good way to get started in the sport of gliding is to take a holiday course at one of the many clubs and schools that offer this tuition. These courses usually run from April through to September. For full details of gliding clubs and

Gliding is a team activity, as this busy launch scene shows (Photo: Keith Carey)

schools in this country see pp. 183–8. Alternatively, contact the British Gliding Association, whose telephone and fax numbers can be found on page 203.

Some of these clubs and schools have residential accommodation at the gliding field; others will arrange for you to stay at a nearby pub or hotel. A tent or caravan may also be allowed on to the gliding site. The individual club or school of your choice will be happy to provide further details. For the newcomer to the sport who wishes to fly solo during his course, two consecutive weeks are recommended. An intensive gliding course is without doubt the fastest way to reach solo standard in a limited time, but you will still need to keep flying regularly to remain competent. Also, just like the weekend flyer, the holiday student will be expected to help with the various ground tasks such as cable retrieving and glider rigging.

WHAT TO WEAR

In the summer, although it may be warm on the ground, the air temperature at a couple of thousand feet can be very much cooler; sunbathing gear is not therefore all that suitable. Don't forget that gliding sites and airfields are quite often exposed and windy places, so take care not to get sunburned. Sunglasses are almost essential and, in really hot weather, a hat (without too floppy a brim – the instructor in the rear seat has to see around you!) will protect your head from the heat and glare coming through the perspex canopy. In colder months a warm anorak or jacket, jeans or trousers and cap and gloves will be required to keep you warm. Mittens are not advisable, because when it is your turn to fly they can restrict the 'feel' of the glider's controls. For the same reason very heavy shoes or boots are not to be recommended, although it is essential to have warm, comfortable and waterproof footwear. Cold, wet feet on a gliding site will quickly ruin your enjoyment of the day's flying.

SOCIAL ACTIVITIES

All gliding clubs offer a variety of lectures, film shows, dances, and barbecue and disco parties throughout the year. Most gliding clubs have meals and refreshments available in the clubhouse at reasonable prices, and some also have a licensed bar.

HOW MUCH WILL IT COST?

With the exceptions of hang gliding and microlight flying (once you have qualified for a licence!), club gliding is one of the most cost-effective, if time-consuming, ways to take up an active airsport. With facilities varying among the many clubs and schools there can be no set price structure. At the time of writing, an average, one-day introductory gliding course costs around £95. For a five-day, all-inclusive course in Scotland prices are around £285; in the Midlands around £300; and at clubs in the southern counties around £350. For a 'Flying Only' course, which comprises all gliding instruction and club fees but does not include any meals or accommodation, weekly prices start at around £169.

THE GLIDER

Most modern gliders are now made of glass fibre. The vast majority of clubs and schools are equipped with modern gliders, and their fleets may include a mix of all glass-fibre, all-metal or glass-fibre/wood/fabric constructions. Those gliders constructed of a number of different materials are often less expensive than the glass-fibre models, and are easier for the inexperienced student to learn on due to their higher drag designs and docile handling qualities. These simpler types of gliders do not give as high a performance as the more sleek plastic machines with lower drag designs, but they are quite adequate for basic training and general club flying where speed and cross-country soaring are not the prime requirements. These aircraft usually have a fixed undercarriage and airbrakes only, not being fitted with the more advanced features such as flaps, comprehensive instrumentation or retractable landing gear.

For the student who really takes to the sport and is interested perhaps in owning his own glider, the usual form is to join a syndicate. For a sum ranging

Awaiting launch. An old car tyre is used to prevent a gust of wind from lifting the glider's wing (Photo: Keith Carey)

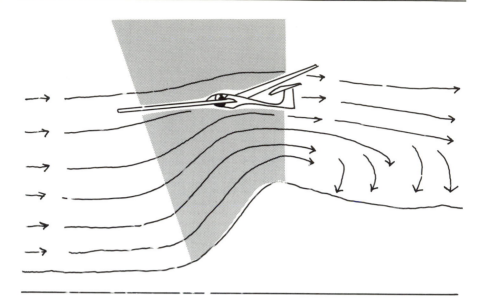

Figure 31 *Shaded area shows best area of lift when ridge soaring*

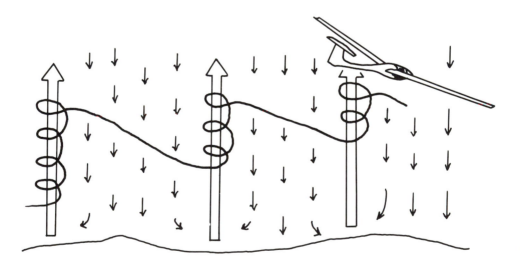

Figure 32 *Glider pilots gain altitude in thermals, and aim to lose as little height as possible in descending air whilst searching for their next area of lift*

from a few hundred pounds to several thousand pounds, depending on the age, condition and complexity of the glider, a pilot can buy for example a one-eighth share in a machine and take turns with the other syndicate members in flying it. This really is the cheapest way to fly. Depreciation of the sum invested is low and, share purchase aside, operating costs will certainly undercut the rental rate of a club-owned glider. Becoming a syndicate member will also mean looking after the glider and its trailer, and you will be expected to put in a good few hours work on ground maintenance. Whilst gliders are immensely strong in the air they can be easily damaged on the ground; they should therefore never be leaned on or held by the trailing edges of the wings or tail-plane. If in doubt as to where to hold them, ask.

PARACHUTES

New students often wonder why glider pilots wear parachutes when light aircraft pilots do not. This is because although modern gliders are very safe, the seat is often designed as a sort of 'bucket' (rather like some sports car seats) into which a parachute fits, thus becoming the cushion on which to sit. Moreover, although gliders are strongly constructed, they may fly near storm clouds when soaring across country, so the wearing of a parachute is really a safe and sensible precaution.

GLIDING CODE OF PRACTICE

The gliding fraternity owes a great deal to farmers for the help that pilots have received when the thermals have run out and a glider has had to make a field landing on private property. When this occurs all due care must be taken to cause as little damage as possible. Gates should always be kept shut and standing crops and livestock should be avoided at all costs. Interested members of the public who may have witnessed the glider's landing should be restrained from trying to enter the field and trampling the farmer's crop. The farmer or landowner should be notified of your arrival in his field, and vehicles must be kept out until permission to proceed has been obtained. Remember, it is in all pilots' interests, whatever their chosen branch of airsport, to follow the country code at all times.

Chapter 5

HANG GLIDING

M an has long dreamed of the day when he might pull on wings and fly like the birds. The jet engines and ever-increasing commercialisation of modern aviation has moved considerably beyond this original vision of simple flight. Although the basic concept of the hang glider as a flying machine dates back many hundreds of years, the modern soaring craft flown by today's

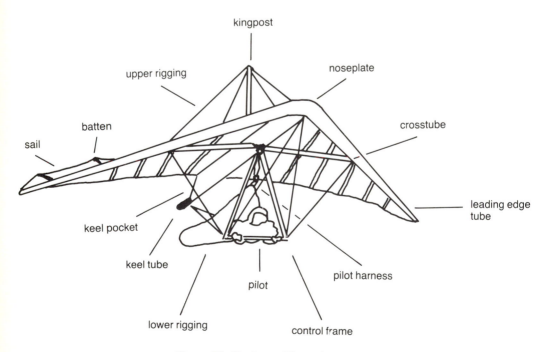

Figure 33 *The hang glider and its components*

pilots has been developed from an early 1960s' initiative in the American space programme. The *Rogallo glider*, as it became known, was Dr Francis Rogallo's design for a type of folding wing intended to assist National Aeronautics and Space Administration (NASA) manned capsules to make safe and 'steerable' recoveries to earth (instead of being forced to parachute to a splashdown in the ocean). Although the design was abandoned in favour of developing the re-useable Space Shuttle, airsport enthusiasts quickly realised that it offered a means of getting into the air with a minimum of cost.

When the new sport of hang gliding first started to become popular, on the Californian sand dunes of west-coast America in the 1960s, it was on Rogallo's delta-wing design that the early pioneers based their machines. Construction techniques were simple: a braced V-shaped frame made of tubing, sometimes even of bamboo poles, was covered with cloth or polythene sheeting. This was then fastened together – often with little more than string, wire and sellotape. It is no wonder that many pilots were injured and sometimes killed attempting to fly these primitive, untried and untested aircraft.

Since then, however, great strides have been made in the sport. Hang gliding has become immensely popular all over the world, and manufacturers from more than a dozen countries now turn out a vast range of commercially constructed machines of an extremely safe and strong design.

FIRST STEPS

For the pilot, hang gliding is an immensely challenging and very 'personal' sport. Although subject to exactly the same laws and responsibilities as any other airsport, hang gliding offers its thousands of participants the freedom of the sky.

The first step is to visit your local library and read everything you can find on hang gliding, which in reality may not be all that much. Although there have been a number of books written on the sport, most local lending libraries tend to stock only one or two of the available titles and even these are likely to be some years out of date. You should therefore contact the British Hang Gliding Association for more up-to-date information. You will find their address, telephone and fax numbers on page 203.

They will then post off to you their information pack, which includes: a list of hang gliding clubs nationwide so that you can find the nearest one to your home; a list of approved training schools; some details on flying training and the pilot rating system; a BHGA membership application form; and a colour leaflet giving some general information on the sport. If you have not flown any sort of aircraft before you will have to put aside for a while the charming thought of 'stepping lightly off a grassy hilltop and gliding out into the valley'. Learning to fly involves hard work, application and study.

First you will need to find a good club or school from which to take instruction. This should be as near to your home as possible to save any unnecessary travelling – although if you choose to train in another part of the country many schools can arrange residential accommodation in a nearby B & B or hotel. Basic training at a registered club or school is essential for your safety and the good name of the sport. All the registered clubs and schools in this country have to meet the very strict training requirements set out by the BHGA, and all are subject to periodic inspection by BHGA Training Officers.

Most clubs and schools run two- and four-day training courses. Both are very useful ways of learning how to hang glide, but, if you can spare the time, the four-day course will train you up to your 'Elementary Pilot Certificate' – the basic award of the BHGA. The fast way to learn is to take one of these full-time courses of instruction and then follow it up by flying every weekend for a few months thereafter to become more proficient. Concentrated learning of this sort will give you useful experience of hang gliding in different wind and weather conditions. It *is* possible to learn to fly just by coming along at weekends – many people do learn to hang glide in this manner – but this can at times be slow and frustrating.

At the hang gliding club or school you will probably spend a good part of your first day on the ground, learning the various procedures of flight in a suspended mock-up of the hang glider harness. Almost without exception

Figure 35 *Launching a hang glider*

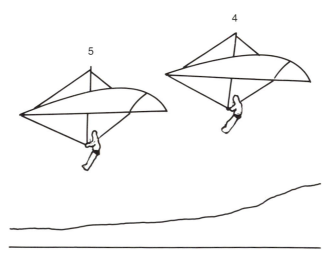

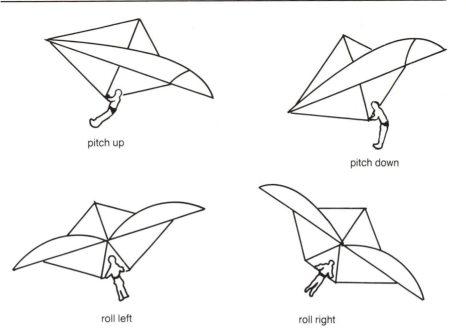

pitch up

pitch down

roll left

roll right

Figure 34 *Effects of the hang glider control bar. Pulling the body-weight forwards makes the nose pitch down and the glider fly faster. Pushing the body-weight back pitches the nose up and reduces speed. To roll left, move body-weight to the left. To move right, move body-weight to the right*

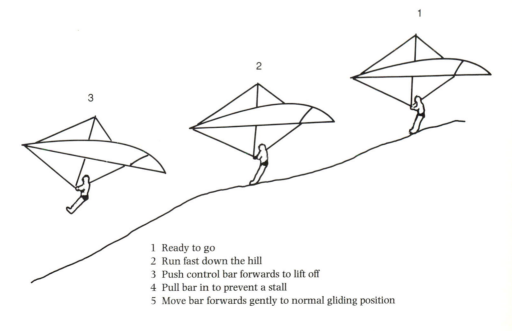

1 Ready to go
2 Run fast down the hill
3 Push control bar forwards to lift off
4 Pull bar in to prevent a stall
5 Move bar forwards gently to normal gliding position

Figure 36 *A hang glider stall and recovery*

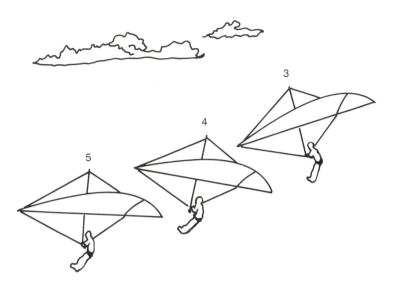

Figure 37 *Landing a hang glider*

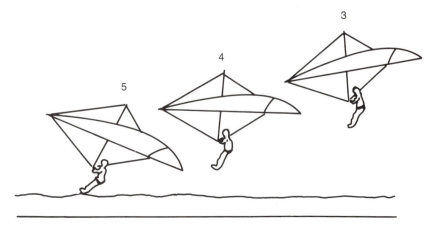

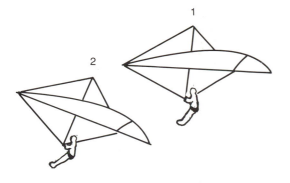

1 Ready to go
2 Nose of glider too high, glider stalls
3 Bar pulled in to dive glider and increase speed
4 Bar pushed forwards when flying speed regained
5 Resumption of normal glide

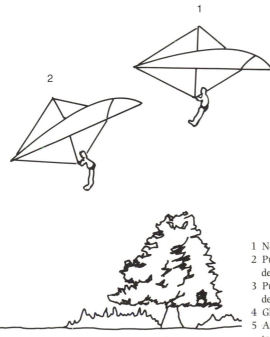

1 Normal glide
2 Pull bar in to increase speed and descend
3 Push bar forwards to reduce rate of descent
4 Glider flying level with the ground
5 As glider stalls, bar is pushed forwards to angle the glider and allow landing

97

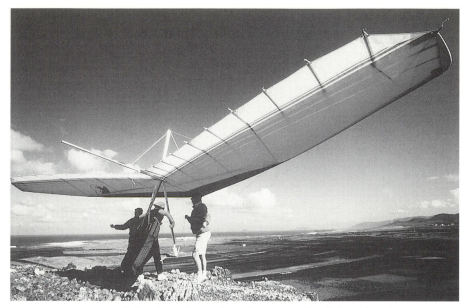

Assistants help a hang glider pilot as he prepares for a hill-top launch
(Photo: Keith Carey)

hang gliders are controlled by what is known as *weight shift*. The pilot is suspended in a harness from a point very close to the wing's centre of gravity. By pushing, pulling or swinging his body-weight relative to the control bar he can initiate any desired manoeuvre in any chosen direction. For instance, if he pulls on the control bar his weight will move forwards and the hang glider will speed up and descend. If he pushes it forwards his body-weight will move backwards and the glider will slow and pull up. If he pushes the control bar to the left, simultaneously swinging his body-weight to the right, increased wing loading will turn the hang glider to the right. Conversely, pushing the bar to the right and swinging left will load the left wing, enabling the glider to bank left. By training in this way the various control techniques can be learned without risk to yourself or others on your course. Many clubs and schools also make extensive use of videos and training films; these can be very useful learning aids as they show how instructors and other experienced hang-glider pilots take off, control the glider and land. Your instructor should also give you a basic lesson on aerodynamics and the theory of flight. He will demonstrate, probably with the use of a small model of a hang glider, how the craft flies, how airflow over and under the wing provides lift, and what happens if you fly too slowly, thereby destroying that lift and stalling the craft.

When you first start learning you will begin with a series of small, bird-like hops, gradually working your way up the launching hill as your ability increases. Although some schools do have the odd dual-seat hang glider that

Taking off. The hands and feet should be placed firmly and comfortably to exert control (Photo: Airwave)

enables a pupil to fly alongside an experienced instructor, the vast majority of training is done solo from day one. There is nothing dangerous about this, as the school gliders are very easy to handle. Their docile flying characteristics enable operation at flying speeds as low as 12 mph. With any amount of headwind the forward speed of the glider is reduced further, effectively giving a forward airspeed of little more than a fast walking pace.

To help the new pilot fly on his own as soon as possible, most hang-gliding clubs and schools use a method of instruction called 'tethered flying' for the first dozen or so flights. Long lines or 'tethers' are attached to the glider's nose and wing leading edges; these lines are held by the instructor and two other pilots, usually students from your own course. When the hang glider is flown off the hillside the line handlers run down the slope, pulling the tethers tight thus enabling the student to make a controlled, straight-line flight. As you become more competent your instructor will move you further up the hill and you will make progressively longer hops. When he is satisfied that you have mastered a straight-line descent he will remove the tethers attached to the wing leading edges and you will have a go at attempting some very gentle turns before landing. The advantage of this system is that training can be carried out when less than ideal wind conditions would otherwise put a stop to any beginner flying. Without tethers, a beginner should only fly on days when the winds are less strong. Constant wind strengths are quite satisfactory, but sudden gusting can present a real danger, particularly at the point of take-off or landing. As well as tethers, many clubs and schools now use a small VHF radio to talk to the student pilot in flight. This is done via a small radio receiver fitted inside the pupil's safety helmet.

THE GLIDER

As we have already mentioned, the hang glider is a basic aircraft of an extremely simple design. Means of control vary from weight shift on the vast majority of gliders to simple aerodynamic controls on some of the more advanced models. The average hang glider does not take very long to rig for flying, most pilots taking about 10 minutes. The primary frame is made of aluminium tube and braced with stainless steel flying wires; the sails are made from top quality sailcoth, often with leading edges of a very smooth material called *mylar* (on all but the most basic of gliders). The wing area of the machine will probably be somewhere between 130 and 175 square feet, with lighter pilots flying the smaller wings and heavier pilots the larger wings. Stalling speed of the glider will be around 12 – 14 mph mark, its most efficient gliding speed around 30 mph, and a top speed of perhaps 45 mph. Various clips and catches enable the glider to be assembled by one man without the use of any tools. It is extremely important that the hang glider be rigged according to the manufacturer's instructions, and that no experimental adjustments or additions are made. When flying has finished for the day the glider will break down in a little more than five minutes, and pack away into its own bag which may then be transported back home on the roof-rack of your car.

THE PILOT'S LICENCE

The British Hang Gliding Association does not issue any sort of formal licence, awarding instead a series of certificates as the pilot climbs up the ratings ladder. These range from the Elementary Pilot Certificate up to the dizzy heights of the *Federation Internationale Aeronautique* (FAI) Delta Gold, which requires the pilot to complete a distance flight of 186 miles (300 kilometres).

MEDICAL REQUIREMENTS

There is no formal medical examination. All the prospective pilot is required to do when booking a course of instruction is declare himself free of any major disorders such as chest or heart trouble, high blood pressure, diabetes, blackouts, fits or dizzy spells. As for any energetic sport, you must be reason-ably fit and active, especially since the first few days will involve a considerable amount of running up and down hills. If you do have any doubts about your general fitness, or if it is some time since you took part in any physical exercise, get the advice of your GP before you start flying.

WHAT TO WEAR

Even in summer it can be quite chilly up on the hills, so take enough warm, wind-proof clothing along with you. Wear comfortable waterproof shoes or boots with good grip and some ankle support (but not of the lace-hook variety), and gloves which will not slip on the control bar. While you are in training the club or school will probably provide you with a crash helmet, but it is up to you to check that it fits properly and it is wise thereafter to try to purchase your own.

THE PILOT RATING SCHEME

The Pilot Rating Scheme serves two purposes. First, it provides a student with a structured learning path, integrating safe, progressive flying lessons with explanatory theory sessions and tests to enable newcomers to make swift and enjoyable progress within the sport. At the same time, it provides the BHGA with an educational system to ensure that hang glider pilots fulfil their legal and moral responsibilities as regards other airspace users. As we have seen, basic training is undertaken at a BHGA-registered club or school under the guidance of qualified and experienced instructors. Here the training syllabus allows the student to progress up from the Elementary Pilot Certificate through to the Club Pilot Certificate and beyond. Once CPC level has been reached, further training is undertaken within your local club. As well as being tested on all the various listed tasks which make up the Pilot Rating Scheme, you will need to consolidate your learning and gain as much flying experience as possible. The only way to do this is to get out to the flying site and get yourself up into the air. For this reason you will only be able to apply for a higher rating when you have held the previous one for a period of no less than four months. The only exception to this rule is the progression from Elementary Pilot Certificate to Club Pilot Certificate holder, which should be made as quickly as possible. The full Pilot Rating Scheme is as follows.

- Contact a BHGA-registered club or school and book yourself on to a course of instruction. There are 20 such establishments throughout the country.
- Arrive at your chosen club or school ready for the course and join the BHGA Training Membership Scheme. This introductory four-month membership will include a training pack, third-party insurance cover, and three issues of *Skywings* magazine. At the time of writing it costs £30.

A hang glider pilot launches into wind from a hill side (Photo: Airwave)

- Start training on your course. An average of four days flying tuition should enable you to gain your Elementary Pilot Certificate.
- Join the Pilot Rating Scheme through the BHGA head office or your club or school. This currently costs £8. You will receive a training pack including a flying handbook.
- Start your Club Pilot Certificate course at your club or school. This should be done directly after you have qualified for your Elementary Pilot Certificate. A longish gap between the two courses will result in a longer total tuition time and therefore increased eventual cost.
- Tasks 9 – 11 of the Club Pilot Certificate may be completed at your local members' club, provided that an experienced pilot or instructor is on hand and able to supervise you.
- After a total of eight or nine days of flying tuition – assuming that you have been learning on a full-time course – you will be awarded your Club Pilot Certificate. You may now legally purchase your own hang glider, and apply to join your local members' hang gliding club as a flying member.
- Continue your flying as a member of your local BHGA club. Progress further with the help of club coaches and fellow club members. Instruction is free, but you will need to have your own hang glider.
- If you wish you may now begin to train as a coach or instructor and help to teach others to learn to fly. Further details of this scheme are available from the BHGA head office.
- By this stage you will have qualified for your Cross-Country Pilot Certificate and will be free to enjoy the delights of cross-country hang gliding.

● Complete your Advanced Pilot Certificate. This qualification is the highest the BHGA can award.

This is as far as most club hang glider pilots will wish to progress. For those who aspire to still greater heights, however, there are national and international competitions. Selection procedures for the British Hang Gliding Team are rigorous. The FAI Delta Silver Certificate requires the pilot to perform a distance flight of not less than 50 kilometres (30 miles), this distance being measured in a straight line; a height of not less than 1,000 metres (3,280 ft) must be gained above launch height, and a flight of at least five hours duration must be completed. All of these tasks may be performed separately or attempted on a single occasion. Finally there is the pinnacle of hang gliding achievement, the FAI Delta Gold. For this a distance flight of 300 kilometres (186 miles) and an out-and-return or *triangle* flight of 200 kilometres (122 miles) must be completed.

FLYING WITH A CLUB

If you have enjoyed your training course you will want to continue to fly. The way to do this is to join a club. At the time of writing there are 43 UK local members' clubs in operation, so there is bound to be one not too far from your home. When you join, tell the club coach how much flying you have done; if you have already purchased your own hang glider tell him what sort it is. He and other experienced members of the club will tell you when it is safe to fly and when it is best to stay on the ground. Expect to progress reasonably slowly at first: you may have a new hang glider to get used to and a new site to explore. Your experience up to this point will have been limited, so don't try to rush things; and don't fly just anywhere there is a hill. You could endanger yourself, and jeopardise the right to fly for others. Remember: no sites, no flying!

SOARING FLIGHT

Soaring flight is achieved by flying the hang glider in *thermals* or in *hill lift*. Thermals are currents of warm air rising from the sun-heated ground. They rise progressively higher until they cool to the temperature of the surrounding air. A good indication of thermal activity is the formation of cumulus cloud. Unless the surrounding air is very dry, it is likely that one of these clouds will form at the top of a thermal. When thermal soaring, the hang glider pilot must stick to the 'inner core' of maximum lift by circling around inside the thermal. If 'thermal turbulence' occurs – caused by large warm-air masses moving upwards and being replaced by cooler descending air – performance of both pilot and craft is put to the test. Because of its extremely light construction a

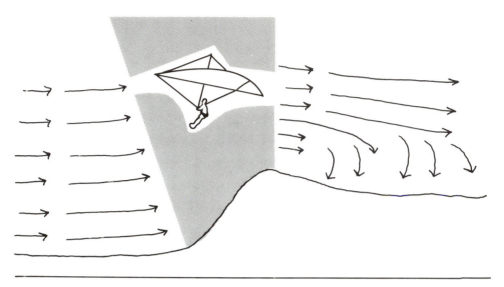

Figure 38 *Shaded area shows the best area of lift when ridge soaring*

To obtain the best performance from a hang glider, the pilot flies in the prone position to reduce drag from the body (Photo: Citroën UK)

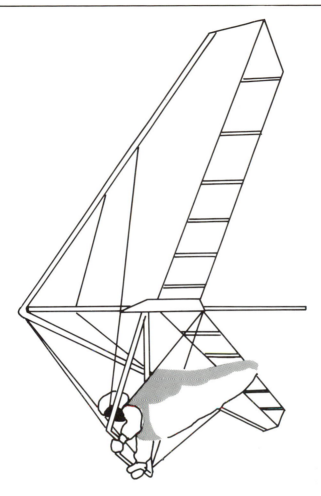

Figure 39 *To obtain the best performance from a hang glider, the pilot flies in the prone position to reduce the drag from his body*

hang glider is far more sensitive to turbulence than any other form of aircraft.

The other way to soar a hang glider is by using *hill* or *ridge lift*. As wind blows through a valley it encounters a hill and rises up over it. The best type of hill for soaring flight is therefore one with a rounded crest and a flatish top on which to land. The theory is that the pilot flies back and forth along the hill: flights of several hours have been achieved in this way.

If the hill falls away to the rear of the crest, however, beware; it is likely that you will encounter vicious downdraughts that may throw you and your glider to the ground very hard indeed. The top of cliffs, especially when jagged, also produce such strong eddies and wind rotors which are easily capable of smashing hang gliders to pieces and are therefore best left to the experts.

Something you will notice when observing hang gliders in flight is that the pilot appears to be lying flat or 'prone' behind the control bar. This is in direct contrast to your own early gliding training, which will have taught you to assume a sitting position. (You may have been supported by a 'belly' harness that allowed you half to sit and half to hang beneath the glider.) Once you have been flying for a short while, however, like all serious hang glider pilots you will start to use an *enclosed prone harness* when you glide. This comfortable pilot support is a 'mini-cockpit' for the hang glider. It will contain a parachute bag (*see* below) and a number of zip-up pockets to enable a small radio, maps and a Mars Bar to be carried. The pilot's legs are pushed into the bag through a zippered opening which is then pulled shut using a strong nylon cord. Flying in this way is very comfortable, even after several hours of gliding. Don't forget, though, that when you are coming in to land you must lower the wheels – a case of simply unzipping the bag and lowering your legs. It is not unknown for a pilot to forget to do this, the subsequent landing being considerably harder than he intended.

When you do begin to make soaring flights you will discover that air, even in summertime, can be cold. Flying in cold air is not only uncomfortable; it can also be dangerous. For the same reason that a swimmer immersed in cold water will get fatigued, so will a hang glider pilot be affected in cold air. The cold slows his reactions and creeps into his muscles. On a very cold day it is better to make several short flights rather than attempt one long one.

PARACHUTES

It has become increasingly common in recent years for all serious hang glider pilots to carry a parachute, and on several occasions they have saved lives. These parachutes are not of the large back-pack type worn by sport parachutists, but are small, hand-activated devices carried in a bag fastened to the glider's harness. In the event of an emergency the pilot pulls the handle of the bag and throws the parachute as hard and far away from the glider as he can. The canopy then opens at the end of a long strop, which ensures that the parachute itself does not obstruct the airframe, and both pilot and hang glider then descend to safety under the nylon umbrella.

HOW MUCH WILL IT COST?

The cost of learning to hang glide varies enormously from school to school, but at the time of writing the average cost for a four-day, full-time course is between £30 and £40 per day (including the use of a glider and all equipment). So a four-day training course that takes you up to Elementary Pilot Certificate level will cost between £120 and £160, and an eight- or nine-day course leading to the Club Pilot Certificate will cost between £270 and £360. Training need not be on a full-time basis; it can be undertaken on a daily basis or just at weekends if you so wish. If you can manage to form a small group, discounts on the above prices may be obtained: individual clubs and schools will be pleased to give further details. After that you will need to purchase your own glider with which to continue club flying.

A typical 'intermediate' hang glider will cost around £600 second-hand, or between £1,200 and £1,500 new. High-performance models may cost as much as £3,000.

SAFETY

To some, the mere mention of hang gliding conjures forth an image of dangerous 'thrill seekers' risking life and limb by throwing themselves foolishly from the tops of cliffs and hills. Like any physical activity, hang gliding involves a degree of risk, but in practice serious accidents during initial training are very, very rare indeed. Running up and down hills may leave you short of breath, and the nature of the terrain that is used for hang gliding may produce the odd sprained ankle, but if you are properly trained and obey all the rules you will not go far wrong.

RULES

There are not many rules as such in hang gliding. You will be expected to know about air law: after all, general aviation and low-level military aircraft will be operating in the same airspace as you. You must also learn about navigation, meteorology and the theory of flight. There are a few BHGA rules, but it is mostly a matter of applying plenty of common sense and remembering what you have been taught. The minimum age for hang gliding is 16.

A hang glider manufacturer will not sell you a new or used hang glider unless you hold a Club Pilot Certificate. Obsolete or dangerous hang gliders are occasionally offered for sale, so for your own sake get advice before you buy. Have the glider inspected by the club or manufacturer's technical officer to make sure that it is fully airworthy and that no previous owner has made any unorthodox or illegal modifications to it. The BHGA publishes its own, very good monthly colour magazine *Skywings*, which carries a selection of new and used hang gliders for sale in its small advertisements pages. This is available on joining the BHGA, whose address may be found on page 203.

As in the world of conventional gliding, a code of good hang gliding practice has been set up and is in operation. A flight should never be attempted alone, either by expert or beginner, for even a minor injury sustained in a remote area could quite quickly develop into a serious situation if there were no help readily to hand. Finding a suitable and accessible site from which to fly is not always easy. Permission to glide must always be obtained in advance

This is what it's all about – a hang glider in soaring flight (Photo: Citroën UK)

or there may be opposition from local people. Do not fly from a site where there are livestock in the intended landing area. Use only recognised gates and close them after you – do not climb through hedges. Avoid standing crops wherever possible, and if you do have to land in them minimise your movements and cause the least amount of damage possible. Keep members of the public out. Designate landing areas and take-off points and keep them free of spectators. Finally, for your own safety, wear a good quality crash helmet on every flight. The BHGA has an advice sheet on which types of helmet are suitable for hang gliding.

Chapter 6

PARAGLIDING

Paragliders are, as their name suggests, a combination of both parachute and hang glider. Modern developments in design and materials have resulted in a minimal 'aircraft' that is exceptionally light and yet possesses a glide ratio rivalling that of many hang gliders. Flying one demands no strength on the part of the pilot, only adroit handling, and that will come with instruction and practice. The sport inspires a tremendous feeling of freedom and is a satisfyingly economical way of taking to the air.

Paragliding as an airsport in its own right evolved from the earlier sport of *parascending*, which is still a popular activity at the newer paragliding clubs and on holiday beaches. Parascending began with Lemoigne's 1961 multi-slotted parachute canopy: this was towed aloft on a wire by a car or boat, and thus a new airsport was born. By 1967 the para-foil self-inflating wing had superseded the multi-slotted parachute, and flying with this new canopy continued for some years until self-launching from mountain tops in the French Alps became very popular. This new twist to the sport of parascending quickly spread, and it was not long before paragliders (as they were to become known) were jumping from small hills and even sea-cliffs in their attempts to become airborne and emulate the birds.

Since then, however, great advances in the performance of these self-inflating wings have taken place, and pilots can now enjoy the delights of soaring in slope-lift and in thermals with 'sailplanes' or 'hang gliders' that can be folded and packed away into a normal hiking rucksack.

FIRST STEPS

The sport of paragliding is closely linked with hang gliding, and indeed the respective sports even have their headquarters in the same building. Much of the previous chapter on hang gliding is applicable to paragliding, and so potential pilots should read the two chapters in conjunction.

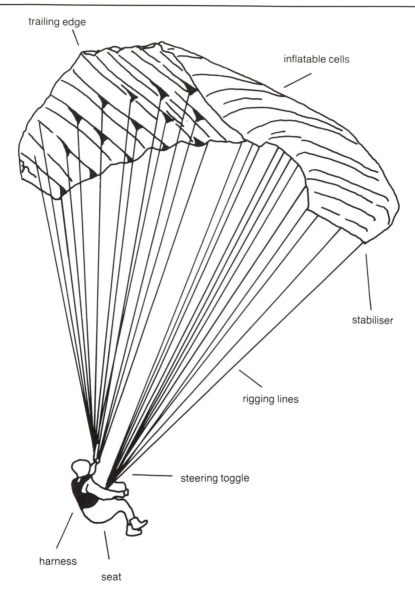

trailing edge

inflatable cells

stabiliser

rigging lines

steering toggle

harness

seat

Figure 40 *The paraglider and its components*

The chief difference between hang gliders and paragliders is that of weight. A typical hang glider weighs around 28 kilos (60 lb), while a typical paraglider weighs in at only 4 kilos (8 lb). This is because a hang glider has an airframe of aluminium covered with dacron sailcoth and braced with stainless steel flying wires; while a paraglider is really little more than an adapted parachute, its wing held in shape simply by air pressure inflating a series of cells incorporated within its design. The craft is easy to land and has a great deal of inbuilt pendulum stability in flight. The colourful fabric wing can be made ready for flight in just a few moments, and then it really is a case of taking a few fast steps down a grassy hillside until you are walking on air. So how do you begin?

Like the hang glider pilot you could start by visiting your local library; but, whilst you may find one or two books on hang gliding, you will almost certainly find nothing at all on the sport of paragliding. Although reading through hang gliding manuals will not be time wasted (after all, much of the training, theory, rules and regulations are almost identical), a better step would probably be to contact the British Association of Paragliding Clubs whose address, telephone and fax numbers may be found on page 203.

The BAPC make a small charge for their information pack (which can be purchased over the telephone with your credit card if you so wish). This pack contains: a membership application form; details of the various options of insurance that form a part of the membership; a shop order form for purchase of clothing, badges and accessories; details of the Pilot Rating Scheme; a directory of paragliding clubs; several colour leaflets from individual paragliding clubs; and a copy of the BHGA/BAPC joint monthly colour magazine *Skywings*.

If after reading this book and obtaining the BAPC information pack you decide that you would like to have a go at paragliding, you will need to find a club from which to take instruction. As with other forms of airsport, this should be as near to your home as possible in order to cut down on any unnecessary travelling time (*see* pp. 191–4 'Where to Paraglide'). Most clubs offer a wide range of courses including one-day introductory days, two-day weekend courses and full four-day Student Pilot Rating or Club Pilot Rating courses. All begin by teaching you how to fall over properly on landing – the *parachute landing fall* – although this is only a basic emergency procedure (most of your landings should be gentle and controlled). You will also be taught the following: how to perform the daily safety check of a paraglider prior to flying; how to appraise flying sites and weather conditions; the basic theory of flight; air law; airmanship; and simple meteorology. You will have the BAPC rating system explained to you and finally be shown how to inflate and ground-handle a paraglider.

The one-day course is intended as a fun day out. Ground training is kept to a minimum, and by the end of the morning you should have several flights to your credit (short hops of between 7 and 29 metres (20–80 ft). The rest of the day is spent developing your new skills and flying under the supervision of your instructor. The general aim of the one-day course is to give the newcomer a taste of the sport and to get him flying quickly and safely. This often means a student/instructor ratio of one to one.

The two-day weekend course gives a student more time to practise his flying. Like the one-day student, after some short hops he will move progressively up the hill to attempt higher and longer flights. Radio contact often

You will start your paraglider flying on the beginner's slope, making a series of small, bird-like hops and working your way up the hill as you improve with practice (Photo: Airwave)

You will get lots of ground handling practice at a paragliding school (Photo: Airwave)

assists students during this early training: a receiver is fitted into their safety helmet and an instructor stands at the bottom of the slope to ensure that they make a safe, soft landing. As an approximate guide, by the second day a student of average ability can expect to be making flights of around 73–110 metres (200–300 ft). The four-day course is for the person seriously interested in the sport and is designed to cover the BAPC curriculum for the Student Pilot Rating, the first step on the ladder to becoming an independent paraglider pilot. By the end of this course you should be fully conversant with all the necessary theory, be able to handle and check the equipment confidently, and to take off, turn and land safely.

THE PARAGLIDER LICENCE

Like its close cousin, the British Hang Gliding Association, the BAPC does not issue a formal pilot's licence. Instead, a series of certificates or 'ratings' are awarded as the pilot progresses. These start with the Student Pilot Rating and range through Club Pilot and Pilot up to Advanced Pilot.

MEDICAL REQUIREMENTS

Not surprisingly, these are identical to the standards required of a potential hang gliding student. You do not need to be very fit to take up paragliding, but you will be walking up and down hills and will need to be able to run for short distances. Anyone with any form of disability should consult their doctor before taking part in paragliding, and the club should be made aware of any special requirements by telephone when you book your course of instruction.

WHAT TO WEAR

Clothing requirements are identical to those of the hang glider pilot: warm, windproof garments and a stout pair of boots (or any other type of footwear that offers ankle support and has no lacehooks.) A crash helmet will be provided by your club.

THE PILOT RATING SCHEME

Today's paraglider pilots often move from site to site and from club to club, so it is necessary to have common standards to provide a basis for the assessment (by both clubs and instructors) of visiting pilots and students. These are offered by the four main levels of the Pilot Rating Scheme. Together with the

Figure 41   *Launching a paraglider*

A well-equipped and well-dressed paraglider pilot prepares his canopy for launch during a paragliding competition (Photo: Airwave)

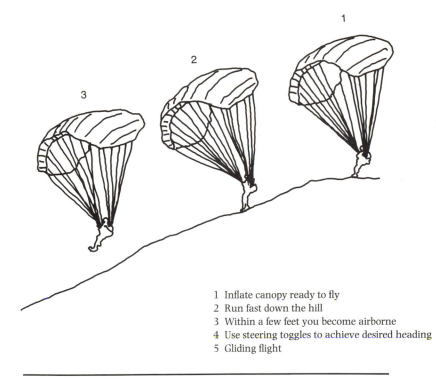

1 Inflate canopy ready to fly
2 Run fast down the hill
3 Within a few feet you become airborne
4 Use steering toggles to achieve desired heading
5 Gliding flight

use of simple written examinations, the scheme ensures that paraglider pilots are sufficiently 'airminded' to take their place alongside other airspace users. The full Pilot Rating Scheme is as follows.

Student Pilot rating

To achieve Student Pilot rating the *ab-initio* entrant must complete a Student Training Card and achieve a pass standard in the following tasks:

- correctly carry out pre- and post-flight routines;
- safely carry out launch assistant duties for other pilots;
- carry out pre-flight checks;
- *self launch* – complete a minimum of six low flights and a further six to a height of at least 36 metres (100 ft);
- complete four appropriate controlled landings in a designated area;
- demonstrate safe airspeed control;
- complete left and right turns;
- describe and evaluate a site and give a flight plan appropriate for the conditions;
- pass the Student Pilot written examination;
- satisfy an instructor as to attitude and airmanship.

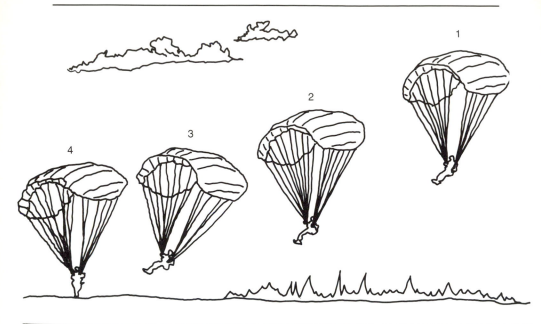

Figure 42 *Landing a paraglider*

1 Approaching touchdown
2 Ground is getting close
3 Pull steering toggles down to slow descent of canopy
4 Make a soft stand-up landing

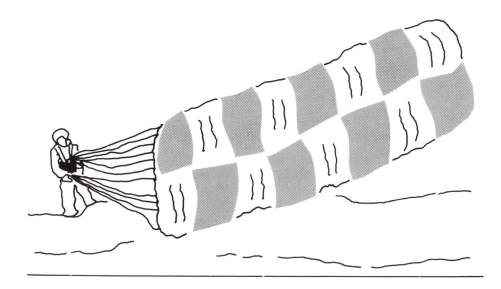

Figure 43 *A paraglider's first step towards becoming airborne lies in the preparation of the canopy. This is sometimes known as 'building the wall'*

Club Pilot rating

To achieve Club Pilot rating the student pilot must achieve a pass standard in the following tasks:

- *self launch* – complete a minimum of 20 flights (subsequent to attaining Student Pilot status) to a height of at least 72 metres (200 ft), and two soaring flights of at least five minutes duration above take-off height. Two of the flights must be for top landing;
- experience take-offs in wind speeds not exceeding 5 mph and in wind speeds of between 10 and 15 mph;
- execute stable 180° turns;
- complete five appropriate landings in a designated area of not more than 20 metres (55 ft) in radius;
- maintain the standards of the Student Pilot rating;
- pass the Club Pilot written examination;
- complete the appropriate log-book entries;
- join a BAPC club;
- satisfy an instructor as to attitude and airmanship.

Figure 44 *You will be taught how to inflate and ground-handle a paraglider safely . . . as well as receive tuition in flight planning and pre-take-off checks*

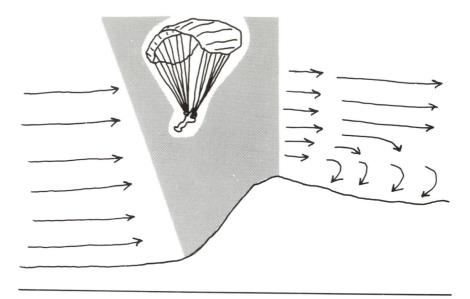

Figure 45 *Shaded area shows the best area of lift when ridge soaring*

Pilot rating

To achieve Pilot rating the candidate must have held the Club Pilot rating for at least four months and must achieve a pass standard in the following tasks:

- *self launch* – complete a minimum of 50 flights subsequent to attaining Club Pilot status with at least 15 flights to a height above that of take-off; at least 15 flights in wind speeds over 15 mph; and at least five flights in thermal conditions. At least five minutes of each flight must be above take-off height, and a minimum of 15 hours of flying must be completed subsequent to obtaining Club Pilot rating;
- complete a full dynamic stall with stall recovery, spins and spiral dives;
- carry out controlled 360° turns in both directions;
- complete at least five flights of over five minutes duration;
- fly in accordance with the rules of the air and air-traffic rules;
- carry out five controlled landings in a designated area of not more than 10 metres (28 ft) in radius;
- *self launch* – carry out two top landings at each of two sites;
- experience flying in four different wind directions and at two sites;
- pass the Pilot written examination;
- satisfy an instructor as to attitude and airmanship.

Advanced Pilot rating

To achieve Advanced Pilot rating the candidate must have held the Pilot Rating for at least four months and achieve a pass standard in the following:

118

Figure 46 *You will be taught how to fall over properly using the parachute landing fall. This is a basic emergency procedure – most landings will be gentle, controlled stand-up landings*

- complete a minimum of 150 flights subsequent to attainment of Pilot rating;
- complete at least 35 hours of flying time subsequent to attainment of Pilot rating;
- complete *Federation Aeronautique Internationale* (FAI) Bronze Eagle Badge (consisting of a 15 km flight, a 500 metre (1,375 ft) height gain, or a flight lasting one hour);
- complete a 20 km cross-country flight;
- complete a 20 km out-and-return flight;

A paraglider in thermalling flight (Photo: Airwave)

- pass the Advanced Pilot written examination;
- satisfy the instructor as to attitude and airmanship.

THE GROUND EXAMINATIONS

Paragliding is flight in its most simple form, and therefore it follows that the written examinations are of a fairly basic nature. They are much less comprehensive than those sat by applicants for any of the 'power' licences. To prepare for the written examinations you should study the following subject areas, details of which can be found in the BAPC Student Pilot's Handbook and Club Pilot's Handbook.

Student Pilot rating examination
Rules of the air; the relationship between air, ground and wind speed; flight theory; local weather conditions; general weather; emergencies; and general regulations.

Club Pilot rating examination
Rules of the air; flight theory; airmanship; and meteorology.

Pilot rating examination
Airspace matters; flight theory; and meteorology.

Paragliding allows a man or woman to take to the sky with a minimum of training and expense (Photo: Airwave)

121

Advanced Pilot rating examination

This examination is based on flight planning for cross-country flying and the application of practical meteorology.

HOW MUCH WILL IT COST?

The cost of learning to paraglide, like the cost of most other forms of flying, does vary considerably from club to club depending on where in the country you choose to train. On average a typical one-day course – including insurance cover – will cost around £50. A two-day weekend course including insurance cover will cost around £90, and complete four-day courses for the Student Pilot or Club Pilot rating, including insurance, will cost in the region of £170. All these prices include provision of an individual canopy and helmet, although once trained you will need to purchase your own paraglider and helmet if you are to continue club flying.

A typical second-hand paraglider can be bought for between £500 and £1,000, while new 'wings', such as a Harley Typhoon or Flight Design Dream, cost in the region of £1,500.

SAFETY

Paragliding, like its close relatives parachuting and hang gliding, does carry an element of risk. Running up and down hills in order to launch your paraglider may leave you slightly breathless; beyond this, if you follow your training and fly only when your instructor tells you it is safe to do so, you will not come to much harm.

Chapter 7

BALLOONING

A field full of multi-coloured balloons is a beautiful sight, and there can be few more pleasant ways of experiencing the joys of flying than in a hot-air balloon in the early morning. The sound of bird-song can usually be heard clearly in the still and quiet dawn air as the huge nylon balloon drifts slowly over mist-laden fields: the roaring flame of the burners is the only intrusion into a peaceful world.

In recent years, interest in the sport of hot-air ballooning has mushroomed and there are now a great many companies that operate balloons for film and television work and for advertising and corporate entertainment. Almost every local newspaper now carries advertisments for champagne pleasure flights near to your home. For training, too, the hot-air balloon has become increasingly popular. Where perhaps 10 years ago there were only a dozen operators that could train you for a balloon pilot's licence, today there are well over 50.

Although as an aircraft a balloon may look rather simple – it is after all only a wicker basket and a container of hot air – its construction is in fact quite complex. A standard balloon canopy is made up of 12 vertical panels or *gores*, which run from the base up to the top of the balloon and give the distinctive shape. Each panel is stitched to the next and has load-bearing tapes along its long edges. Each gore is made up of 25 sub-panels, usually 3 ft wide and 12 ft long (but depending of course on the individual size and shape of the balloon). The overall shape of a finished balloon is derived entirely from the effect of the assembled panels which are now almost exclusively designed by computer.

Most modern balloons are quite large, 65,000 cubic feet (1,841 cubic metres) being a popular size for club and syndicate flying. The canopies are made from 'rip-stop' nylon weighing approximately 1.75 ounces per square yard; although the material is light, allowing easy packing away when the flying has finished, it is incredibly strong. Because flame from the burners

*The tranquillity of silent flight – hot-air ballooning offers challenges and rewards
unmatched by any other branch of sport aviation* (Photo: Cameron Balloons)

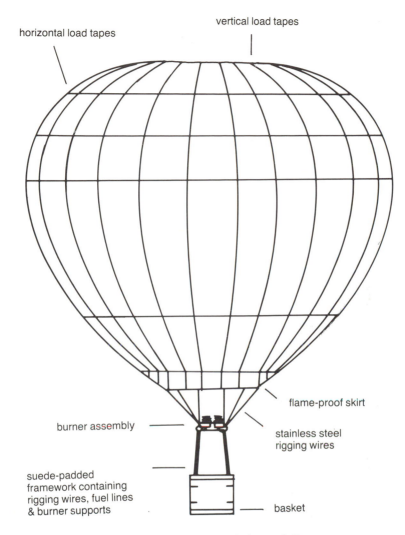

horizontal load tapes

vertical load tapes

flame-proof skirt

burner assembly

stainless steel
rigging wires

suede-padded
framework containing
rigging wires, fuel lines
& burner supports

basket

Figure 47 *The anatomy of a hot-air balloon*

blasts straight into the open mouth of the balloon, the protecting skirt around the canopy's lower edges is usually made of a fire-proof material such as *Nomex*.

The two main flying controls built into the balloon canopy are known as the *ripping panel* and the *discharge* or *dump valve*. The ripping panel is a large triangle of nylon at the very top of the balloon, secured by velcro tape around its edges. This provides the pilot with a means of allowing the hot air to escape quickly on landing, thus deflating the balloon and sparing its crew an uncomfortable drag across the field. To prevent the panel being accidentally opened in flight there is a built-in safety precaution: a coloured line usually has to be broken at three points before the panel can be opened. The other control, the

125

discharge or 'dump' valve, is located on the side of the balloon canopy and can be opened in flight to allow excess hot air to escape. In practice, however, this control is seldom used as the hot air will only have to be replaced later in the flight and the propane gas needed to heat the air costs money.

Underneath the canopy is probably the most important item as far as the crew are concerned – the basket. This is almost always made of genuine, woven willow-cane: whilst other materials and construction techniques have been tried intermittently, the simple, low-technology basket's combination of strength, shock-absorbing qualities and low weight has not yet been surpassed. The basket is suspended from the skirt of the balloon by stainless steel wire ropes, and provides a cockpit for the crew as well as a home for the burners and various other pieces of auxiliary equipment.

The power units of the balloon – the burners – work on the same basic principles as (of all things) a gas camping stove! The liquid propane gas is vapourised via a coil on each burner and passed through a set of four jets on each unit to form a flame. The supplies of propane from the cylinders to the main jets are entirely independent, each having its own on/off cock. This is a safety measure; cocks have been known to fail to open when they have been most needed. The cylinders are usually made of aluminium for lightness and

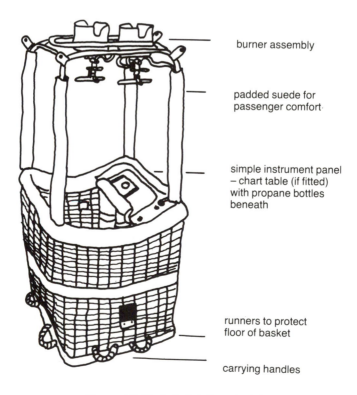

burner assembly

padded suede for
passenger comfort

simple instrument panel
– chart table (if fitted)
with propane bottles
beneath

runners to protect
floor of basket

carrying handles

Figure 48 *The hot-air balloon basket*

each holds approximately 20 kg (44 lb) of liquid propane. Each burner unit is controlled by a single on/off tap connected to the fuel bottles by strong, high-pressure hoses. The burners are not left on continually, as you may think, but are ignited for short bursts of heat approximately 30 seconds apart. These bursts are around the 1,900 degree centigrade mark and combustion is almost perfect, so there is very little chance of a build-up of explosive gases in the balloon canopy. Besides the fuel bottles and burners the basket may carry very basic instrumentation – usually in the form of an altimeter, a vertical speed indicator and perhaps an envelope temperature gauge. Also carried is a trail of rope of around 45 metres (150 ft) in length, coiled on the outside of the basket, and a dry-powder fire extinguisher.

FLYING A BALLOON

Like conventional gliding, ballooning is a team affair and a pilot needs several helpers to prepare a hot-air balloon for flight. Rigging usually starts by assembling the burners and basket. The two lightweight propane gas containers are lifted into the basket and strapped firmly into position. The burners are then installed. These are usually supported by four fibreglass or metal rods, one rod being slotted into each corner of the basket. Stainless steel cables running from each corner of the basket to the burner frame make sure the rods are held in position and help to absorb the tension loads between the basket and the balloon. Each of these rods is enclosed in a zip-fastened and padded sleeve made of leather or suede to protect the pilot and his passengers from any knocks during a less-than-perfect landing. With the burners and support rods fixed to the basket, all that remains is to connect up the fuel hoses before attention may be turned to the balloon canopy itself.

This is now pulled from its storage bag (how does all that material fit into such a small container?) and spread out on the ground. The flying wires that attach the canopy to the basket are untangled and clipped to the burner frame assembly, and the balloon is ready for inflation. At this stage expensive, propane-generated hot air is not used; cold air is driven into the balloon envelope by petrol-powered inflator fans. A helper or two holds open the mouth of the balloon and the fan (which is really nothing more than a large version of a typical desk-top air conditioning fan) is used to fill half of the balloon with cold air. When this has been done the basket is laid on its side and, after fuel pressures have been checked, the burners are ignited and jets of flame shot into the balloon. To allow for a symmetrical inflation of the canopy the burners are mounted on *gimbals* that allow the pilot to direct the blasts of heat in any direction.

With the hot air now being shot into the canopy the balloon seems to come to life; it rises from the ground slowly until it is floating vertically above the basket. All hands are now required to stop the balloon from lifting off

Most balloon launches tend to take place at or close to dawn, when the still and silent air allows for easy inflation and safe, smooth flying
(Photo: Cameron Balloons)

prematurely. As all the helpers hang on to the basket, pulling it to the earth, final preparations for flight are made by the pilot. Passengers are helped aboard and – with a roar from the burners and perhaps a gentle bump or two of the basket – the balloon is released from its moorings and takes to the air.

You decide to level off at 610 metres (2,000 ft) and check to see what the wind is doing today. Visibility is good, and flying at 5 or 6 knots you estimate that you are drifting to the south. A quick check of your map reveals that you are roughly on course. Navigation in good weather is a simple affair, basic map reading being the only skill required. How far you go depends solely on the wind. In the United Kingdom the air is seldom absolutely calm, but it does happen very occasionally that your balloon is becalmed and you must wait for the wind to pick up (or use the burner to climb higher where there is likely to be a drift of wind to transport you on your way).

If you do have to terminate the flight, select a landing place. Needless to say, since your course cannot be altered, only those fields directly ahead may be considered. Pick a nice green field where the grass looks soft and there is no livestock wandering about. Then initiate a long, shallow descent that enables you to check that road access is available to the retrieve crew's vehicle. As the balloon descends, frequent blasts of the burners will be required to check the loss of height and ensure a smooth approach. Still using blasts of burner, bend your knees and brace your handholds for landing. When you are down, the ripping panel is pulled away and the hot air trapped in the canopy escapes

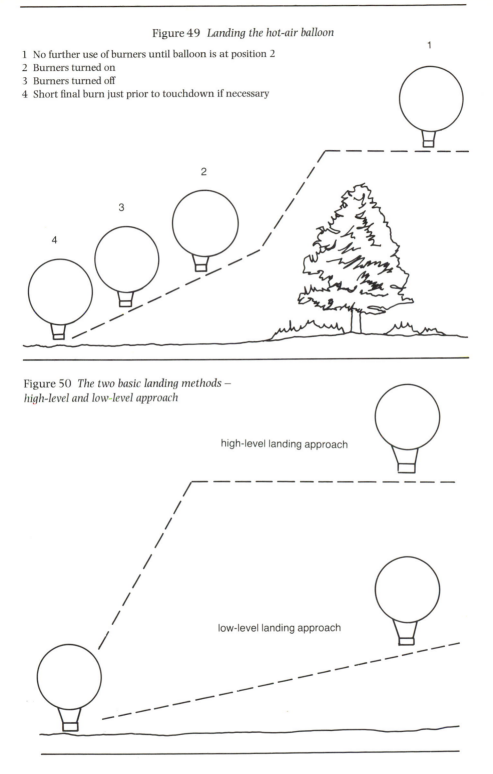

Figure 49 *Landing the hot-air balloon*

1 No further use of burners until balloon is at position 2
2 Burners turned on
3 Burners turned off
4 Short final burn just prior to touchdown if necessary

Figure 50 *The two basic landing methods –*
high-level and low-level approach

high-level landing approach

low-level landing approach

with a whoosh, the brightly coloured balloon slowly collapsing on to the ground around you. With any luck the retrieve crew will already be waiting at the side of the field and packing away can begin. Remember, though, that not all of your balloon landings will take place on calm days! On a day when the wind has gathered strength since lift-off the landing can be much more exciting and you must be prepared for a bit of a rough ride. A tight hold on the basket is essential as the balloon may be dragged several hundred feet across a wet and bumpy field before finally coming to a stop.

WHAT MUST I DO TO GET A LICENCE?

You must receive balloon flying tuition from a qualified pilot. However, unlike the training for any of the powered pilot's licences, not *all* of the required tuition need be with a qualified instructor. The minimum flying experience for a licence is 12 hours – comprising not less than six flights – under instruction. Two of these flights must be under the supervision of a British Balloon and Airship Club approved instructor, but the remainder may be with any licensed balloon pilot (although it is recommended that this pilot have at least 10 hours of pilot-in-command flying experience). Each of your flights must be recorded and signed off by the instructing pilot in a balloon pilot's flying log-book (obtainable from the BBAC sales department whose address may be found on page 203.) When you are considered ready you will have a test flight with an examiner and make a solo balloon flight.

The examination flight is really the airborne equivalent of a driving test and must be conducted by one of the 12 registered BBAC flight test examiners. The test is not difficult and the examiner will not expect you to have all the qualities of an experienced balloon pilot; simply the ability to operate the balloon safely through a normal flight. The solo flight will last no less than 30 minutes, and you will be required to repeat all the actions of the examination flight, this time on your own. It will be made under the supervision of the testing examiner or a delegated instructor. In addition to your flying instruction examination and solo flight, you will also be required to pass a series of written examinations. You should not be daunted by these as they are based on common sense, not academic brilliance.

Like those of the more conventional branches of powered flying, these written examinations must be passed before your Private Pilot's Licence (Balloons and Airships) can be issued. They are simple multiple-choice papers which present you with three possible answers. Two of these will be plausible but wrong, leaving one correct answer for you to identify with a tick. The usual pass-mark required is 70%. The subjects for the ground examinations are navigation, meteorology, air law, human performance and limitations, and balloon systems. The textbooks you will have been reading since beginning balloon lessons, plus lots of tips from your pilots and instructors along the way, will more than adequately have prepared you to achieve good pass-marks – but a commitment to some hard study will be required on your part. The examination subjects in more detail are as follows.

Navigation

The ability to navigate accurately and safely is of prime importance in all types of flying. Although the balloon pilot has no real choice as to his direction of flight, being at the mercy of the prevailing wind, he will be expected to demonstrate an elementary understanding of map reading, cross-country flying and the effects of wind on track and groundspeed.

Meteorology

A hot-air balloon is less weather tolerant, especially during launch and land-ing, than any other type of aircraft, so a good understanding of weather systems and the conditions required for their formation is vitally important. You can expect to be asked about cloud types, the conditions required for the formation of different types of fog, temperature and humidity, and the forma-tion of frontal systems.

Air law

As a balloonist you will not be flying into airfields or making much use of the various air-traffic facilities, but, in common with other air users, you must have a good understanding of air law. The paper on this subject may include questions on types of airspace, operating rules and regulations, airways and control zones.

Human performance and limitations

Like the examination for the microlight pilot in this subject, this is a simplified version of the paper taken by applicants for light aircraft and helicopter licences. It covers a very general understanding of human capabilities and limitations and the factors affecting their ability to fly safely.

Balloon systems

Similar to the aircraft technical examination sat by light aircraft students, this paper requires the candidate to demonstrate a general understanding of balloons and ballooning.

MEDICAL REQUIREMENTS

There is no longer any need to take an aviation medical to fly a balloon. All that is required is that you submit a declaration of fitness countersigned by your own doctor. You do not need to have your declaration of fitness signed *before* you start taking ballooning instruction, but (since it also serves the

131

purpose of being a student pilot's licence) you must have had your doctor sign it before you will be allowed to fly solo. The form will ask you to declare to the best of your knowledge and belief that you are in good health, that you are not receiving any medical care, and that as far as you are aware you do not suffer from any of the following conditions: epilepsy; fits; a recent, severe head injury; recurrent fainting, giddiness or blackouts; high blood pressure; coronary artery disease; insulin-controlled diabetes; any psychiatric disorder; or any other disorder liable to cause incapacitation. The declaration is valid for five years if you are aged under 40; for two years if you are between 40 and 50; for one year if you are between 50 and 70; and for six months if you are 70 years or over.

HOW LONG DOES IT TAKE TO GET A LICENCE?

This depends on the weather, on your financial situation, and on balloon availability. British weather being what it is you may have to be patient, as a good balloon pilot/instructor will not want you to start your flying career in anything except the right conditions. If funds permit, an intensive two-week package course to full PPL standard may be taken with a company such as the Anglo Alpine Balloon School. Flying in the picturesque scenery and exceptional ballooning conditions of Bavaria in Southern Germany, a concentrated course like this is undoubtedly the quickest way to get your licence. Whichever method you choose, and however long it takes you (though the course only requires a minimum of 12 flying hours, remember!), the time spent is well worth it.

CIVIL AVIATION AUTHORITY CURRICULUM FOR
FLIGHT TRAINING EXERCISES

- Preparation for flight: explain the meteorological forecast; select a suitable launch site; carry out flight planning to include load chart calculations and navigation.
- Preparation for flight; brief crew and passengers.
- Rig the balloon for flight.
- Inflate the balloon.
- Take off in wind strengths of more than 5 knots from shelter.
- Take off in wind strengths of less than 5 knots without shelter.
- Take off in wind strengths of more than 5 knots without shelter.
- Climb and make the transition to level flight.
- Level flight.
- Descend and make the transition to level flight.
- Approach and overshoot from a high level.

132

- Approach and overshoot from a low level.
- Navigation.
- Fuel management.
- Emergency procedures – burner system and fire.
- Emergency procedures – fast climb/descent.
- Landing and action after flight.
- Tethered flight and use of the handling line.
- Flight in wind strengths greater than 12 knots.
- Demonstrate airmanship.

AIRSHIP AND BALLOON SYSTEMS EXAMINATIONS

- Pre-inflation checks; post-inflation checks; crew and passenger briefing; pre-flight checks; and in-flight checks.
- Criteria for take-off sites and weather conditions.
- Launching; in-flight and landing hazards and precautions; problems of immediate touch-downs.
- Flying in convection – hazards and precautions.

The Cameron one-man balloon suspends its pilot in a harness, rather than in a traditional willow basket. You need a good head for heights in order to fly a balloon like this
(Photo: Cameron Balloons)

- Landing criteria for landing fields; crowd control; relationship with land-owners.
- Emergency procedures in the event of failure of the burner system or pilot system; premature descents in downdraughts; miscalculation of take-off angle or approach glide path; emergency use of burner, ripping line, ballast and trail rope.
- Canopy: controls; definition and purpose of primary and secondary elements; permissible damage.
- Propane: properties in liquid and gaseous form; ground handling and transfer; storage and fire prevention; laws and regulations.
- Burners: principles of operation; main elements and controls; output in different ambient conditions; care and maintenance.

ARE THERE ANY BALLOONING FACILITIES NEAR ME?

Affiliated to the British Balloon and Airship Club are a number of regional clubs which organise local ballooning meets, social gatherings with guest speakers, slide/video evenings, and visits to manufacturers, air-traffic control centres and meteorological stations. Once you have joined the BBAC it is recommended that you also join the nearest regional club (*see* pp. 195–9). This will put you in touch with balloon pilots and crews who are flying locally and give you the opportunity to participate in their activities.

WHERE CAN I FLY?

You can fly a balloon from any reasonably open ground, given the land-owner's permission and taking into account any local controlled airspace and heavily built-up areas. Most of the regions within the British Balloon and Airship Club have favourite flying sites with regular take-offs. On most weekends throughout the year an organised balloon meet takes place some-where in the country; these are organised by the BBAC, by a regional club, or perhaps by a commercial or corporate sponsor.

WHAT IF I JUST WANT A SINGLE FLIGHT?

If you are not yet sure that ballooning is the right choice of airsport for you, why not do as prospective light aircraft, helicopter, microlight and glider pilots do and get yourself a 'trial' flight? A one-hour pleasure flight costs around £90 at the time of writing, and will give you an ideal introduction to the sport. You will see how the balloon is inflated, crewed, flown, controlled and landed, and by the end of the flight you will know for sure whether or not

*Few sights can compare with that of an early morning mass balloon launch,
particularly when the backdrop includes the beautiful grounds of Leeds Castle in
Kent, a popular site for ballooning venues* (Photo: Cameron Balloons)

this is the sport for you. Most balloon schools offer these pleasure flights, so for
further details see pp. 195–9 of this book or send for the BBAC's excellent free
1994 Ballooning Directory which contains a list of operators and pilots who
carry out commercial work.

THE BRITISH BALLOON AND AIRSHIP CLUB

The British Balloon and Airship Club (BBAC) is the national club for British balloon pilots, crew members and enthusiasts. It is recognised as the representative and governing body for ballooning in the United Kingdom by the Royal Aero Club, the *Federation Aeronautique Internationale* and the Civil Aviation Authority. The club was founded in 1965 with the following objectives:

- the formation of an association of persons interested in the practice and encouragement of developing lighter-than-air flight, hot-air ballooning, gas ballooning and airship flying;
- the encouragement of the study of ballooning and airship flying, pilotage, navigation and the improved design of balloons and airships;
- the holding and arrangement of meetings and competitions in ballooning, and the offering and granting of contributions towards the provision of prizes, awards and distinctions;
- the promotion of social events involving members and their friends.

The BBAC is very active in representing the interests of its members in discussions with such organisations as the Civil Aviation Authority (Airworthiness Division and Private Aviation Committee) and general aviation bodies such as GAMTA and AOPA and the Sports Council (which recognises ballooning as a growing sport and gives the club financial assistance for the organisation and promotion of competitive ballooning both nationally and internationally).

HOW CAN I BECOME INVOLVED?

The answer is simple: join the BBAC! An application form can be obtained from their information office or from the new members' secretary (*see* page 203). On joining you will receive a colourful membership certificate, a membership card, a lapel badge, a sew-on badge and a car sticker. Every two months you will receive a copy of the club's full-colour magazine *Aerostat* which contains news of ballooning events both at home and abroad, topical and historical features, technical and safety articles, a calendar of balloon meetings, and pages of classified advertising. At the time of writing membership subscriptions are as follows: junior member (under 18 years of age) £5; full member £15; family member (two members at the same address) £18.

HOW MUCH WILL IT COST?

It is possible to become a balloon pilot by taking a course of instruction with a commercial school, or by joining a regional flying group. A typical example of

Hot-air balloons come in every size and shape imaginable
– so if you like a drink while you fly, this one is for you!
(Photo: Cameron Balloons)

a commercial school is the British School of Ballooning based at Petworth in West Sussex, whose instructors are qualified and experienced professional balloonists. Amongst the usual champagne pleasure flights, corporate balloon operations and flying for film and television work, they offer a complete Private Pilot's Licence (Balloons and Airships) course for around £2,000 (plus VAT).

An alternative to learning with a school, and a route chosen by many prospective balloon pilots, is joining a regional flying group. Several interested persons club together to purchase a balloon and share its running costs. This is an ideal way for a newcomer to begin training and, since the average balloon basket is large enough to carry three or four people at a time, you will pick up a lot of useful experience whilst flying as a passenger.

A word of caution, however: as a general rule, the smaller the group the better. Putting together a large group, while financially advantageous, will have the result of too many members wanting to spend time in the air and therefore less flying time for each individual.

Like cars, balloons come in many shapes and sizes. Balloon manufacturers listed in BBAC Commercial Directory will be happy to provide more details of the models available and their current prices. The annual and hourly operating costs of running a balloon, especially when shared among the members of a flying group, put the sport among the cheapest available ways of getting into the air.

BALLOONING CODE OF PRACTICE

The British Balloon and Airship Club is well aware of the necessity for maintaining good public relations with farmers and other landowners. Like the British Gliding Association and the British Hang Gliding Association, it has drawn up a code of good conduct with the National Farmers Union for the guidance of balloon pilots and crew members. A copy of this code is issued free to all balloonists. Among the more important points to note are the following.

Flight planning
Do not fly unless you are reasonably certain that your flight path will be over country suitable for landing a balloon. For example, during the summer months you should avoid flying over standing crops, particularly corn. Avoid any known stables, stud farms, large concentrations of livestock and noise-sensitive areas.

Taking off
Always obtain permission from the farmer or landowner before driving your equipment into a field. *Never* just pick somewhere to fly from and set up without permission. Brief all ground crew and other helpers to make absolutely sure all gates are closed after use.

In the air
Always fly high enough to avoid disturbing horses or livestock as you pass over. In practice, this means a height of at least 304 metres (1,000 ft) with the burners off. If it looks as though the animals may have been disturbed for any reason, note the location of the incident and check the cause with the farmer after landing. If you cannot locate him, consider informing the local police.

Landing and retrieval
Where possible, select a field that causes the least possible inconvenience to the farmer, landowner or other members of the public. Particular care must be taken during the summer months when standing crops cover large areas of the countryside. Remember too that the risk of fire during this period can be

Figure 51 *The effects of wind on a hot-air balloon take-off*

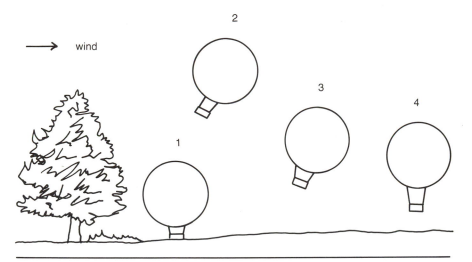

1 Sheltered from the wind behind trees, balloon takes off
2 As balloon clears the top of the trees, prevailing wind distorts canopy – causes loss of hot air and balloon descends
3 Pilot applies burner and re-establishes climb
4 Climb-out continues at a shallower angle, taking account of the wind

very great. Before deploying the trail rope, check that the ground both ahead and below is clear of power-lines, buildings and livestock. When the balloon has landed, discourage any onlookers from entering the field and trespassing on the farmer's property. Contact the farmer or landowner as soon as possible after landing and obtain his permission before bringing recovery vehicles on to the land.

Never make tethered flights or reinflate the balloon in the landing field unless you have obtained permission to do so from the farmer or landowner. If the farmer or landowner cannot be contacted directly on landing you must try to locate him as soon as possible afterwards. If any damage has been caused by the landing, or if the farmer wishes to take further action over your arrival on his land, exchange names and addresses (including those of your insurers).

HOT-AIR AIRSHIPS

The shape of ballooning has changed in recent years, and craft known as hot-air airships are now appearing in increasing numbers. Instead of the more conventional 'teardrop' shape, these airships are cigar shapes, nearly 30 metres (100 ft) in length and require over 2,688 cubic metres (96,000

139

cubic feet) of hot air for inflation. The main difference between an airship and a conventional balloon is that the former has forward motion thanks to a small 1,600 cc petrol engine driving a pusher propeller.

In place of the traditional wicker basket these airships usually have a light, fibreglass gondola amidships that carries a crew of two. As a practical means of transport they are not really effective, with a cruising speed of only around 20–25 knots. When operated just for pleasure, however, three or four enthusiasts could have a very enjoyable time taking turns to fly one.

GLOSSARY OF BALLOONING TERMS[1]

Bullet A metal peg attached to the top of the rip line.

Burn To turn on the on/off control and allow the main burner to work at full power.

Burner The unit consisting of the coiled stainless steel tubing that feeds the propane fuel to the jets.

Car lines Stainless steel wires running around and under the basket and emerging at the top, extending upwards and attached to the underside of the burner offload ring.

Copybook landing A perfect landing, without tipping the basket over and with the minimum of vertical speed.

Crew Chief The senior ground crew member who is responsible for the inflation and launching of the balloon.

Crown The top of the balloon.

Crown line A strong line attached to the top or crown of the balloon and used to hold the canopy down during inflation.

Doghouse landing A very fast landing which results in the balloon basket turning upside down.

Dump To open the dump valve in order to lose hot air and thus height.

Dump line The line made of stainless steel wire attached to the dump valve or window and running down to the basket.

Dump valve A fabric window which can be opened by means of the dump line to allow sufficient hot air to escape to allow the balloon to descend.

False lift When the balloon lifts off and starts to climb and then begins to descend again. This is usually due to incorrect weighing off or being assisted off the ground by enthusiastic but unskilled helpers.

Good landing A landing that you can walk away from.

Handling line A thin rope approximately 61 metres (200 ft) long.

Hands off During the 'hands off' helpers stand around the balloon basket firmly holding it to the ground. In order to tell if the balloon has enough lift to rise from the ground all helpers raise their hands vertically above the basket. If the balloon is ready for flight the basket will rise and the order 'hands on' will be given. When the pilot is ready for lift off he will say 'hands off and stand back'.

---

[1]Due to the number of terms specific to the sport of ballooning, this glossary has not been integrated into the general glossary on pp. 214–22.

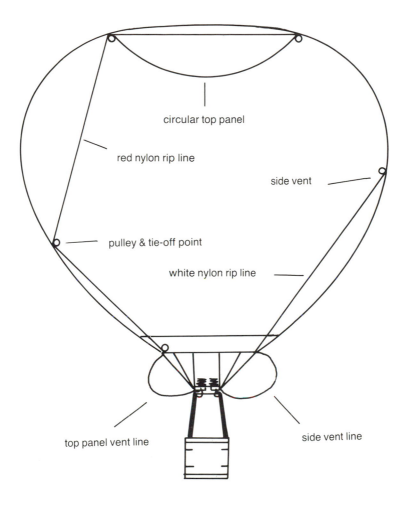

Figure 52 *The components of a hot-air balloon*

Heavy When the air in the balloon is not hot enough to keep it in equilibrium and the balloon starts to descend.

Light When the balloon is ready to leave the ground or is ascending.

Load ring The metal surround which holds the burner unit suspended by the rigging lines beneath the mouth of the balloon.

Mouth The bottom, open part of the balloon.

Pilot light A small pipe and jet which enables a constant flame to be available for re-igniting the main burners.

Rigging lines Stainless steel wires running from the load tapes to the burner ring.

Rip To pull open the rip panel to deflate the balloon.

Rip line A line attached to the top of the rip panel and running down to the basket.

Rip panel A large triangular section of a balloon canopy laced or fixed in place with velcro tape, which can be pulled open to deflate the balloon.

Skirt Fire-resistant material hung around the mouth of the balloon.

Tie-off thread Breaking thread of 14 kg (30 lb) used to secure rip.

Vigorous landing A term used by a pilot who has come in to land far too fast and the balloon has bounced back into the air before coming to rest.

Weighing off Checking for positive lift, making sure that the balloon will fly when the 'hands off' command is given.

Workperson All helpers and ground crew other than the pilot and crew chief.

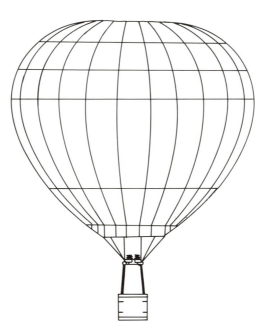

Chapter 8

PARACHUTING

The ancient Chinese and the Italian artist, philosopher and engineer Leonardo da Vinci are credited with the concept of the parachute. In fact, it was in France in the 18th century that the first man-carrying parachutes were actually made and used.

In 1797 the Frenchman André Jacques Garnerin made the first, historic descent by parachute (from a balloon). He used an open canopy of silk, stiffened with supporting poles. The next development was the invention of the limp parachute which had no stiffening poles to hold it open, and a trapeze bar instead of a basket for the parachutist. The first descent with one of these new 'chutes was made in 1897 by an American, Tom Baldwin. In 1919, another of Baldwin's countrymen, Leslie Irvin, made the first (intentional) free-fall parachute descent near Dayton, Ohio using his own hand-operated parachute. This revolutionised parachuting and gave birth to a new sport.

The modern parachute, however, has distinctly military origins. It was developed as a means of escaping from a balloon and, later, from a disabled aircraft in flight. Indeed, early sport parachutists used this ex-military equipment to experiment with the aerodynamics of the parachute by cutting holes in it to improve the qualities of steering and flight. Today, the parachute of the first-time student and of the top competitor has been designed intentionally for use within the sport.

Skydiving is now one of the most exciting of currently available airsports. Dynamic and colourful, it offers both men and women a chance to enjoy total mastery of the air and the freedom to make the skies their own – if only for a short while! At the highest level it is a competitive sport requiring finely tuned skills, intimate knowledge of the air, and perfect body control. As one of the fastest growing adventure sports in the United Kingdom today it offers not only access to the freedom of the sky but also unlimited opportunities to make and meet new friends and to enjoy a wide range of social activities. Many skydivers go on to join or form display teams, entertaining the public throughout the summer months by jumping into fêtes and country shows.

IS IT FOR YOU?

This is obviously the first question that the would-be parachutist must ask. When you are thousands of feet up in the sky, about to throw yourself into the

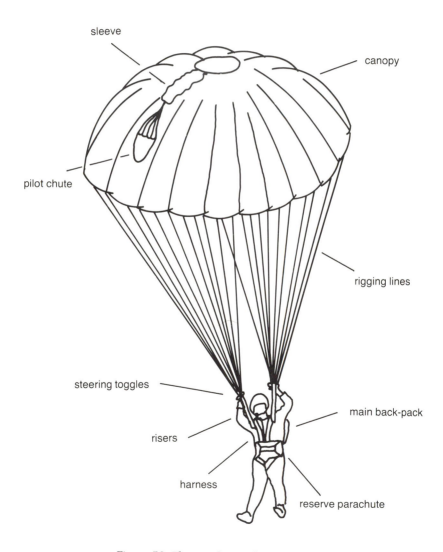

Figure 53 *The parachute and its components*

emptiness of space, you cannot afford to have any self-doubts. This sport calls for confidence, both in oneself and in one's training. The controlling body of the sport in the United Kingdom is the British Parachute Association. This association is responsible to the Civil Aviation Authority for the training and safety standards of all civilian parachutists and skydivers. All parachutists are required to observe the strict rules laid down for their own safety and the safety of others. The current membership of the Association is in excess of 40,000, and well over 150,000 parachutists have joined since its formation in 1962.

The BPA is funded by membership subscriptions, shop sales and sports council grants, and has an annually elected council of 12 full members who control all aspects of the sport. It represents all UK skydivers, and anyone who parachutes within the UK is a member. The control of the sport, including safety, training, competition, finance and development, is looked after by its full-time officers (two national coaches, safety officers and a full administrative staff). The Association is represented on the council of the Royal Aero Club, the *Federation Aeronautique Internationale* and the *Commission Internationale de Parachutisme*. There are approximately 40 parachute clubs in operation at the time of writing. A number of service clubs and associations also exist in the United Kingdom, Cyprus, Germany and Hong Kong. In Scotland, which has its own Scottish Parachute Association, there are currently three clubs in operation. A full list of all the parachute schools may be found on pp. 200–04.

AVAILABLE JUMPS

There are basically three ways of making that intrepid first parachute descent.

Static line parachute

The traditional, most widespread and least expensive way of making your first parachute jump is known as *static line* parachuting, in which the parachute opens automatically as soon as you leave the aircraft. The training course for this is at least six hours. The jump is made from an aircraft flying at between 610 and 1,060 metres (2,000 and 3,500 ft); the parachute or 'canopy' can be either round or square. During your training course you will be taught how to wear the equipment, exit the jump aircraft, steer your parachute, land safely and master associated emergency procedures. The course is designed to give you an introduction to the sport of parachuting: when you have completed your first drop you can progress to free fall by only your sixth jump! After a minimum of 22 jumps you can achieve British Parachute Association Category 8, which qualifies you to jump from 3,050 metres (10,000 ft) by yourself. Progression to Category 8 is the same regardless of which type of parachute you choose to use.

Formation skydiving is just one of the many different disciplines available
(Photo: The Red Devils)

In free fall at 120 mph. Surely there can be no other airsport more exhilarating
(Photo: The Red Devils)

Static line round parachute

Using the traditional round parachute you will jump from 610 metres (2,000 ft). Most courses take place at weekends, the training on the Saturday and the jump on the Sunday, weather permitting. Some clubs also train midweek, training and jumping on the same day (daylight *and* weather permitting). This type of course is ideal for groups such as those taking part in a charity fund-raising jump, but are equally suitable for the individual who would like to take part in a group activity and have lots of fun.

Static line square parachute

The use of square parachutes for static line parachuting is being developed at selected centres throughout the country. A more expensive method of making that first jump, it offers the opportunity of using an experienced skydiver's parachute from the outset. Using one of these more advanced *ram air* parachutes your first jump will be from 1,060 metres (3,500 ft). Courses for this type of drop are frequently run midweek, training and jumping taking place on the same day (daylight and weather permitting). The instruction on this type of course is more personalised and courses are therefore often limited to a maximum of three people.

Tandem jump

Tandem parachuting offers a quick and easy introduction to the art of free fall using a dual harness system. You jump with an instructor who controls the free fall, the parachute deployment and the landing. Tandem parachuting allows many disabled people to experience the thrills of skydiving, and is ideal for the person who would like to experience the sport without taking any of the responsibility. It is also particularly suitable for people only wishing to make the one jump. The jump is made from 3,050 metres (10,000 ft); the instructor opens the parachute at 1,515 metres (5,000 ft), giving you the excitement of approximately 30 seconds of free fall. Once the canopy has been opened you can have a go at steering the parachute if you wish. From a tandem jump you can move on to AFF (see below) or to static line jumping if you wish to stay with the sport.

Accelerated free fall

Commonly known as AFF, this is for the person who is confident enough (or perhaps brave enough) to go straight into a high-level, free-fall descent. The course provides free-fall instruction that will enable you to skydive from 3,660 metres (12,000 ft) on your first jump. At the end of the course you will be a British Parachute Association recognised parachutist, qualified to jump at any drop zone in the world. It is called the *accelerated free-fall course* because it accelerates the learning process. There are eight levels which can be achieved in as many jumps, and the course can be completed in three to nine days depending on the weather. All the jumps on the course are carried out

147

Figure 54 *'Stable spread' in free fall*

Figure 55 *The stable spread position. The static-line student will learn this position in basic training. It ensures that he always falls to earth face-first*

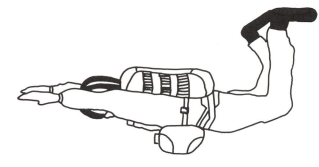

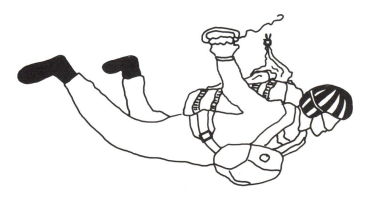

Figure 56 *The 'frog' free-fall position is less tiring than the stable spread position, but the rate of descent is usually faster. The parachutist looks down and reaches for the rip-cord handle; he then pulls it and recovers to the stable spread position*

Figure 58 *Tandem jumping*

from 3,050 metres (10,000 ft) or higher, which gives maximum time in free fall in which to relax and carry out your practice exercises. On your first three jumps you will be securely held by two instructors who will help and guide you throughout the skydive. At the correct height you will deploy the parachute; the instructors will not leave you until this has been safely completed. One instructor will remain with you on your jumps through the next four levels as you learn the more advanced skills of turning, looping and tracking. The eighth level is a shorter delay jump from a lower altitude.

The equipment used on an AFF course is of the most up-to-date type and has a couple of added safety features. Both the main and reserve parachutes are of the square or ram air type, which have the advantage of being stable and manoeuvrable (and thus easy to land). As an additional back-up the parachute is fitted with an automatic activation device, and you will also wear a radio receiver so instructions can be passed to you once you are under your open parachute.

GROUND TRAINING

Assuming that you have now made up your mind that you want to give parachuting a try, you will turn up at your local club on the appointed day ready for your course of instruction. Before the actual instruction starts, however, you will need to have the proper clothing and equipment. All parachute

150

courses involve a degree of physical activity, so a tracksuit and training shoes are ideal. If your training is taking place during the winter months, two or three layers of clothing and a pair of warm gloves are recommended. At most clubs a helmet and overalls are provided for a first jump (although you can bring your own along if you wish – an open-faced motorcycle type will do).

Although a number of parachute clubs are located on quite busy general aviation airfields, quite a few use little more than a large grass field with a take-off strip for the aircraft and one or two hangers for equipment storage. If you train during the summer months most initial instruction will be given outside. You will have lectures and practical training in subjects such as safety regulations, parachute packing and aircraft exit procedures. The full training programme as recommended by the British Parachute Association is as follows.

A   Orientation
- Documentation: check restricted permit BPA classification card.
- Outline of the training syllabus.
- Routine safety instructions to be observed with aircraft.
- Orientation flight (if needed).

B   Introduction
- Safety regulations.
- Equipment and clothing.
- Introduction to the type of aircraft in use.
- Determination of wind drift.
- Exit technique (stability).
- Emergency procedures.
- Canopy handling.
- Landing techniques.
- Parachute packing.

C   Familiarisation with parachutes
- The anatomy of the main chute.
- The anatomy of the reserve chute.
- The functioning of the main and reserve parachutes.
- Parachute fitting.
- Preplanning a parachute descent.
- Equipment-checking procedure.

D   The jumping aircraft
- Safety checks
- Procedure for entering and exiting the aircraft.
- Static line procedure.

- Signals and words of command in the air.

E   Aircraft exits
- Commands, signals and actions.
- Move into exit position.
- Position after exit (stable position).
- Counting, count follow-through and rip-cord procedure.

F   Emergency procedures
- Verbal count static line.
- Verbal count free fall.
- Check of main canopy immediately after opening.
- Recognition of malfunction.
- Corrective action.
- Drill period using suspended harness.

G   Canopy handling
- Checking canopy.
- Orientation with the ground: grasp toggles; check location over target and drift; work to wind (zig-zag method); check vertical angle of descent; avoid obstacles; harness drill period.

H   Preparing to land
- Altitude to adopt landing position.
- Body position (face into wind).
- Obeying ground instructions.

I   **Parachute landing falls**
- Normal.
- Tree.
- Power line.
- Water.
- Points of body contact.

J   **Field packing the parachute**
- Chain lines.
- Sleeve over canopy.
- Close one side flap with side opening bands.

- Secure all equipment and go to parachute packing area.

K   **Drop zone**
- Responsibility.
- Control.
- Rotation of ground personnel.

L   **Parachute packing instruction**
- Backpacks only.

M   **Testing all phases**

This is the British Parachute Association recommended training schedule. Its aim is to turn you into a safe and competent parachutist. During the parachute packing phase, backpacks only will be packed. Reserves are packed only by instructors and other qualified parachutists.

JUMPING

The first few jumps that you make as a beginner will be with the assistance of a static line. When you push yourself out of the jump aircraft you will fall to the full length of the static line – about 5 metres (15 ft). As the line is pulled tight by the weight of your body it will snap out the pins in the main backpack and the *drogue* or pilot chute will pull the sleeve-wrapped main parachute into the air. The sleeve will then be pulled up, allowing the main canopy to deploy. And you will be floating high above the earth beneath your nylon umbrella. To assist the smooth and safe opening of the canopy you should assume the *full-spread* or 'stable' position on leaving the jump aircraft. This position, in which the body is arched into the shape of a cross or star, will ensure that you do not spin and thus entangle the rigging lines of your parachute – a most unpleasant situation should you ever encounter it.

As you fall away you count as you have been taught: '1,000, 2,000, 3,000, 4,000, check canopy'. If on looking up you see that the main parachute has not opened for some reason, you must waste no time in deploying the chest-mounted reserve parachute. This smaller reserve parachute is approximately 7 metres (24 ft) in diameter; bearing a 91 kg (200 lb) parachutist it will stabilise the rate of fall to roughly 8 metres (25 ft) per second. The reserve pack has no drogue chute or sleeve: a large handle on the front of the pack is pulled open and the parachute packed within is grabbed and physically thrown away from the body by the parachutist. This enables rapid deployment and saves vital seconds in an emergency.

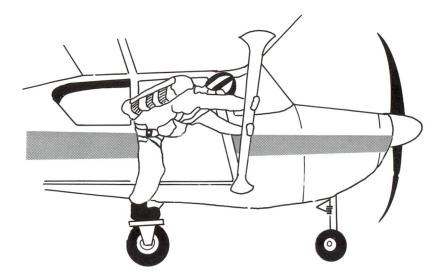

Figure 57 *Step jump used on the Cessna 172/180/182 series aircraft*

After you have made a minimum of six descents with your parachute opened automatically by a static line, you will be allowed to jump and open the parachute yourself. As you gain more experience you will delay the opening more and more. If you leave the jump aircraft at a height of 3,660 metres (12,000 ft), for instance, you will be able to free fall for 60 seconds. This is the highest practicable height from which to jump without using oxygen.

When you eventually become an experienced parachutist you may wish to enter competitions, either at your own club or further afield. There are five main specialisations in competition parachute jumping.

Accuracy landings
Jumping from a height of 915 metres (3,000 ft), competitors attempt to land on a 5 cm (2 in) disc situated on an electronic recording surface. Distance from the disc is measured in centimetres up to 16 cm (6.5 in). The aggregate distance over a number of rounds donates placement, with the lowest total distance being placed first. This category is the oldest of the competitive disciplines, and parachute development has enabled competitors to achieve great accuracy. Ten years ago the disc was 10 cm (4 in) in diameter. Today's top competitors train to land on a 3 cm (1.5 in) disc.

Style free-fall gymnastics
An individual free-fall event, during which competitors are judged on how quickly and precisely they perform a set routine of loops and turns. This is the loneliest of all the disciplines, demanding a high degree of skill and control.

Relative work – team formation skydiving

A team competition for between four and eight persons. During a set free-fall time (35 seconds for a team of four; 50 seconds for a team of eight) the team has to perform a series of predetermined formations as many times as possible. This discipline is probably the most popular at club level. The first world championships in relative work were held in 1975.

Canopy contact

Popularly known as *canopy stacking*, teams of four or eight link their parachutes together to form predetermined designs as many times as possible within a set time. This, the newest of parachuting disciplines, grew out of the advent of the square parachute development explosion of the 1970s. British teams have consistently won world championship medals in this event.

Paraski

The latest recognised discipline, paraski combines slalom skiing and accuracy landing parachuting as two separate competitions, with scores from each added together to determine the winner. Landing on a snow-covered slope adds a new dimension to accuracy competitions.

Competition in all the above events takes place at club, regional, national and international level. Unlike most competitive sports, skydiving allows men and women to compete on an equal footing: the only limiting factor is your own determination to win. At the annual national championships in Britain, parachutists compete over the first four disciplines at which the national team for that year's European and world championship disciplines are selected. It is hoped that skydiving will soon have full Olympic status.

GRADES OF COMPETENCE

Students progress initially within the sport via one of two category systems; which one depends on how they made their first jump. Static line parachuting, with either round or square canopies, takes you through category system 1 to 10 (reproduced below). For those receiving training in the accelerated free-fall (AFF) programme, a level system of 1 to 8 is used. As you progress you can also qualify for the *Federation Aeronautique Internationale* licences A to D.

Category 1

The student has attended a basic ground training course (a total of at least six hours of instruction) and is ready for a first static line parachute descent.

Category 2

The student has performed under observation a minimum of three absolutely stable static line descents in the full-spread position, counting throughout;

These parachutists are practising canopy stacking against a setting sun
(Photo: The Red Devils)

and has completed a total of 13 hours of ground training in accordance with the BPA minimum ground training programme.

Category 3
The student has performed under observation a minimum of three consecutive and successful static line descents with dummy ripcord pulls (counting throughout).

Category 4
The student has performed a minimum of five 5-second-delayed openings (counting throughout); has remained stable throughout opening on each descent; has looked at the ripcord handle before and during the 'reach and pull'; and has achieved a reasonable standard of canopy handling.

Category 5
The student has performed a minimum of five (stable) 10-second-delayed openings (counting throughout), and has learned to maintain heading during the aircraft exit and in subsequent free fall.

Category 6
The student has performed a minimum of five (stable) 15-second-delayed openings in the following sequence: (a) two flat stable; (b) three flat stable descents using instruments (after instruction) but continuing to count throughout. After successful completion of the above the student has demonstrated the ability to perform 360° turns in each direction, stopping the turn on the heading of the jump aircraft.

Category 7
The student has performed a minimum of five (stable) 20-second-delayed openings; has demonstrated the ability to recover from an unstable position on leaving the jump aircraft; and has been introduced to spotting.

Category 8
The student has landed within 46 metres (150 ft) of the centre of a target on a minimum of three 30-second-delayed opening descents; has learned to track and turn in during a track; and has been cleared for self-spotted descents of up to 2,135 metres (7,000 ft).

Category 9
The student has demonstrated to an instructor in free fall that he is fully in control of his movements, is aware of other parachutists around him, and is capable of taking evasive action if necessary; has demonstrated the ability to perform forward loops and barrel rolls; and has been introduced to relative-work parachuting.

Category 10

The student has demonstrated his ability in unsupervised relative work, having successfully executed the following: (a) a link followed by a backloop and a second link (with another Category 10 parachutist approved by the club chief instructor) on a single jump; (b) closure (third) on a three-man group on two separate occasions; (c) self-spotted descents of up to 3,660 metres (12,000 ft).

Note Up to and including category 6, all parachute students are observed and timed – from exiting the aircraft until full canopy deployment – by the jump-master in the aircraft.

The following FAI British Standard Certificates are issued by the Royal Aero Club of the United Kingdom.

- 'A' Certificate – Category 3: 10 jumps.
- 'B' Certificate – Category 5: 25 jumps, to include 10 jumps landing within 50 metres (164 ft) of the target.
- 'C' Certificate – Category 8: 50 jumps, to include 20 jumps landing within 20 metres (66 ft) of the target.
- 'D' Certificate – Category 10: 200 free-fall jumps, to include 20 jumps landing within 15 metres (49 ft) of the target.

AGE LIMITATIONS

The minimum age for parachute training is 16 years, provided that written consent has been obtained from the parent or guardian of under-18s. The maximum training age, excepting tandem jumping, is usually 50 years unless you can convince the club's chief instructor that you are very fit.

MEDICAL REQUIREMENTS

If you are under the age of 40 no formal medical examination is necessary in the United Kingdom. Instead, would-be skydivers are required to sign on the day of their course a declaration of fitness stating that they suffer from no serious illness or disabilities. The questions are similar to those asked of glider pilots, mainly concerning freedom from faintness or giddiness and one or two other general medical questions. If you are aged over 40, you will need to have a certificate of fitness signed by your doctor. The relevant form is available on request from the parachute club when you book your course of instruction. Whatever your age, if you are in any doubt about your fitness to parachute, please contact the parachute club concerned or your doctor for further advice.

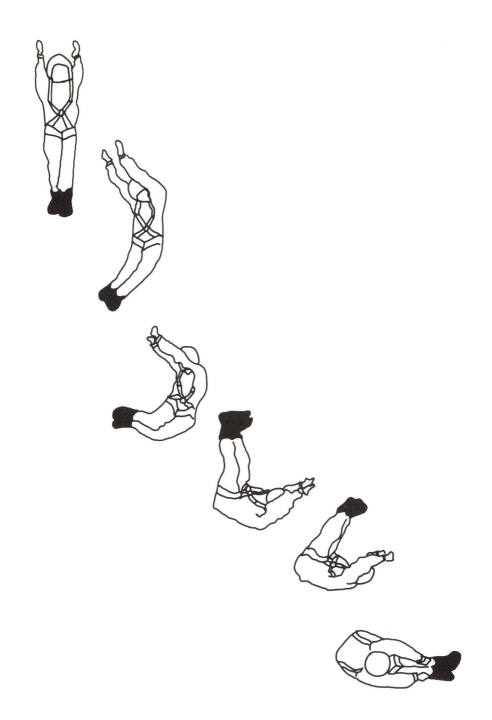

Figure 59 *Parachute training includes learning how to land safely*

HEIGHT/WEIGHT RESTRICTIONS

Some operators will not accept students who are overweight in relation to their height. As an example, Headcorn Parachute Club in Kent use the following table for their Static Line Round Parachute Course.

Male		Female	
Height	Max. weight	Height	Max. weight
5'2"	9st 12 lb	4'10"	8 st 6 lb
5'3"	10 st 2 lb	4'11"	8st 9 lb
5'4"	10 st 6 lb	5'00"	8 st 12 lb
5'5"	10 st 10 lb	5'1"	9 st
5'6"	11 st 1 lb	5'2"	9 st 3 lb
5'7"	11 st 5 lb	5'3"	9 st 6 lb
5'8"	11 st 9 lb	5'4"	9 st 10 lb
5'9"	11 st 13 lb	5'5"	10 st
5'10"	12 st 4 lb	5'6"	10 st 4 lb
5'11"	12 st 10 lb	5'7"	10 st 8 lb
6'00"	13 st 1 lb	5'8"	10 st 13 lb
6'1"	13 st 6lb	5'9"	11 st 4lb
6'2"	13 st 11 lb	5'10"	11 st 8 lb
6'3"	14 st 2 lb	5'11"	11 st 13 lb
6'4"	14 st 7 lb	6'00"	12 st 4 lb

For static line square, tandem and accelerated free-fall (AFF) courses Headcorn apply a maximum weight limit of 15 stone, regardless of height.

HOW MUCH WILL IT COST?

With facilities varying among the many parachute clubs, there can be no set pricing structure. Some clubs are run as full-time commercial operations with sophisticated twin-engined aircraft capable of carrying a large number of parachutists in a single lift. Others are small, weekend-only clubs operating a single Cessna light aircraft which can only carry three or four jumpers at a time. All of this has a final bearing on the cost of the courses on offer. With regard to payment, a number of operators will accept the popular credit cards such as Access and Barclaycard, and most will require a deposit of around £50 on booking (balance payable on the day of your course). Discounts for group bookings are usually available, since many people choose to parachute as a means of fund-raising for a favourite charity. As a guide, the following shows prices currently charged at the time of writing (1992) for static line, tandem and accelerated free-fall (AFF) courses by two Kent-based clubs, Headcorn Parachute Club and Slipstream Adventures.

Headcorn Parachute Club

- Static line round parachute course: midweek, £95; weekend, £120. Continuation jumps, £20.
- Static line square parachute course: midweek only, £150. Continuation jumps, £25.
- Tandem jump: any day, £150.

Slipstream Adventures

- Accelerated free-fall (AFF) course: eight jumps, £1,200. Jump-by-jump breakdown:-

First level £300	Rejump £150
Second level £250	Rejump £150
Third level £200	Rejump £150
Fourth level £105	Rejump £100
Fifth level £105	Rejump £100
Sixth level £105	Rejump £100
Seventh level £105	Rejump £100
Eighth level £30	Rejump £30

PHOTOGRAPHS AND VIDEO FILMS

A number of parachute clubs will offer you the opportunity of having your first jump photographed or recorded on video film. Whilst not strictly necessary (although a video can prove a wonderful teaching aid to students on an AFF course, clearly showing technique or lack of it during their drop), they are never the less fine mementos of a no-doubt adventurous and enjoyable day. They will cost in the region of £65.

AIRCRAFT IN USE

If you have ever watched a military display team such as the army's 'Red Devils' or the RAF 'Falcons' run and throw themselves out into space from the gaping ramp of a Hercules transport, forget it! The aircraft in use at most parachute clubs is one of the Cessna family of single-engined, high-winged light aircraft. This aeroplane will probably be the parachute club's property, or it may be leased from the local flying club. The great advantage of the Cessna range is its ability to fly at the low speeds at which parachuting takes

The Short Skyvan is probably the largest aircraft a civilian parachutist will jump from. Peterborough parachute centre operate one for advanced skydiving training
(Photo: Shorts Aircraft)

place. With the passenger seats taken out and the starboard door removed, Cessnas make perfect jumping aircraft.

The Cessna 172 can lift three parachutists plus its pilot. If fuel costs are to be kept down it must waste no time in reaching the required jump height before returning to land. In the hands of a skilled pilot, the aircraft is often likely to be back on the ground before the parachutists. Its larger brother, the Cessna 182, can lift four jumpers plus a pilot. Larger still than the Cessna series are the twin-engined BN Islander and single-turbine-powered Pilatus PC-6 Turboporter. The Islander is used by a number of parachute clubs and enables nine jumpers to be lifted in a single flight; whilst the Pilatus PC-6 carries eight parachutists plus its pilot. Later on, if you progress beyond static line parachuting, you may have the opportunity to jump from all sorts of large aircraft including Skyvans, Twin Otters, DC3s and even helicopters.

Appendix 1

Where to Fly

Avon

Bristol Flying Centre
Lulsgate Airport
Telephone (0275) 474601
Fax (0275) 474851
PPL, IMC, NIGHT, MULTI, PPL/IR

Bristol & Wessex Aeroplane Club
Lulsgate Airport
Telephone (0275) 472514
Fax (0275) 472412
PPL, RT, IMC, NIGHT, RADIO NAV

ABS Aviation Services
Lulsgate Airport
Telephone (0275) 474440
Fax (0275) 474794
PPL, RT, IMC, NIGHT

Bedfordshire

Bedfordshire School of Flying
Cranfield Apirport
Telephone (0234) 751403
Fax (0234) 751363
PPL, RT, IMC, NIGHT, MULTI,
PPL/IR, AEROS

Sandra's Flying Group
Cranfield Airport
Telephone (0933) 53870
Fax (0933) 59199
SELF FLY HIRE ONLY

Osprey Flying Club
Cranfield Airport
Telephone (0234) 750197
PPL, IMC, NIGHT, MULTI, AEROS

Phoenix Aviation Ltd
Cranfield Airport
Telephone (0234) 750592
Fax (0234) 751523
PPL, IMC, NIGHT, TAILWHEEL

Cabair College of Air Training
Cranfield Airport
Telephone (0234) 751243
Fax (0234) 751363
PPL, RT, IMC, NIGHT, MULTI, PPL/IR

Luton Flight Training
Luton Airport
Telephone (0582) 24426
Fax (0582) 24426
PPL, RT, IMC, NIGHT, MULTI, AEROS

Henlow Flying Club
RAF Henlow
Telephone (0462) 851936
Fax (0462) 851936
PPL, RT, IMC, NIGHT, MULTI, PPL/IR

Fordaire Aviation
Little Gransden
Telephone (0767) 51950
Fax (0767) 51665
PPL, IMC, NIGHT, MULTI, RADIO NAV,
AEROS, TAILWHEEL

Berkshire

West London Aero Club
White Waltham Aerodrome
Telephone (0628) 823272
Fax (0628) 826070

PPL, RT, IMC, NIGHT, MULTI,
AEROS, TAILWHEEL

Buckinghamshire

British Airways Flying Club
Wycombe Air Park
Telephone (0494) 529262
Fax (0494) 461237
PPL, RT, IMC, NIGHT

Wycombe Air Centre
Wycombe Air Park
Telephone (0494) 443737
Fax (0494) 465456
PPL, RT, IMC, NIGHT, PPL/IR,
AEROS, TAILWHEEL

Air Training Services
Wycombe Air Park
Telephone (0494) 445412
SIMULATOR COURSES FOR RT, IMC,
PPL/IR, RADIO NAV

Denham School of Flying
Denham Aerodrome
Telephone (0895) 833327
Fax (0895 835048
PPL, RT, IMC, NIGHT, MULTI, PPL/IR

Denham Cessna Flight Centre
Denham Aerodrome
Telephone (0895) 834730
Fax (0895) 835048
PPL, RT, IMC, NIGHT, MULTI, RADIO NAV

Cambridgeshire

Rural Flying Corps
Bourn Aerodrome
Telephone (0954) 719602
PPL, RT, IMC, NIGHT, MULTI, AEROS,
RADIO NAV, TAILWHEEL

Klingair Flying Club
Conington Aerodrome
Telephone (0487) 832022
Fax (0487) 832614
PPL, RT, IMC, NIGHT, MULTI, AEROS

Walkbury Flying Club
Sibson Airfield
Telephone (0832) 280289
Fax (0733) 238041

PPL, RT, IMC, NIGHT, MULTI, AEROS,
RADIO NAV, TAILWHEEL

Cambridge Flying Group
Cambridge Airport
Telephone (0223) 053343
PPL, IMC, TAILWHEEL

Cambridge Aero Club
Cambridge Airport
Telephone (0223) 373214
Fax (0223) 321032
PPL, RT, IMC, NIGHT

Cheshire

Ravenair
Manchester International Airport
Telephone (061) 436 8848
Fax (061) 499 1632
PPL, RT, IMC, NIGHT, MULTI, PPL/IR

MSF Aviation UK
Manchester International Airport
Telephone (061) 499 1444
Fax (061) 499 1445
PPL, RT, IMC, NIGHT, MULTI,
RADIO NAV, TAILWHEEL

Cornwall

Lands End Aero Club
Lands End Aerodrome
Telephone (0736) 788771
Fax (0736) 787274
PPL, RT, IMC, AEROS,
RADIO NAV, TAILWHEEL

Cornwall Flying Club
Bodmin Airfield
Telephone (0202) 882 419
PPL, RT, IMC, NIGHT, AEROS, RADIO NAV

Bournemouth Flying Club
Bournemouth Airport
Telephone (0202) 578558
Fax (0202) 570203
PPL, RT, IMC, NIGHT, MULTI, AEROS

SFT Aviation
Bournemouth Airport
Telephone (0202) 499888
Fax (0202) 499119
PPL, RT, IMC, PPL/IR, AEROS

Cumbria

Carlisle Flight Centre
Carlisle Airport
Telephone (0228) 573333
PPL, IMC, NIGHT, MULTI

Border Air Training
Carlisle Airport
Telephone (0228) 573490
PPL, IMC

Cumbria Aero Club
Carlisle Airport
Telephone (0228) 573633
PPL, RT, IMC, NIGHT, MULTI

Devon

Exeter Flying Centre
Exeter Airport
Telephone (0392) 67653
PPL, RT, IMC, NIGHT, MULTI, AEROS

Airways Flight Training
Exeter Airport
Telephone (0392) 64216
Fax (0392) 68255
PPL/IR, MULTI

Devon School of Flying
Dunkeswell Aerodrome
Telephone (0404) 891643
Fax (0404) 891465
PPL, RT, IMC, NIGHT, MULTI, RADIO NAV

Plymouth School of Flying
Plymouth City Airport
Telephone (0752) 773335
PPL, RT, IMC, NIGHT, MULTI, PPL/IR,
AEROS, RADIO NAV, TAILWHEEL

Eaglescott School of Flying
Eaglescott Airfield
Telephone (07693) 404
PPL, IMC, TAILWHEEL

Dorset

Interair Flight Centre
Bournemouth Airport
Telephone (0202) 593377
Fax (0202) 581984
PPL, RT, IMC, NIGHT, MULTI, PPL/IR,
AEROS, RADIO NAV, TAILWHEEL

Leading Edge Aviation
Southend Airport
Telephone (0702) 544057
Fax (0702) 544057
PPL, RT, IMC, NIGHT, MULTI,
RADIO NAV, TAILWHEEL

Essex Flying School
Earls Colne Aerodrome
Telephone (0787) 223676
PPL, RT, IMC, NIGHT, MULTI, PPL/IR

Stapleford Flying Club
Stapleford Aerodrome
Telephone (04028) 380
PPL, RT, IMC, NIGHT, MULTI, PPL/IR

Clacton Aero Club
Clacton Airfield
Telephone (0255) 424671
Fax (0255) 473832
PPL, RT, MULTI, AEROS, TAILWHEEL

Andrewsfield Flying School
Saling Airfield
Telephone (0371) 856500
Fax (0371) 856769
PPL, IMC, NIGHT, TAILWHEEL

East Midlands

Donair Flying Club
East Midlands
Telephone (0332) 810444
Fax (0322) 812726
PPL, RT, IMC, NIGHT, AEROS

East Midlands Flying School
East Midlands Airport
Telephone (0332) 850383
Fax (0332) 853088
PPL, RT, IMC, NIGHT

Derby Aero Club
Tatenhill Aerodrome

Telephone (0283) 75407
Fax (0283) 75407
PPL, RT, IMC, MULTI,
RADIO NAV, TAILWHEEL

Essex

Skylane Flight Centre
Southend Airport
Telephone (0702) 546156
Fax (0702) 546491
PPL, RT, IMC, NIGHT, MULTI,
PPL/IR, AEROS, RADIO NAV

Seawing Flying Club
Southend Airport
Telephone (0702) 545420
PPL, IMC, NIGHT, AEROS

Southend Flying Club
Southend Airport
Telephone (0702) 545198
Fax (0702) 543756
PPL, RT, IMC, NIGHT, MULTI,
TAILWHEEL, AEROS, RADIO NAV

Thames Estuary Flying Club
Southend Airport
Telephone (0702) 542497
Fax (0702) 542497
PPL, RT, IMC, NIGHT

Gloucestershire

Swallow Flight Centre
Gloucester Airport
Telephone (0452) 713555
Fax (0452) 712808
PPL, IMC, NIGHT, MULTI, PPL/IR

Staverton Flying School
Gloucester Airport
Telephone (0452) 712388
Fax (0452) 713565
PPL, RT, IMC, NIGHT, MULTI, AEROS

Cotswold Aero Club
Gloucester Airport
Telephone (0452) 713924
Fax (0452) 856771
PPL, RT, IMC, NIGHT, AEROS,
RADIO NAV, TAILWHEEL

Archer Flight Training
Gloucester Airport
Telephone (0452) 713830
Fax (0452) 857021
PPL, RT, IMC, NIGHT, MULTI, AEROS,

Gloucester School of Flying
Gloucester Airport
Telephone (0452) 857153
PPL, RT, IMC, NIGHT, MULTI, RADIO NAV

Aeros Flying Club
Gloucester Airport
Telephone (0452) 857419
Fax (0452) 856741
PPL, RT, IMC, NIGHT, MULTI,
AEROS, RADIO NAV

Hampshire

Wiltshire Aeroplane Club
Thruxton Airport
Telephone (0264) 773900
PPL, RT, IMC, NIGHT

Thruxton Flight Centre
Thruxton Airport
Telephone (0264) 773425
Fax (0264) 773426
PPL, IMC, NIGHT, AEROS

BM Aviation
Southampton Airport
Telephone (0962) 854931
PPL, RT, IMC, NIGHT, MULTI, AEROS

Solent Flight
Southampton Airport
Telephone (0703) 650300
Fax (0703) 617623
PPL, RT, IMC, NIGHT, TAILWHEEL

Carill Aviation Flying School
Southampton Airport
Telephone (0703) 643528
PPL, RT, IMC, NIGHT, MULTI, RADIO NAV

Top Flight
Southampton Airport
Telephone (0703) 629360
Fax (0703) 616690
PPL, RT, IMC, NIGHT

165

Premi-Air Aviation UK
Southampton Airport
Telephone (0703) 650600
Fax (0703) 283964
PPL, IMC, NIGHT, MULTI

1 to 1 Aviation Flight Training
Southampton Airport
Telephone (0703) 617641
PPL, IMC, NIGHT, MULTI

Herefordshire

Herefordshire Aero Club
Shobden Airfield
Telephone (0568) 708369
PPL, RT, IMC, NIGHT

Hertfordshire

Firecrest Aviation
Leavesden Airport
Telephone (0923) 662794
PPL, RT, IMC, NIGHT, RADIO NAV

Leavesden Flight Centre
Leavesden Airport
Telephone (0923) 671411
Fax (0923) 893141
PPL, RT, IMC, NIGHT, MULTI,
PPL/IR, AEROS, RADIO NAV

Panshanger School of Flying
Panshanger Aerodrome
Telephone (0707) 335021
PPL, RT, IMC, NIGHT

London School of Flying
Elstree Aerodrome
Telephone (081) 953 4343
PPL, RT, IMC, NIGHT, MULTI, PPL/IR

Modern Air Self Fly Rental
Fowlmere Aerodrome
Telephone (0763) 208281
Fax (0763) 208861
PPL, IMC, NIGHT, MULTI, RADIO NAV

Humberside

Humber Flying Club
Humberside Airport

Telephone (0652) 680746
Fax (0652) 688492
PPL, RT, IMC, NIGHT, MULTI

Frank Morgan School of Flying
Humberside Airport
Telephone (0652) 688859
PPL, RT, IMC, NIGHT, MULTI, AEROS,
RADIO NAV, TAILWHEEL

Soloflight Captains Club
Humberside Airport
Telephone (0652) 688833
Fax (0652) 688833
PPL, RT, IMC, NIGHT, MULTI, AEROS

Hull Aero Club
Linley Hill Airfield
Telephone (0964) 544944
Fax (0964) 544944
PPL, RT, IMC, RADIO NAV, TAILWHEEL

Isle of Wight

Airborne School of Flying
Sandown Airport
Telephone (0983) 403355
PPL, RT, IMC, RADIO NAV, TAILWHEEL

Kent

London Flight Centre
Headcorn Aerodrome
Telephone (0622) 890997
Fax (0622) 891105
PPL, RT, IMC, NIGHT, MULTI, PPL/IR

North Kent Flying Club
Rochester Airport
Telephone (0634) 863436
PPL, IMC, NIGHT, TAILWHEEL

Rochester Aviation Flying Club
Rochester Airport
Telephone (0634) 816340
PPL, RT, IMC, NIGHT, TAILWHEEL

Medway Flight Training
Farthing Corner Airfield
Telephone (0634) 389757
PPL, RT, IMC, NIGHT, TAILWHEEL

Thanet Flying Club
Manston Airport
Telephone (0843) 823520
PPL, RT, IMC, NIGHT, MULTI, TAILWHEEL

Cinque Ports Flying Club
Lydd Airport
Telephone (0679) 21818
Fax (0679) 21888
PPL, RT, IMC, NIGHT, MULTI, RADIO NAV

SEACOAT
Manston Airport
Telephone (0843) 822022
Fax (0843) 821288
PPL, RT, IMC, NIGHT, MULTI, PPL/IR,
AEROS, RADIO NAV

London Flight Centre
Lydd Airport
Telephone (0679) 21549
Fax (0679) 21947
PPL, RT, IMC, NIGHT, MULTI, PPL/IR

Surrey & Kent Flying Club
Biggin Hill Airport
Telephone (0959) 72255
PPL, IMC, NIGHT

Kingair Flying Club
Biggin Hill Airport
Telephone (0959) 75088
Fax (0959) 72163
PPL, RT, IMC, NIGHT, MULTI, AEROS,

Hall Aviation
Biggin Hill Airport
Telephone (0689) 855359
PPL, RT, IMC, NIGHT, RADIO NAV

Civilair Flying Club
Biggin Hill Airport
Telephone (0959) 73853
PPL, RT, IMC, NIGHT, MULTI, AEROS

Alouette Flying Club
Biggin Hill Airport
Telephone (0293) 524772
Fax (0959) 73243
PPL, RT, IMC, NIGHT, AEROS

Biggin Hill School of Flying
Biggin Hill Airport
Telephone (0959) 73583
Fax (0959) 72163
PPL, RT, IMC, NIGHT, MULTI

EFG Flying School
Biggin Hill Airport
Telephone (0959) 540054
PPL, RT, IMC, NIGHT, MULTI

Air Touring Club & School
Biggin Hill Airport
Telephone (0959) 73133
Fax (0959) 75782
PPL, RT, IMC, NIGHT, RADIO NAV

Man Air
Biggin Hill Airport
Telephone (081) 647 7742
Fax (081) 669 9199
MULTI

Metropolitan Police Flying Club
Biggin Hill Airport
Telephone (0959) 72350
PPL, RT, IMC, NIGHT

Lancashire

ANT Flying Club
Blackpool Airport
Telephone (0253) 43102
Fax (0253) 45396
PPL, RT, IMC, NIGHT, MULTI

Comed Aviation
Blackpool Airport
Telephone (0253) 49072
Fax (0253) 49072
PPL, RT, IMC, NIGHT, MULTI, AEROS

Blackpool Air Centre
Blackpool Airport
Telephone (0253) 41871
Fax (0253) 41567
PPL, RT, IMC, NIGHT, MULTI

Westair Flying School
Blackpool Airport
Telephone (0253) 404925
Fax (0253) 401121
PPL, RT, IMC, NIGHT

Lancashire Aero Club
Barton Aerodrome
Telephone (061) 737 7326
Fax (061) 787 8782
PPL, RT, IMC, NIGHT, MULTI,
AEROS, RADIO NAV

West Lancashire Aero Club
RAF Woodvale
Telephone (07048) 72610
PPL, RT, IMC, NIGHT

Woodvale Aviation Co
RAF Woodvale
Telephone (07048) 74497
Fax (07048) 32327
PPL, RT, IMC, NIGHT, MULTI, AEROS,
RADIO NAV, TAILWHEEL

Air Nova Flight Centre
Liverpool Airport
Telephone (051) 427 7907
Fax (051) 427 8093
PPL, RT, IMC, NIGHT, MULTI

Deltair
Liverpool Airport
Telephone (051) 494 2040
PPL, RT, IMC, NIGHT

Cheshire Air Training School
Liverpool Airport
Telephone (051) 486 8383
Fax (051) 486 7228
PPL, RT, IMC, NIGHT, MULTI, PPL/IR

Merseyside Aviation
Liverpool Airport
Telephone (051) 547 3362
PPL, IMC, NIGHT, MULTI

Liverpool Flying School
Liverpool Airport
Telephone (051) 427 7449
Fax (051) 427 8816
PPL, RT, IMC, NIGHT, MULTI, TAILWHEEL

Liverpool Aviation Services
Liverpool Airport
Telephone (051) 494 0365
Fax (051) 440 0087
PPL, RT, IMC, NIGHT, MULTI

Leicestershire

Leicestershire Aero Club
Leicester Airpoirt
Telephone (0533) 592360
Fax (0533) 592712
PPL, RT, IMC, NIGHT, MULTI, AEROS,
RADIO NAV, TAILWHEEL

Lincolnshire

Skegness Aero Club
Skegness Aerodrome
Telephone (0754) 762240
Fax (0754) 767087
PPL, RT, IMC, NIGHT, MULTI, TAILWHEEL

Lincoln Aero Club
Sturgate Airfield
Telephone (042783) 305
Fax (042783) 423
PPL, IMC, NIGHT

Wickenby Flying Club
Wickenby Airfield
Telephone (06735) 346
Fax (06735) 391
PPL, IMC, NIGHT, MULTI, PPL/IR,
AEROS, TAILWHEEL

Fenland Aero Club
Fenland Airfield
Telephone (0406) 34461
PPL, IMC, NIGHT, AEROS

Norfolk

The Norwich School of Flying
Norwich Airport
Telephone (0603) 403107
PPL, RT, IMC, NIGHT, MULTI

Arrow Air Centre
Shipdham Airfield
Telephone (0362) 820162
Fax (0362) 820162
PPL, RT, IMC, NIGHT, MULTI, AEROS,
RADIO NAV, TAILWHEEL

Waveney Flying Group
Seething Airfield
Telephone (0508) 50453
PPL, RT, IMC, NIGHT, MULTI

Norfolk & Norwich Aero Club
Swanton Morley Airfield
Telephone (0362) 637274
Fax (0362) 637764
PPL, RT, IMC, NIGHT, MULTI,
RADIO NAV, TAILWHEEL

Northamptonshire

Northamptonshire School of Flying
Sywell Aerodrome
Telephone (0604) 644678
Fax (0604) 495324
PPL, IMC, NIGHT, MULTI, AEROS,
RADIO NAV, TAILWHEEL

Turweston Flying Club
Turweston &
Hinton-in-the-Hedges Airfields
Telephone (0327) 62148
Fax (0327) 62148
PPL, RT, IMC, NIGHT

Nottinghamshire

The Sherwood Flying Club
Nottingham Apirport
Telephone (0602) 811402
Fax (0602) 332442
PPL, RT, IMC, NIGHT, AEROS,
RADIO NAV, TAILWHEEL

Trumanair Flying School
Nottingham Airport
Telephone (0602) 815050
Fax (0602) 811444
PPL, RT, IMC, NIGHT, MULTI,
PPL/IR, RADIO NAV

Sheffield Aero Club
Netherthorpe Aerodrome
Telephone (0909) 475233
PPL, RT, IMC, NIGHT

Oxfordshire

Oxford Air Training School
Oxford Airport

Telephone (0865) 844260
Fax (0865) 841807
PPL, RT, IMC, NIGHT, MULTI, PPL/IR,
AEROS, RADIO NAV, TAILWHEEL

Enstone Flying Club
Enstone Airfield
Telephone (0608) 678204
PPL, RT, IMC, NIGHT, AEROS, TAILWHEEL

Shropshire

Shropshire Aero Club
Sleap Airfield
Telephone (0939) 232882
PPL, RT, IMC, NIGHT, AEROS

Suffolk

Ipswich School of Flying
Ipswich Airport
Telephone (0473) 729510
Fax (0473) 716128
PPL, RT, IMC, NIGHT, MULTI,
AEROS, RADIO NAV

Suffolk Aero Club
Ipswich Airport
Telephone (0473) 713312
PPL, RT, IMC, NIGHT, AEROS,
RADIO NAV, TAILWHEEL

Horizon Flying Club
Ipswich Airport
Telephone (0473) 714840
Fax (0473) 718365
PPL, RT, IMC, NIGHT, AEROS,
RADIO NAV, TAILWHEEL

Crowfield Flying Club
Crowfield Airfield
Telephone (0449) 711017
PPL, RT, IMC, RADIO NAV

Surrey

Redhill Flying Club
Redhill Aerodrome
Telephone (0737) 822959
Fax (0737) 822163
PPL, RT, IMC, NIGHT, MULTI, PPL/IR,
AEROS, RADIO NAV, TAILWHEEL

Cabair Flight
Redhill Aerodrome
Telephone (0737) 822166
Fax (0737) 822147
PPL, RT, IMC, NIGHT

Cubair
Redhill Aerodrome
Telephone (0737) 822124
PPL, TAILWHEEL

Fairoaks Flight Centre
Fairoaks Airport
Telephone (0276) 858075
PPL, RT, IMC, NIGHT, MULTI, RADIO NAV

Cabair School of Flying
Blackbushe Airport
Telephone (0252) 870999
Fax (0252) 871975
PPL, IMC, NIGHT

European Flyers
Blackbushe Airport
Telephone (0252) 873747
Fax (0252) 876177
PPL, RT, IMC, NIGHT, MULTI, AEROS

Sussex

Southern Aero Club
Shoreham Airport
Telephone (0273) 462457
PPL, RT, IMC, NIGHT, MULTI, RADIO NAV

Mercury Flight Training
Shoreham Airport
Telephone (0273) 462277
Fax (0273) 440310
PPL, RT, IMC, NIGHT, MULTI,
RADIO NAV, TAILWHEEL

Southern Air
Shoreham Airfield
Telephone (0273) 461661
Fax (0273) 464474
PPL, RT, IMC, NIGHT

Barry Aviation
Shoreham Airport
Telephone (0403) 60189
PPL, RT, IMC, NIGHT

Goodwood Flying School
Goodwood Aerodrome
Telephone (0243) 774656
Fax (0243) 536497
PPL, RT, IMC, NIGHT, RADIO NAV

Vectair
Goodwood Aerodrome
Telephone (0243) 781652
PPL, RT, IMC, NIGHT, AEROS, TAILWHEEL

Teeside

Teeside Aero Club
Teeside Airport
Telephone (0325) 332752
Fax (0325) 333916
PPL, IMC, NIGHT, MULTI

Cleveland Flying School
Teeside Airport
Telephone (0325) 332855
Fax (0325) 332855
PPL, RT, IMC, NIGHT, MULTI

Tyne & Wear

Newcastle-upon-Tyne Aero Club
Newcastle Airport
Telephone (091) 286 1321
PPL, RT, IMC, NIGHT, MULTI

Warwickshire

Coventry Aeroplane Club
Coventry Airport
Telephone (0203) 301428
PPL, RT, IMC, NIGHT, MULTI, AEROS

Airwing Services
Coventry Airport
Telephone (0203) 639254
Fax (0203) 307192
PPL, IMC, NIGHT, MULTI

Beagle Pup Flying Group
Coventry Airport
Telephone (0672) 62631
Fax (0672) 62631
PPL, RT, IMC, NIGHT, AEROS

AWA Flying Group
Coventry Airport
Telephone (0203) 301498
PPL, RT, NIGHT

Sandwell Valley Aero Club
Coventry Airport
Telephone (0922) 648556
PPL, IMC, NIGHT

Tudor Flying Group
Coventry Airport
Telephone (0203) 301341
PPL, RT, IMC, NIGHT

Senair
Coventry Airport
Telephone (0203) 302553
Fax (0203) 639348
PPL, IMC, NIGHT, MULTI, RADIO NAV

Midland Air Training School
Coventry Airport
Telephone (0203) 304914
PPL, RT, IMC, NIGHT, MULTI

Solihull Flying Club
Coventry Airport
Telephone (0564) 826235
Fax (0564) 823012
PPL, IMC, NIGHT, MULTI

Central Flight Training
Coventry Airport
Telephone (0203) 307003
Fax (0203) 639348
PPL, IMC, NIGHT, MULTI

West Midlands Police Flying Club
Coventry Airport
Telephone (021) 422 0785
PPL, RT, IMC, NIGHT, RADIO NAV

South Warwickshire Flying School
Wellesbourne Mountford Aerodrome
Telephone (0789) 840094
Fax (0789) 842593
PPL, RT, IMC, NIGHT, RADIO NAV

Wellesbourne Aviation
Wellesbourne Mountford Aerodrome
Telephone (0789) 841066
PPL, RT, IMC, NIGHT, MULTI

RS Pilot Training
Wellesbourne Mountford Aerodrome
Telephone (0789) 470434
Fax (0789) 470434
PPL, RT, IMC, NIGHT

West Midlands

Warwickshire Flying Centre
Birmingham International Airport
Telephone (021) 782 7755
Fax (021) 782 2094
PPL, RT, IMC, NIGHT, MULTI

Birmingham Airport Flying Group
Birmingham International Airport
Telephone (021) 782 2045
PPL, RT, IMC, NIGHT

Warwickshire Aero Centre
Birmingham International Airport
Telephone (021) 782 1011
Fax (021) 782 4256
PPL, RT, IMC, NIGHT, MULTI, AEROS,
RADIO NAV, TAILWHEEL

Bobbington Air Training School
Halfpenny Green Airport
Telephone (0384) 88292
PPL, RT, IMC, NIGHT, MULTI

Exec-H Flying Centre
Halfpenny Green Airport
Telephone (0384) 88456
Fax (0384) 88459
PPL, RT, IMC, NIGHT, RADIO NAV

Wiltshire

Abbas Air
Compton Abbas Airfield
Telephone (0747) 811767
Fax (0747) 811161
PPL, RT, IMC, NIGHT, MULTI,
PPL/IR, TAILWHEEL

Yorkshire

Doncaster Aero Club
Doncaster Airport
Telephone (0302) 535666
Fax (0302) 537890
PPL, RT, IMC, NIGHT, MULTI, RADIO NAV

Yorkshire Aeroplane Club
Leeds-Bradford Airport
Telephone (0532) 503840
PPL, RT, IMC, NIGHT, MULTI,
AEROS, RADIO NAV

Knight Air
Leeds-Bradford Airport
Telephone (0532) 501401
PPL, RT, IMC, NIGHT

Sherburn Aero Club
Sherburn-in-Elmet Aerodrome
Telephone (0977) 682674
Fax (0977) 683699
PPL, RT, IMC, AEROS, RADIO NAV

Sandtoft Air Services
Sandtoft Aerodrome
Telephone (0427) 873676
Fax (0427) 874680
PPL, RT, IMC, NIGHT, MULTI

Channel Islands

Jersey Aero Club
Jersey Airport
Telephone (0534) 43990
Fax (0534) 41290

Guernsey Flight Training
Guernsey Airport
Telephone (0481) 65254
PPL, RT, IMC, NIGHT, AEROS, RADIO NAV

Channel Aviation
Guernsey Airport
Telephone (0481) 37217
Fax (0481) 38886
PPL, RT, IMC, NIGHT, MULTI, RADIO NAV

Stratair Flight Training
Alderney Airport
Telephone (0481) 822549
Fax (0481) 823480

Isle of Man

Manx Flyers Aero Club
Ronaldsway Airport
Telephone (0624) 822926
PPL, RT, IMC, NIGHT, MULTI, RADIO NAV

Ashley Gardner School of Flying
Ronaldsway Airport
Telephone (0624) 823454
Fax (0624) 825744
PPL, RT, IMC, NIGHT, RADIO NAV,
TAILWHEEL

Northern Ireland

Woodgate Air Services
Belfast Airport
Telephone (08494) 22789
PPL, RT, IMC, NIGHT, MULTI, AEROS,
RADIO NAV, TAILWHEEL

Eglinton Flying Club
Eglinton Airport
Telephone (0504) 810962
PPL, RT, IMC, NIGHT

Ulster Flying Club
Newtownards Aerodrome
Telephone (0247) 813327
PPL, IMC, NIGHT

Catalina Seaplanes
St Angelo Airport
Telephone (0365) 322771
PPL, IMC, TAILWHEEL

Scotland

Turnhouse Flying Club
Edinburgh Airport
Telephone (031) 339 4706
PPL, RT, IMC, NIGHT, MULTI

Edinburgh Air Centre
Edinburgh Airport
Telephone (031) 339 4059
Fax (031) 317 7265
PPL, IMC, NIGHT, MULTI

Edinburgh Flying Club
Edinburgh Airport
Telephone (031) 339 4990
PPL, RT, IMC, NIGHT, MULTI, RADIO NAV

Glasgow Flying Club
Glasgow Airport
Telephone (041) 889 4565
PPL, RT, IMC, NIGHT, MULTI, AEROS,
RADIO NAV, TAILWHEEL

West of Scotland Flying Club
Glasgow Airport
Telephone (041) 889 7151
PPL, RT, IMC, NIGHT, MULTI, AEROS,
RADIO NAV, TAILWHEEL

Renfrew Flying Club
Glasgow Airport
Telephone (041) 887 3398
PPL, RT, IMC, NIGHT

Scottish Airways Flyers
Prestwick Airport
Telephone (0292) 75583
PPL, RT, IMC, NIGHT

Prestwick Flying Club
Prestwick Airport
Telephone (0292) 75583
PPL, RT, IMC, NIGHT, AEROS

Prestwick Flight Centre
Prestwick Airport
Telephone (0292) 76523
Fax (0292) 75991
PPL, RT, IMC, NIGHT, MULTI

Air Alba
Inverness Airport
Telephone (0667) 462664
PPL, RT, IMC, NIGHT, MULTI

Highland Flight Centre
Inverness Airport
Telephone (0667) 462230
PPL, RT, IMC, NIGHT, AEROS

Cumbernauld Aviation
Cumbernauld Airfield
Telephone (0236) 722100
PPL, RT, IMC, NIGHT

AST Training College
Perth Aerodrome
Telephone (0738) 52311
Fax (0738) 51539
PPL, RT, IMC, NIGHT, MULTI, AEROS

Fife Airport Management
Fife Airport
Telephone (0592) 753792
PPL, RT, IMC, NIGHT, MULTI

Tayside Flying Club
Dundee Airport

Telephone (0382) 644372
Fax (0382) 644531
PPL, RT, IMC, NIGHT, MULTI, AEROS

Far North Flight Training School
Wick Aerodrome
Telephone (0955) 2201
Fax (0955) 2201
PPL, RT, IMC, NIGHT, MULTI

Aberdeen Flying Club
Aberdeen Airport
Telephone (0224) 725333
Fax (0224) 725458
PPL, RT, IMC, NIGHT, AEROS

Wales

Falcon Aero Club
Swansea Airport
Telephone (0792) 205241
PPL, RT, IMC, NIGHT, MULTI

Swansea Aero Club
Swansea Airport
Telephone (0792) 204063
Fax (0792) 297923
PPL, RT, IMC, NIGHT, MULTI, RADIO NAV

Cumbrian Flying Club
Swansea Airport
Telephone (0792) 297275
PPL, RT, IMC, NIGHT, RADIO NAV

Flite-Aids
Swansea Airport
Telephone (0792) 297883
PPL, RT, IMC

Swallow Flight Centre
Cardiff-Wales Airport
Telephone (0446) 711942
Fax (0446) 710213
PPL, RT, IMC, NIGHT, MULTI

Cardiff-Wales Flying Club
Cardiff-Wales Airport
Telephone (0446) 710000
PPL, RT, IMC, NIGHT, MULTI, RADIO NAV

Pool Aerocentre
Welshpool Airfield
Telephone (0938) 555062
Fax (0928) 555487
PPL, RT, IMC, MULTI, RADIO NAV

Haverfordwest School of Flying
Haverfordwest Aerodrome
Telephone (0437) 760822
PPL, IMC, NIGHT, MULTI, TAILWHEEL

Snowdon Aviation
Caernarfon Airport

Telephone (0286) 380800
PPL, RT, IMC, NIGHT

Mona Flying Club
RAF Mona, Anglesey
Telephone (0407) 720581
PPL, RT, IMC, NIGHT,
RADIO NAV, TAILWHEEL

Appendix 2

Where to Fly Helicopters

Avon

Bristol Flying Centre
Lulsgate Airport
Telephone (0275) 474601
Fax (0275) 474851
PPL(H), RT

Bedfordshire

Burman Helicopters
Cranfield Airport
Telephone (0234) 752220
Fax (0234) 752221
PPL(H), RT, NIGHT, TURBINE

Bedfordshire School of Flying
Cranfield Airport
Telephone (0234) 751403
Fax (0234) 751363
PPL(H), RT

Cabair College of Air Training
Cranfield Airport

Telephone (0234) 751243
Fax (0234) 751363
PPL(H), RT

Delta Helicopters
Luton Airport
Telephone (0582) 405250
Fax (0582) 401884
PPL(H), RT, RADIO NAV, LONDON
HELICOPTER ROUTES TRAINING

TPS Helicopters
Little Gransden Airfield
Telephone (0462) 894533
Fax (0462) 896169
PPL(H), RT, NIGHT

Buckinghamshire

Skyline Helicopters
Wycombe Air Park
Telephone (0494) 451111
Fax (0494) 450627

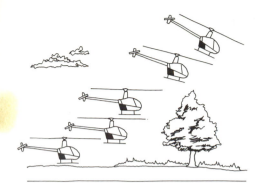

PPL(H), RT, IMC, MOUNTAIN FLYING,
ADVANCED HANDLING, TURBINE

Cheshire

Ranger Helicopters
Manchester International Airport
Telephone (061) 4989013
Fax (061) 4988344
PPL(H), RT, MOUNTAIN FLYING,
HELICOPTER SAFETY COURSE

Cornwall

Cornwall Flying Club
Bodmin Airfield
Telephone (020) 882 419
PPL(H), RT, GYROPLANES

Dorset

Interair Flight Centre
Bournemouth Airport
Telephone (0202) 593377
Fax (0202) 581984
PPL(H), RT

Essex

Andrewsfield Flying School
Saling Airfield
Telephone (0371) 856500
Fax (0371) 856769
PPL(H), RT

Leading Edge Aviation
Southend Airport

Telephone (0702) 544057
Fax (0702) 544057
PPL(H), RT

Gloucestershire

Aeros Flying Club
Gloucester Airport
Telephone (0452) 857419
Fax (0452) 856741
PPL(H), RT

Staverton Flying School
Gloucester Airport
Telephone (0452) 857419
Fax (0452) 713565
PPL(H), RT

Hampshire

FAST Helicopters
Thruxton Airport
Telephone (0264) 772508
Fax (0264) 773824
PPL(H), RT, NIGHT, MOUNTAIN FLYING,
ADVANCED HELICOPTER HANDLING,
TURBINE

Thruxton Flight Centre
Thruxton Airport
Telephone (026) 477 3425
Fax (026) 477 3426
PPL(H), RT

Hertfordshire

Cabair Helicopter Training
Elstree Aerodrome
Telephone (081) 953 4411
Fax (081) 207 0995
PPL(H), RT

London School of Flying
Elstree Aerodrome
Telephone (081) 953 4343
PPL(H), RT

RM Helicopters
Leavesden Airport
Telephone (0923) 894368
Fax (0923) 674931
PPL(H), RT, TURBINE, MULTI

Leavesden Flight Centre
Leavesden Airport
Telephone (0923) 671411
Fax (0923) 893141
PPL(H), RT

Kent

Thurston Helicopters
Headcorn Aerodrome
Telephone (0622) 891158
Fax (0622) 890876
PPL(H), RT, NIGHT, TURBINE

Lancashire

The Helicentre
Blackpool Airport
Telephone (0253) 43082
PPL(H), RT, NIGHT, MOUNTAIN FLYING,
HELICOPTER SAFETY COURSES, TURBINE

ANT Flying Club
Blackpool Airport
Telephone (0253) 43102
Fax (0253) 45396
PPL(H), RT

Lancashire Aero Club
Barton Aerodrome
Telephone (061) 737 7326
Fax (061) 787 8782
PPL(H), RT

The Manchester Helicopter Centre
Barton Aerodrome
Telephone (061) 787 7125
Fax (061) 787 7892
PPL(H), RT, TURBINE

Leicestershire

Meridian Helicopters
Leicester Airport
Telephone (0533) 593789
Fax (0533) 592712
PPL(H), RT, NIGHT, TURBINE

Northamptonshire

CJ Helicopters
Sywell Aerodrome
Telephone (0604) 760760
Fax (0604) 702902

PPL(H), RT, NIGHT,
MOUNTAIN FLYING, TURBINE

Sloane Helicopters
Sywell Aerodrome
Telephone (0604) 790595
Fax (0604) 790988
PPL(H), RT, NIGHT, TURBINE

Nottinghamshire

East Midlands Helicopters
Nottingham Airport
Telephone (0509) 856464
Fax (0509) 856444
PPL(H), RT, IF

Sheffield Aero Club
Netherthorpe Aerodrome
Telephone (0909) 4785233
PPL(H), RT

Sherwood Helicopter Centre
Netherthorpe Aerodrome
Telephone (0909) 475233
PPL(H), RT

Oxfordshire

Oxford Air Training School
Oxford Airport
Telephone (0865) 844239
Fax (0865) 841807
PPL(H), RT, TURBINE

Suffolk

Ipswich School of Flying
Ipswich Airport
Telephone (0473) 729510
Fax (0473) 716128
PPL(H), RT

Surrey

Alan Mann Helicopters
Fairoaks Airport
Telephone (0276) 857471
Fax (0276) 857539
PPL(H), RT, NIGHT, TURBINE, MULTI

Cabair Flight Centre
Redhill Aerodrome
Telephone (0737) 822166

Fax (0737) 822147
PPL(H), RT

Bristow Helicopters
Redhill Aerodrome
Telephone (0737) 822353
PPL(H), RT, IF, NIGHT, TURBINE, MULTI

Sussex

Southern Air
Shoreham Airport
Telephone (0273) 461661
Fax (0273) 464474
PPL(H), RT, TURBINE

FAST Helicopters
Shoreham Airport
Telephone (0273) 465389
PPL(H), RT, NIGHT, MOUNTAIN FLYING,
ADVANCED HELICOPTER HANDLING,
TURBINE

Watkinson Helicopters
Goodwood Aerodrome
Telephone (0243) 530344
Fax (0243) 531240
PPL(H), RT, NIGHT, TURBINE

Heli-Flair
Goodwood Aerodrome
Telephone (0243) 779222
Fax (0243) 531420
PPL(H), RT, TURBINE

Teeside

Tyne Tees Helicopter Centre
Teeside Airport
Telephone (0325) 333823
Fax (0325) 333278
PPL(H), RT, NIGHT,
MOUNTAIN FLYING, IF, TURBINE

Warwickshire

Osprey Helicopters
Coventry Airport
Telephone (0203) 639297
Fax (0203) 639311
PPL(H), RT, MOUNTAIN FLYING, TURBINE

Dollar Helicopters
Coventry Airport
Telephone (0236) 457567
Fax (0236) 457550
PPL(H), RT, TURBINE, MULTI

Heliair
Wellesbourne Mountford Aerodrome
Telephone (0789) 470476
Fax (0789) 470466
PPL(H), RT, NIGHT,
MOUNTAIN FLYING, TURBINE

West Midlands

Warwickshire Aero Centre
Birmingham International Airport
Telephone (021) 782 1011
Fax (021) 782 4256
PPL(H), RT

Exec-H Flying Centre
Halfpenny Green Airport
Telephone (0384) 88456
Fax (0384) 88459
PPL(H), RT, TURBINE

Yorkshire

Northern Helicopters
Leeds-Bradford Airport
Telephone (0532) 500588
Fax (0532) 508161
PPL(H), RT, NIGHT,
MOUNTAIN FLYING, TURBINE

Yorkshire Helicopter Centre
Doncaster Airport
Telephone (0302) 370670
Fax (0302) 537890
PPL(H), RT, NIGHT, IF,
MOUNTAIN FLYING, TURBINE

Heliyorks Flight Training
Sherburn-in-Elmet Aerodrome
Telephone (0937) 833448
Fax (0937) 835793

Sandtoft Air Services
Sandtoft Aerodrome
Telephone (0427) 873676
Fax (0427) 874680
PPL(H), RT

Scotland

Merlin Helicopters
Edinburgh Airport
Telephone (031) 317 7181
Fax (031) 317 7334
PPL(H), RT, NIGHT, IF

Appendix 3

Where to Fly Microlights

Bedfordshire

Bedford Microlight Centre
Sandy, Beds
Telephone (0767) 692350

Berkshire

Berkshire Microlight Club
Reading, Berks
Telephone (0734) 423137

Buckinghamshire

Buckinghamshire Microlight Club
Oakley, Bucks
Telephone (0844) 237508

Cambridgeshire

Cambridge Microlight Club
Sutton, Cambs
Telephone (0353) 778446

Pegasus Flight Training
Sutton Meadows Airfield
Telephone (0487) 842360

Air School Instruction
March, Cambs
Telephone (0354) 740953

Cheshire

Cheshire Microlight Centre
Sandbach, Cheshire
Telephone (0270) 764713

Cheshire Flyers
Nr Crewe, Cheshire
Telephone (0270) 71345

Cornwall

Cornwall Microlight Club
Bodmin, Cornwall
Telephone (0208) 72601

Southwest Airsports
Camelford, Cornwall
Telephone (08406) 517

Moorland Flying Club
Davidstow Aerodrome
Telephone (08406) 517

Cumbria

Lorton Aero Club
Cockermouth, Cumbria
Telephone (0900) 822535

Morris Airsports
Great Orton Airfield
Telephone (0228) 42109

Cumbria Microlights
Keswick, Cumbria
Telephone (07687) 72762

Derbyshire

North Derby Microlights
Chesterfield, Derbyshire
Telephone (0246) 260047

Devon

Wright Flight
South Molton, North Devon
Telephone (076) 97762

Western Counties Microlight Club
Torquay, South Devon
Telephone (0803) 612668

Devon Airsport Microlight Centre
Eaglescott Airfield
Telephone (0363) 82480

Dorset

The Microlight Aviation Club
Verwood, Dorset
Telephone (0202) 822486

Newton Peverell Flying Group
Redlands, Weymouth
Telephone (0305) 812342

Essex

Essex Airsports
Grays, Essex
Telephone (0375) 371172

West Essex Microlight Group
Nr Harlow, Essex
Telephone (0378) 813449

Slipstream Aviation
Romford, Essex
Telephone (0371) 856744

Andrewsfield Flying Club
Saling Airfield
Telephone (0371) 856744

Hertfordshire Flying Club
Nr Harlow, Essex
Telephone (0279) 792151

HVA Partnership
Harlow, Essex
Telephone (0279) 419873

Gloucestershire

Seven Valley Microlight Club
Hartpury, Glos
Telephone (045270) 314

Hampshire

Airborne Aviation
Basingstoke, Hants
Telephone (0202) 822486

Hampshire Microlight Club
Lyndhurst, Hants
Telephone (0703) 813480

Sussex Microlight Club
Emsworth, Hants
Telephone (0243) 377356

Herefordshire

Sabre Air Sports
Shobden Airfield
Telephone (056881) 8168

Hereford Airsports Flying Club
Madley, Hereford
Telephone (0981) 251242

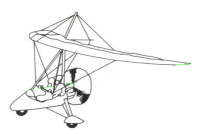

Kent

Medway Microlights
Rochester, Kent
Telephone (0634) 270780

Kent Microlight Aircraft Club
Nr Canterbury, Kent
Telephone (0227) 70463

SEMAC
Nr Canterbury, Kent
Telephone (0227) 720400

The Wealden Microlight Club
Tonbridge, Kent
Telephone (0732) 364569

Medway Airsports Club
Gillingham, Kent
Telephone (0634) 43679

Lancashire

Northwest Microlight Aviation
Accrington, Lancs
Telephone (0254) 395956

Ribble Valley Microlight Club
Blackburn, Lancs
Telephone (0254) 60235

Northwest Microlight Aircraft Club
Prestwich, Manchester
Telephone (061) 798 0690

Northern Microlight School
Preston, Lancs
Telephone (0995) 604694

Leicestershire

Central Airsports Flying Club
North Kilworth, Leics
Telephone (0860) 334920

Lincolnshire

B Wright Fenland Microlight School
Nr Spalding, Lincs
Telephone (0406) 34330

Norfolk

David Clark Microlight Aircraft
Worthing, Norfolk
Telephone (0362) 637405

Northrepps Aero Club
Aylsham, Norfolk
Telephone (0263) 732003

Northamptonshire

C10 Airsports
Brackley, Northants
Telephone (0295) 712462

Northampton Microlight Club
Earls Barton, Northants
Telephone (0604) 812290

North Beds Microlight Club
Earls Barton, Northants
Telephone (0604) 812290

Nottinghamshire

Derby & Nottingham Microlights
Burton Joyce, Nottingham
Telephone (0602) 312254

Oxfordshire

Chilton Park Microlight Club
Wallingford, Oxon
Telephone (0491) 874242

Pegasus Flight Training
Enstone Airfield
Telephone (06087) 8741

Somerset

Jim Greenshields Somerset Micros
Taunton, Somerset
Telephone (0823) 442391

Staffordshire

Staffordshire Aero Club
Cannock, Staffs
Telephone (0922) 416381

Midlands Microlight School
Fradley Aerodrome
Telephone (0543) 414613

Trent Valley Microlight Club
Little Haywood, Staffs
Telephone (0836) 363370

Midland Microlight Flying Club
Cannock, Staffs
Telephone (0543) 275756

Suffolk

Microlight Aircraft Flight Training
Ipswich, Suffolk
Telephone (0860) 774078

Tyne & Wear

Northumbria Flying Club
Bedlington, Northumbria
Telephone (0670) 825427

Northumbria Microlights
Tynemouth, Tyne & Wear
Telephone (091) 258 0982

Warwickshire

Aerolite
Long Marston Airfield
Telephone (0789) 299299

Aerolite Flying Club
Alcester, Warks
Telephone (0789) 400900

Avon Microlight Centre
Long Marston Airfield
Telephone (0789) 204010

Long Marston Microlight Club
Bidford on Avon, Warks
Telephone (0789) 490388

Leicestershire Microlight Club
Nuneaton, Warks
Telephone (0203) 340160

Wiltshire

Pegasus Flight Training
Long Newnton Airfield
Telephone (0836) 591596

Chilbolton Flying Club (Micros)
Salisbury, Wilts
Telephone (0794) 390638

GS Aviation
Nr Marlborough, Wilts
Telephone (0672) 512578

M4 Microlight Club
Swindon, Wilts
Telephone (0793) 740854

Wiltshire Microlight Centre
Nr Marlborough, Wilts
Telephone (0672) 86554

Yorkshire

Meridan Ultralights
Pocklington, East Yorks
Telephone (0759) 304337

Doncaster Airsports
Doncaster, South Yorks
Telephone (0302) 782564

Yorkshire Dragons Microlight Club
Thongsbridge, Huddersfield
Telephone (0484) 687479

Full Sutton Flying Club
Wilberfoss, Yorks
Telephone (075) 95583

Flightpath Microlights
Rufforth, Yorks
Telephone (0860) 871638

Baxby Airsports Club
Hustwaite, Yorks
Telephone (03476) 572

Baileys Ultralights
Shadwell, Leeds
Telephone (0532) 650530

Yorkshire Microlight Aircraft Club
Pudsey, Leeds
Telephone (0532) 563049

West Riding Microlight Aircraft Club
Hawksworth Estate, Leeds
Telephone (0532) 588401

Yorkshire Eagles Microlight Club
Wetherby, West Yorks
Telephone (0937) 842562

Northern Lites
Pudsey, Leeds
Telephone (0532) 563049

North Yorkshire Flying Club
Whitby, North Yorks
Telephone (0947) 603010

Windsports Centre Club
Wombleton Aerodrome
Telephone (0751) 32356

Isle of Man

Manx Eagles Club
Laxey, Isle of Man
Telephone (0624) 781300

Northern Ireland

Thruster Ireland
Woodview, County Armagh
Telephone (0762) 871125

Scotland

Strathclyde Microlight Club
Shieldhill, Nr Falkirk
Telephone (0324) 28989

Connel Flying Club
Oban, Argyll
Telephone (0631) 66079

Grampian Microlight Flying Club
Rosemount, Aberdeen
Telephone (0224) 642520

East of Scotland Microlights
Gorebridge, Midlothian
Telephone (0875) 20102

North Scottish Microlight Flying Club
Dyce, Aberdeen
Telephone (0224) 722517

Wales

Swansea Airsports
Swansea Airport
Telephone (0792) 297665

Skylines Microlight School
Swansea Airport
Telephone (0792) 290476

Pembrokeshire Microlight Flying Club
Narberth, Pembrokeshire
Telephone (0834) 861510

Aeromoth
Swansea Airport
Telephone (0729) 290476

Appendix 4

Where to Glide

Bedfordshire

Cranfield Institute of Technology
Gliding Club
Cranfield Airport
Cranfield, Beds
Telephone (0234) 750111

London Gliding Club
Tring Road
Dunstable, Beds
Telephone (092) 7422358

RAE Bedford Flying Club
RAE Bedford, Beds
Telephone (0234) 261079

Sackville Gliding Club
Sackville Lodge
Risley, Beds
Telephone (0234) 708877

Buckinghamshire

Booker Gliding Club
Wycombe Air Park
Marlow, Bucks
Telephone (0494) 442501

Upward Bound Trust Gliding Club
Aylesbury/Thames Airfield
c/o Airtech Ltd
Haddenham, Bucks
Telephone (0442) 61747

Cambridgeshire

Cambridge University Gliding Club
Duxford Airfield
Duxford, Cambs
Telephone (07677) 7077

Nene Valley Gliding Club
RAF Upwood
Ramsey, Cambs
Telephone (0480) 301316

Cornwall

Cornish Gliding Club
Travellas Airfield
Perranporth, Cornwall
Telephone (0872) 572124

Cumbria

Lakes Gliding Club
Walney Airfield
Barrow In Furness, Cumbria
Telephone (0229) 471458

Devon

Dartmoor Gliding Society
Burnford Common
Heathfield, Brentor
Tavistock, Devon
Telephone (0822) 613892

Devon & Somerset Gliding Club
North Hill Airfield
Broadhembury
Honiton, Devon
Telephone (040) 484 386

North Devon Gliding Club
Eaglescott Airfield
Burrington
Umberleight, North Devon
Telephone (7693) 404

Derbyshire

Derby & Lancashire Gliding Club
Camphill
Great Hucklow
Tideswell, Derbyshire
Telephone (0298) 871270

Essex

Essex Gliding Club
North Weald Airfield
North Weald, Bassett
Nr Epping, Essex
Telephone (0378) 82222

Essex & Suffolk Gliding Club
Wormingford Airfield
Fairfields Farm
Colchester, Essex
Telephone (0206) 242596

Gloucestershire

Bristol & Gloucestershire Gliding Club
Nympsfield
Nr Stonehouse, Glos
Telephone (0453) 860342

Cotswold Gliding Club
Aston Down Airfield
Frampton Mansell
Nr Stroud, Glos
Telephone (0285) 760473

Hampshire

Imperial College Gliding Club
Lasham Airfield
Alton, Hants
Telephone (025) 683 270

Lasham Gliding Society
Lasham Airfield
Alton, Hants
Telephone (0256) 381 322

Royal Aircraft Establishment
Farnborough Airfield
Farnborough, Hants
Telephone (0252) 24461 Ext 4352

Surrey & Hants Gliding Club
Lasham Airfield

Alton, Hants
Telephone (025) 381 270

Thruxton Gliding Club
Thruxton Airport
Nr Andover, Hants
Telephone (026) 477 3274

Herefordshire

Herefordshire Gliding Club
Shobden Airfield
Shobden
Nr Leominster, Herefordshire
Telephone (056) 881 8908

Humberside

Trent Valley Gliding Club
The Airfield
Kirton Lindsey
South Humberside
Telephone (0652) 648777

Isle of Wight

Vectis Gliding Club
Isle of Wight Airport
Newport Road
Sandown, Isle of Wight
Telephone (0983) 405125

Kent

Channel Gliding Club
Waldershare Park
Dover, Kent
Telephone (0304) 363111

Kent Gliding Club
Squids Gate
Challock
Nr Ashford, Kent
Telephone (023) 374 307

Lancashire

Blackpool & Fylde Gliding Club
Lower Cock Hill Farm
Fiddlers Lane
Chipping
Nr Preston, Lancs
Telephone (0995) 61267

Leicestershire

Coventry Gliding Club
Husbands Bosworth Airfield
Nr Lutterworth, Leics
Telephone (0858) 880521

Lincolnshire

Buckminster Gliding Club
Saltby Airfield
Saltby Heath Entrance
Skillington
Grantham, Lincs
Telephone (0476) 860385

Peterborough & Spalding Gliding Club
Crowland Airfield
Nr Peterborough
Telephone (0733) 210463

Strubby Gliding Club
The Airfield
Strubby Alford, Lincs
Telephone (0472) 691053

Norfolk

Norfolk Gliding Club
Tibenham Airfield
Long Stratton, Norfolk
Telephone (037) 977207

Northamptonshire

Aquila Gliding Club
The Airfield
Hinton in the Hedges
Brackley, Northants
Telephone (0295) 811056

Brackley Gliding Club
Turweston Airfield
Brackley, Northants
Telephone (0280) 704470

Welland Gliding Club
'Lyvedon'
Harley Way
Brigstock, Northants
Telephone (0406) 22480

Nottinghamshire

Dunkeries Gliding Club
Gamston Airfield
Retford, Notts
Telephone (0909) 501032

Newark & Notts Gliding Club
Winthorpe Airfield
Winthorpe
Newark, Notts
Telephone (0636) 707151

Northumberland

Borders Gliding Club
Galewood Farm
Milfield
Nr Wooler, Northumberland
Telephone (066) 86284

Oxfordshire

Enstone Eagles Gliding Club
The Control Tower
Enstone Airfield
Church Enstone, Oxon
Telephone (0608) 677461

Oxford Gliding Club
RAF Weston on the Green
Weston on the Green, Oxon
Telephone (086) 989 265

Oxfordshire Sportflying Club
Enstone Airfield
Church Enstone, Oxon
Telephone (0608) 677208

Shenington Gliding Club
Edgehill Airfield
Shenington, Oxon
Telephone (0295) 251716

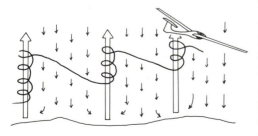

Shropshire

Midland Gliding Club
The Soaring Ground
The Long Mynd
Church Stretton, Shropshire
Telephone (058) 861 206

Shropshire Soaring Group
Sleap Airfield
Nr Wem, Shropshire
Telephone (0939) 32045

Suffolk

Rattlesden Gliding Club
The Airfield
Hightown Green
Rattlesden
Bury St Edmunds, Suffolk
Telephone (0449) 737789

Somerset

Mendip Gliding Club
Halesdown New Road
Draycott, Nr Cheddar
Somerset
Telephone (0749) 870312

Staffordshire

Marchington Gliding Club
Marchington Airfield
Moreton Lane
Marchington
Nr Uttoxeter, Staffs
Telephone (0283) 820108

Staffordshire Gliding Club
Morridge
Thorncliffe
Nr Leek, Staffs
Telephone (053) 834 369

Surrey

Surrey Hills Gliding Club
Kenley Airfield
Kenley, Surrey
Telephone (081) 763 0019

Sussex

East Sussex Gliding Club
Kitsons Field
The Broyle
Rigmer
Lewes, East Sussex
Telephone (0825) 840347

Southdown Gliding Club
Parham Airfield
Cootham
Storrington, West Sussex
Telephone (0903) 742137

Tyne & Wear

Northumbria Gliding Club
Currock Hill
Chopwell
Newcastle upon Tyne
Telephone (0207) 561286

Warwickshire

Avon Soaring Centre
Bidford Airfield
Bidford on Avon, Warks
Telephone (0789) 772606

Stratford on Avon Gliding Club
Snitterfield Airfield, Warks
Telephone (0789) 731095

Wiltshire

Bath & Wiltshire Gliding Group
Keevil Airfield
Nr Trowbridge, Wilts
Telephone (0380) 870411

Dorset Gliding Club
Old Sarum Airfield
Salisbury, Wilts
Telephone (0722) 338479

Shalborne Soaring Society
Rivar Hill Airfield
c/o Moordown Farm
Oxenwood
Marlborough, Wilts
Telephone (0264) 89204

Vale of Whitehorse Gliding Club
c/o Sandhill Farm
Swindon, Wilts
Telephone (0793) 783293

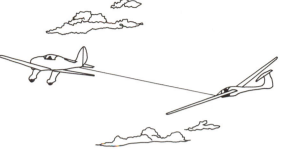

Worcestershire

RSRE Flying Club
RSRE Pershore
Worcestershire
Telephone (03865) 552123

Yorkshire

Burn Gliding Club
Park Lane
Burn
Selby, North Yorks
Telephone (0757) 270296

Carlton Moor Gliding Club
Carlton Moor
Nr Stokesley, North Yorks
Telephone (0642) 778234

Wolds Gliding Club
The Airfield
Pocklington, York
Telephone (0759) 303579

York Gliding Centre
Rufforth Aerodrome
York
Telephone (090) 483694

Yorkshire Gliding Club
Sutton Bank
Thirsk, North Yorks
Telephone (0845) 597237

Highland Gliding Club
Dallachy Airfield
Spey Bay
Fochabers, Morayshire
Telephone (0343) 820568

Scottish Gliding Union
Portmoak Airfield
Scotlandwell
By Kinross, Kinross-shire
Telephone (059) 284 543

Strathclyde Gliding Club
Strathaven Airfield

Couplaw Farm
Strathaven, Lanarkshire
Telephone (0357) 20235

Wales

Black Mountains Gliding Club
Troed Yr Harn Farm
Talgarth
Brecon, Powys
Telephone (0874) 711463

Glyndwr Soaring Club
Lleweni Parc
Mold Road
Denbigh, Clwyd
Telephone (0745) 813774

North Wales Gliding Club
Bryn Gwyn
Bach Farm
Rhuallt, Clwyd
Telephone (051) 327 4760

Over T-Twenty One Club
Highmoor Field
Haffoty Bennet
Roadside
Abergete, Clwyd
Telephone (0492) 650398

Northern Ireland

Ulster Gliding Club
Bellarena
County Londonderry
Northern Ireland
Telephone (05047) 50301

Scotland

Angus Gliding Club
Condor
Arbroath, Angus
Telephone (0241) 74001

Argyll & West Highland Gliding Centre
Connel Airfield
North Connel
Oban, Argyll

Cairngorm Gliding Club
Blackmill Airstrip
Feshiebridge
Kincraig
Inverness-shire
Telephone (05404) 317

Connel Gliding Club
Connel Airfield
North Connel
Oban, Argyll
Telephone (036) 981256

Deeside Gliding Club
Aboyne Airfield
Dinnet

Aboyne, Grampian
Telephone (033) 9885 339

Dumfries & District Gliding Club
Falggunzeon
Dalbeattie, Kircudbrightshire
Telephone (038776) 601

Grampian Gliding Club
Mill of Garvock Farm
Laurencekirk, Grampian
Telephone (05612) 430

South Wales Gliding Club
Gwernsey
Usk, Gwent
Telephone (0291) 690536

Vale of Neath Gliding Club
The Airfield
Rhigos
Aberdare, Mid Glamorgan
Telephone (0639) 637241

West Wales Gliding Association
Templeton Airfield
Templeton
Nr Narbeth, Dyfed
Telephone (0646) 601534

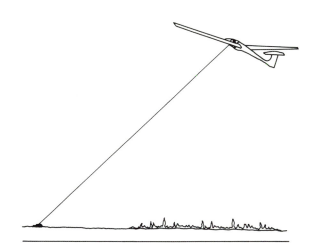

Appendix 5

Where to Hang Glide

There are approximately 40 + hang gliding clubs sited throughout the United Kingdom. Membership of these clubs is only available to trained pilots. If you are not yet trained you must undergo basic training at one of the registered schools listed below before you will be allowed to join one of the clubs as a flying member.

Devon

Devon School of Hang Gliding
1 Dovedale Road
Beacon Park
Plymouth, Devon
Telephone (0752) 564408

Derbyshire

Sheffield Hang Gliding Centre
Cliff Side
Church Street
Tideswell, Derbyshire
Telephone (0298) 872313

Peak School of Hang Gliding
The Elms
Wetton
Nr Ashbourne, Derbyshire
Telephone (033) 527 257

Isle of Wight

Isle of Wight Hang Gliding Centre
Tapnell Farm House
Afton
Nr Yarmouth, Isle of Wight
Telephone (0983) 754042

Kent

Skywing Sports
59 Chelsfield Road

Orpington, Kent
Telephone (0689) 873873

Norfolk

Flexwing Training
Shetland
Chapel Lane
Beeston, Norfolk
Telephone (0328) 701602

Nottinghamshire

South Peak Airsports
3 Kirby Close
Newthorpe, Nottingham
Telephone (0773) 760236

Sussex

Sussex College of Hang Gliding
10 Crescent Road
Brighton, East Sussex
Telephone (0273) 609925

Staffordshire

Peak District Flight Training
Abbey Units
Macclesford Road
Leek, Staffs
Telephone (0538) 383659

Wiltshire

Wiltshire Hang Gliding Centre
The Old Barn
Rhyls Lane
Lockerbridge
Marlborough, Wilts
Telephone (0672) 86555

Yorkshire

Pennine Gliding Centre
18 Scrape View
Golcar
Huddersfield, West Yorks
Telephone (0484) 641306

Airborne Hang Gliding Centre
Hey End Farm
Luddendenfoat
Halifax, West Yorks
Telephone (0422) 834989

Northern Hang Gliding Centre
Dunvegan Lodge
Front Street
Barmby Moor, North Yorks
Telephone (0759) 304404

Wales

Hiway Flight Services
2 Lion Terrace

Gilwern
Abergavenny, Gwent
Telephone (0873) 831667

Skysports
36 Hatherleigh Road
Abergavenny, Gwent
Telephone (0873) 6112

Welsh Hang Gliding Centre
Bryn Bach Park
The Visitor Centre
Tredegar, Gwent
Telephone (0873) 832100

Rhossili Soaring Centre
46 Squirrel Walk
Fforest
Pontardulais, Swansea
Telephone (0792) 885536

Joint Services Hang Gliding Centre
Cwrt-Y-Gollen
Crickhowell, Powys
Telephone (0873) 810386

Scotland

Cairnwell Hang Gliding School
Cairnwell Mountain
By Braemar
Ballater, Aberdeen
Telephone (03397) 41331

Where to Paraglide

Avon

Avon Eagles
Hengrove Park
Bristol
Telephone (0272) 322857

Bedfordshire

BMS CCF PC
Bedford
Telephone (0234) 364331

Cambridgeshire

Venture Flights
Airfield Nr Cambridge
Telephone (0462) 701225

Cheshire

Paraglide PC
Stockport
Telephone (061) 432 7315

Parapente Services
Stockport
Telephone (0663) 743438

Cornwall

Cornwall Paragliding Club
Perranporth
Telephone (0209) 218962

Cumbria

Eagle Quest PC
Penrith
Telephone (07684) 83888

Lakeland Leisure
Windermere
Telephone (05394) 44786

Devon

Paraflight Training
Torbay
South Devon
Telephone (0709) 700475

East Midlands

Derby Mountain Centre
Derby
Telephone (0332) 365650

Essex

The Brigade PC
North Weald
Epping
Telephone (081) 519 7663

North Weald PC
North Weald
Epping
Telephone (0702) 540901

Greater London N Scouts
North Weald
Epping
Telephone (043871) 5510

Green Dragons PC
Wanstead Flats
Nr Ilford
Telephone (081) 517 7945

Gloucestershire

Flight Factory
Cheltenham Race Course
Telephone (0242) 261621

Hampshire

Army Air Corps Centre PC
Stockbridge
Telephone (0703) 637107

Marwell Activity Centre
Marwell
Nr Tichfield
Telephone (0329) 46969

Saints Ascending Team
Southampton
Telephone (0703) 442693

Hertfordshire

Hertford School of PG
Hertfordshire
Telephone (0920) 465781

Isle of Wight

High Adventure PC
Yarmouth IOW
Telephone (0983) 752322

Kent

Ascent International
North Kent Coast
Telephone (0474) 853675

Deal District Scouts PC
North Kent Coast
Telephone (0304) 812782

Fly High (KSPT) PC
West Malling Airstation
Telephone (0622) 728230

Lancashire

Bollington PC
Barton Airfield
Nr Manchester
Telephone (0625) 573983

Mountaineering Paraglide Extreme
Oldham
Telephone (0457) 872080

Lincolnshire

Lincolnshire Scouts
Spitalgate
Nr Grantham
Telephone (0773) 826880

Purple Parrots
Kirton Lindsey Airfield
Gainsborough
Telephone (0742) 478899

Norfolk

2620 Sqn Adventure Training Section
RAF Marham
Kings Lynn
Telephone (0760) 337188

Oxfordshire

Birdwings (South Cerney) PC
Banbury
Telephone (0295) 271718

Shropshire

High Sports Paragliding Club
Shrewsbury
Telephone (0743) 231649

Surrey

GLSW & Surrey PC
Headley Heath
Telephone (0932) 844766

Surrey ACF PC
Chersey
Telephone (0932) 567591

Sussex

East Sussex Scouts PC
East Sussex
Telephone (0342) 21876

Free Flight PC
Steyning
Telephone (0273) 411239

Purple Haze
Beeding Hill
West Sussex
Telephone (0903) 245447

West Sussex Scouts PC
Bognor Regis
Telephone (0243) 823105

Sky Systems Paragliding
Edburton
Nr Henfield
Telephone (0273) 857000

Sunrisers PC
Littlehampton
West Sussex
Telephone (0268) 699225

Sussex College of Paragliding
Brighton
Telephone (0273) 609925

Tyne & Wear

Leading Edge
Berwick Upon Tweed
Telephone (0289) 308013

West Midlands

Chase Parascending Club
Chasewater
Walsal
Telephone (0543) 78312

Midflight PC
Tamworth
Telephone (0827) 280244

Wiltshire

Wiltshire Paragliding Club
Marlborough
Telephone (067286) 555/4

Paravion
Devizes
Telephone (0380) 860348

Yorkshire

Active Edge PC
Settle

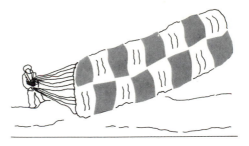

North Yorks
Telephone (0729) 822311

Central Yorks Scouts PC
RAF Topcliffe
Nr Rippon
Telephone (0532) 671711

Dales Paragliding Club
Wensleydale
North Yorks
Telephone (0759) 304404

Peak Paragliding
Sheffield
Telephone (0742) 369296

Channel Islands

Pilot Watersports
Trinity
Jersey CI
Telephone (0534) 63538

Isle of Man

Manx PC
Isle of Man
Telephone (0624) 21328

Northern Ireland

Wild Geese PC
Colraine
Northern Ireland
Telephone (026) 585 669

Scotland

Adventure Parapent Extreme
Aberdeenshire
Telephone (09756) 51207

193

Cloudbusters
Glasgow
Telephone (041) 634 6688

Croft-Na-Caber
Perthshire
Telephone (08873) 236 or 588

Extreme Paragliding Club
Tinto Hills
Orchills
Telephone (0259) 723511

Parapente Ecosse
Edinburgh
Telephone (031) 313 5409

Sky & Air Scotland
Edinburgh
Telephone (0577) 4415

Strathclyde Country Park PC
Motherwell
Telephone (0698) 66155 Ext 139

Wingbeat PC
Minto Hills
Nr Hawick
Telephone (045) 088 215

Wales

Dragonfly (Wales)
Tenby

Dyfed
Telephone (0834) 843553

Enigma
Gwynedd
Telephone (0286) 870334

Harley Chutes PC
Powys
Telephone (0597) 822987

Welsh Borders PC
New Radnor
Powys
Telephone (0544) 21375

Paraglide International
Rhayader
Mid Wales
Telephone (0568) 614086

Skydragons
Vale of Clwyd
Telephone (082) 42 7171

South Wales HG & PC
Bryn Bach Park
Gwent
Telephone (0873) 832100

South East Wales HG & PG Club
New Radnor
Powys
Telephone (0873) 831862

Appendix 7

Where to Balloon

Avon

Cameron Balloons
St Johns Street
Bedminster, Bristol
Telephone (0272) 637216
Fax (0272) 661168

Balloon Base
Vauxhall House
Coronation Road, Bristol
Telephone (0272) 633333
Fax (0272) 632263

Gone With The Wind Ltd
Mulberry House
Front Street
Churchill, Bristol
Telephone (0934) 852359

Bristol Balloons
Parkland Road, Bristol
Telephone (0272) 637858
Fax (0272) 639555

Bedfordshire

Mid Bucks Farmers Balloon Group
Mount Pleasant Farm
Stewkley, Leighton Buzzard
Telephone (0525) 24045

Berkshire

Peter Bish
Haywards Cross, Hungerford
Telephone (0488) 681527
Fax (0488) 681527

Dante Balloon Group
83 Juniper
Birch Hill, Bracknel
Telephone (0344) 59996

Newbury Balloon Company
Millbank
Benham Park
Marsh Benham, Newbury
Telephone (0831) 222158

Buckinghamshire

J Bennett & Son Ltd
The White House
21 High Street
High Wycombe
Telephone (0494) 450450

Christopher Dunkley
3 Sidney Terrace
Wendover
Telephone (0296) 624725

Cumbria

Wind & Water Specialist Sports
23 Church Street
Windemere
Telephone (05394) 44020
Fax (05394) 44020

Devon

Apollo Balloon Company Ltd
Highland House
Highland Street, Ivybridge
Telephone (0752) 690993
Fax (0752) 691182

Essex

Anglo Alpine Balloon School
5 Baynards Crescent
Frinton-on-Sea
Telephone (0255) 673709
Fax (0206) 575479

Quixote Balloons
12 St Austins Lane
Harwich
Telephone (0255) 507661

Gloucestershire

Cotswold Balloons
Jasmine Cottage
The Pitch
Brownshill, Stroud
Telephone (0453) 885187

Skylark Balloons
Walnut House
Old Rectory Road
Kingswood, Wotton
Telephone (0453) 843985
Fax (0453) 843985

Herefordshire

Ross Balloons
Springfield
Walford, Ross on Wye
Telephone (0989) 66034

Wye Valley Aviation
45a Edde Cross Street
Ross on Wye
Telephone (0989) 763134
Fax (0989) 768242

Hertfordshire

Corporate Balloon Company Ltd
Elstree Aerodrome
Elstree
Telephone (081) 905 1826
Fax (081) 953 9445

Leicestershire

Capricorn Balloons Ltd
Threeways, Beacon Road
Woodhouse Eaves, Loughborough
Telephone (0509) 890348
Fax (0509) 890710

Middlesex

Sky Sailor Hot Air Ballooning
4 Lingfield Close
Northwood
Telephone (0923) 824223
Fax (0923) 835649

Norfolk

Anglia Balloons
Peacock Lodge
Marlingford
Telephone (0603) 880819

Wizard Balloons
The Cottage
The Green, Diss
Telephone (0379) 898079
Fax (0379) 890199

Broadland Balloons Ltd
Arboretum House
Scottow Road, Lamas
Telephone (069) 269520
Fax (0603) 279514

Northamptonshire

The Balloon Business Ltd
4 Bock Lane
Hardingstone
Telephone (0604) 768617

Nottinghamshire

Dragon Balloon Company
Redcourt
University Park
Telephone (0602) 473778
Fax (0602) 791336

Shropshire

Airship & Balloon Company
Unit 19
Stafford Park 12, Telford
Telephone (0952) 292945
Fax (0952) 292930

Border Balloon Company
Tyn-a-Coed
The Candy, Oswestry
Telephone (0691) 659429
Fax (0691) 654911

Northern Flights
15 Southfield Road
Much Wenlock
Telephone (0952) 727343

Thunder & Colt
Maesbury, Oswestry
Telephone (0691) 670644
Fax (0691) 670617

Somerset

The European Balloon School
Higher Hare Farm
Hare Lane
Buckland St Mary, Chard
Telephone (0460) 234597
Fax (0460) 54261

Dave Seager-Thomas
41 Boulting
Shepton Mallet
Telephone (074) 988 502
Fax (0860) 511700

Somerset Balloon Safaris
Priory Farm
Wheathill, Somerton

Staffordshire

Wickers World
3 Anson Row
Little Haywood
Telephone (0889) 575575
Fax (0889) 575582

Aerial Promotions
Cannock Chase Ent Centre
Rugeley Road
Hednesford, Cannock
Telephone (0543) 879451
Fax (0543) 879114

Suffolk

Anglia Balloons
Old Romney

Lower Street
Cavendish, Bury St Edmunds
Telephone (0787) 280213

Surrey

Flying Pictures
Montgolfier House
Fairoaks Airport
Chobham, Woking
Telephone (0276) 855111
Fax (0276) 858868

Hot Airlines Ltd
5 Woodstock Close
Cranleigh
Telephone (0483) 268934
Fax (0483) 273279

Reach For The Sky
Sudpre Cottage
Worpledon, Guildford
Telephone (0483) 232662
Fax (0483) 233895

Sussex

The British School of Ballooning
Little London
Ebernoe, Petworth
Telephone (042) 878307

Tyne & Wear

Ballooning Adventures Ltd
Richmond Lodge
Moor Road South, Gosforth
Telephone (091) 2859343
Fax (091) 2130946

Warwickshire

Heart of England Balloons
Cross Lanes Farm
Walcote, Alcester
Telephone (0789) 488219

John Henderson
1 Welford Hill Cottages
Lone Marston Road
Welford-on-Avon
Telephone (0789) 750663
Fax (0789) 750663

Wiltshire

Balloons International
1 Fairview Cottages
Pennsylvania, Chippenham
Telephone (0225) 891884

PSH Skypower Ltd
Bembridge House
Manningford Bruce, Pewsey
Telephone (0672) 63379

Yorkshire

Airborne Adventures Ltd
43 Westwood
Carleton, Skipton
Telephone (0756) 701566
Fax (0860) 548458

Ascents of Satisfaction
3 Main Street
Kelfield
Telephone (0757) 248495
Fax (0757) 249002

Balloon Rides
Leeman Road
York
Telephone (0904) 640007

Scotland

Sky Climber Balloon Adventures Ltd
St Enoch Business Centre
40 St Enoch Square, Glasgow
Telephone (041) 2487767
Fax (041) 2040958

Wales

Balloons Over Wales
236 Mynydd Garnllwyd Road
Morriston, Swansea
Telephone (0792) 774495
Fax (0792) 775626

Regional & Club Representatives

3-4-40 Region
James Dobson
Conifers
Wantage Road
Streatley, Berks
Telephone (0491) 872063

Black Horse Balloon Club
Derek Belton
Alder House
Peters Lane
Whiteleaf

Chiltern Region
Ian Chadwick
92 The Hedges
Higham Ferrers
Wellingborough, Northants

Pennine Region
Alan & Mary Dunning
7 The Crescent
Ormesby
Middlesborough, Cleveland
Telephone (0642) 300266

Mid Hampshire Balloon Club
Paul Hutton
13 Fellows Road
Farnborough, Hants
Telephone (0252) 514396

Eastern Region
Brian Ribbans
Allonsfield House
Campsea Ash
Woodbridge, Suffolk
Telephone (0728) 747095

Western Region
Paul Spellwood
34 Lower Redland Road
Telephone (0272) 742056

Midlands Region
Sue Jones
39 Kenmere Tower
Erdington, Birmingham
Telephone (021) 377 6245

East Midlands Balloon Group
David Davies
21 Popular Avenue
East Leake, Leics
Telephone (0509) 852655

North West Region

Derek Grimshaw
Fleetwood Farm
North Road
Bretherton, Preston
Telephone (0772) 600103

Oswestry Balloon Club
Mike Evans
86 Aston Way

Oswestry, Shropshire
Telephone (0691) 655945

Surrey & Sussex Balloon Group
Neil Lindsay
Tawlbrook
Plaistow Road
Loxwood, West Sussex
Telephone (0483) 574424

Cinque Ports Flying Club
Adrian Greaves
Woobury House
Woodchurch Road
Tenterden, Kent
Telephone (05806) 32864

London Region & Capital Balloon Club
Roger Yorke
4 Nevern Square
London
Telephone (071) 370 3466

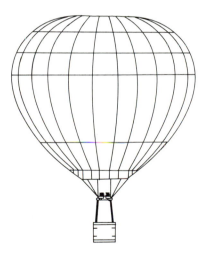

Appendix 8

Where to Parachute

Avon

Badminton Parachute Club
Contact J Davies
Badminton
Avon
Telephone (045) 421 486

Berkshire

London Parachute School
PO Box 18
Goring on Thames
Reading RG8 9EW
Telephone (0249) 651909 (DZ)
Telephone (0860) 559112
(Weekends)

Cambridgeshire

Peterborough Parachute Centre
Sibson Airfield
Wansford
Peterborough
Telephone (0832) 280490

The Free Fall Company
Sibson Airfield
Wansford
Peterborough
Telephone (0832) 280055

Cornwall

Cornwall Parachute Centre
Frans Ranch
Old Naval Airfield
St Merryn, Cornwall
Telephone (0841) 540691

Cumbria

North West Parachute Centre
Cark Airfield
Flookburgh
Nr Grange-Over-Sands
Cumbria
Telephone (05395) 58672/58555
(Airfield)
Telephone (0772) 720848
(Weekdays)

Carlisle Parachute Centre
Carlisle Airport
Crosby-on-Eden
Carlisle
Cumbria CA6 4NW
Telephone (0228) 73633

Devon

Devon & Somerset Parachute School
2 Wyvern Road
Sherford
Taunton
Somerset TA1 4RB
Telephone (0823) 279780

Eaglescott Parachute Centre
Eaglescott Airfield
Ashreighney
Chulmleigh
Devon EX18 7PH
Telephone (07693) 552/0392 75222

Durham

Peterlee Parachute Club
Shotton Colliery Airfield
Peterlee
Co. Durham
Telephone (091) 5171234/
(091) 3865315

Essex

POPS UK
64 Ardleigh Court
Hutton Road
Shenfield
Essex
Telephone (0277) 219717

East Coast Parachute Centre
8 Burns Crescent
Chelmsford
Essex CM2 OTS
Telephone (0245) 268772

Kent

Headcorn Parachute Centre
Headcorn Airfield
Headcorn
Kent TN27 9HX
Telephone (0622) 890862

Slipstream Adventures
Headcorn Airfield
Headcorn
Kent TN27 9HX
Telephone (0622) 890641/890862

Lincolnshire

Freebird Skydiving
Contact Chris Donaldson
3 Reepham
Orton
Brimbley
Peterboroguh PE2 OTS
Telephone (0733) 370863

Lancashire

Black Knights Parachute Centre
Contact Bob Parry
Patty's Farm

Hilliam Lane
Cockerham Nr Lancaster
Telephone (0524) 791820 (Weekends)
Telephone (051) 924 5560 (Midweek)

Northamptonshire

Oxon & Northants Parachute Centre
Hinton-in-the-hedges Airfield
Steane Nr Brackley
Northants
Contact Mike Bolton
85 Oak Park Road
Wordsley Stourbridge
West Midlands DY8 5YJ
Telephone (0384) 393373

Northumberland

Border Parachute Centre
Dunstanburgh House
Embleton
Northumberland NE66 3XF
Telephone (066576) 588

Nottinghamshire

British Parachute School
The Control Tower
Langar Airfield
Langar
Nottingham
Telephone (0949) 60878
Fax (0949) 60878

David Morris Action Sports
41 Ellindon
Bretton North
Peterborough PE3 8RG
Telephone (0733) 266076

Shropshire

The Sport Parachute Centre
Tilstock Airfield
Whitchurch
Shropshire
Telephone (0948) 841111

Suffolk

Ipswich Parachute Centre
Ipswich Airport
Nacton Road
Ipswich
Suffolk IP3 9QF
Telephone (0473) 710044

Sussex

Flying Tigers Skydiving Centre
Goodwood Airfield
Nr Chichester
West Sussex PO18 OPH
Telephone (0243) 533444

Warwickshire

Midland Parachute Centre
Long Marston Airfield
Stratford-Upon-Avon
Warks
Telephone (0789) 297959

West Midlands

Halfpenny Green Skydiving Centre
The Airfield
Bobbington Nr Stourbridge
Telephone (0384) 88293

Yorkshire

Doncaster Parachute Club
Doncaster Airfield
Doncaster
South Yorks
Telephone (0302) 532922 (Weekends)
Telephone (0532) 505600 (Midweek)

Merlin Parachute Centre
Topcliffe Near Thirsk
North Yorks
Telephone (0748) 832521 (Weekends)
Telephone (0845) 524713 (Weekdays)

Scotland

Fife Parachute Centre
Errol Airfield
Grange
Perthshire PH2 7TB
Telephone (0821) 2673

Scottish Parachute Club
Strathallan Airfield
Nr Auchterarder Perthshire
Perthshire PH3 1LA
Telephone (0764) 62572 (Weekends)

Stirling Parachute Centre
Thornhill
Nr Stirling FK8 3QT
Telephone (0786) 87788
Fax (0786) 87748

Northern Ireland

Wild Geese Skydiving Centre
Movenis Airfield
116 Carrowreagh Road
Garvagh Coleraine
Co. Londonderry Northern Ireland
Telephone (0265) 58609/57050 (DZ)
Telephone (0265) 58002 (Dave Penny)

Appendix 9

Useful Addresses

Aircraft Owners & Pilots Association
(AOPA)
50A Cambridge Street
London SW1V 4QQ
Telephone (071) 834 5631
Fax (071) 834 8623

British Microlight Aircraft
Bullring Deddington
Banbury, Oxon OX15 0TT
Telephone (0869) 38888
Fax (0869) 37116

British Parachute Association
5 Wharf Way
Glen Parva
Leicester LE2 9TF
Telephone (0533) 785271
Fax (0533) 477662

British Gliding Association
Kimberley House
Vaughan Way
Leicester
Telephone (0533) 531051
Fax (0533) 515939

British Hang Gliding Association
The Old Schoolroom
Loughborough Road
Leicester LE4 5PJ
Telephone (0533) 612362
Fax (0533) 611323

British Association
of Paragliding Clubs
The Old Schoolroom
Leicester LE4 5PJ
Telephone (0533) 611322
Fax (0533) 611323

British Balloon & Airship Club
New Members Secretary
6 Aplins Close
Harpenden
Herts AL5 2QB
Telephone (0582) 767938

British Aerobatic Association
70 South Road
Handsworth
Birmingham B18 5LD
Telephone (021) 235 3785
Telephone (021) 554 2117

British Helicopter Advisory Board
(BHAB)
Building C2
West Entrance
Fairoaks Airport
Chobham
Surrey GU24 8HX
Telephone (0276) 856100
Fax (0276) 85126

Biggin Hill Ground School
Building 162
Biggin Hill Airport
Kent
Telephone (0959) 71919

Civil Aviation Authority
45-49 Kingsway
London WC2B 6TE
Telephone (071) 379 7311
Fax (071) 240 1153

CAA Flight Crew Licensing
Aviation House
South Area
Gatwick Airport

West Sussex RH6 OYR
Telephone (0293) 573630
Fax (0293) 573999

CAA Medical Department
Aviation House
South Area
Gatwick Airport
West Sussex RH6 OYR
Telephone (0293) 573685
Fax (0293) 573999

Department of Civil Aviation Studies
City of London Polytechnic
100 Minories
London EC3 1JY
Telephone (071) 320 1757
Fax (071) 320 1759

Harry Mendelssoln
Discount Pilot Sales
Merchiston Cottage
16 Colinton Road
Edinburgh EH10 5EL
Telephone (031) 447 7777
Fax (031) 452 9004

Helicopter Club of Great Britain
Rylands House
Aynho Banbury
Oxon OX17 3AT
Telephone (0869) 810646
Fax (0869) 810755

Popular Flying Association
Terminal Building
Shoreham Airport
Shoreham-By-Sea
West Sussex BN43 5FF
Telephone (0273) 461616
Fax (0273) 463390

PPL Home Study Courses
Cranfield Aviation Studies
PO Box 574
Cranfield
Bedford MK43 OYE
Telephone (0234) 750050
Fax (0234) 750839

PPL Ground Studies
East Surry College
Gatton Point
Redhill
Surrey RH1 2JX
Telephone (0737) 762684

Pilot Training Loans
Orion Finance
Freepost
Edgeware
Middlesex HA8 8BR
Telephone (081) 207 4610
Fax (081) 953 8560

Transair Pilot Shop
West Entrance
Fairoaks Airport
Chobham Nr Woking
Surrey GU24 8HX
Telephone (0276) 858533
Fax (0276) 855464

The Aviation Bookshop
656 Holloway Road
London N19 3PD
Telephone (071) 272 3630

The Student Pilots Association
30 Tisbury Road
Hove
East Sussex BN3 3BA
Telephone (0273) 204080

Appendix 10

Overseas Flying Training Organisations

Eire

Irish Aero Club
Dublin Airport
Telephone (010) 3531 424400
Fax (010) 3531 378323

Leinster Aero Club
Dublin Airport
Telephone (010) 353 1 715577
Fax (010) 353 1 725071

Island Helicopters
Dublin Airport
Telephone (010) 353 1 406790
Fax (010) 353 1 406761

Iona Flying Club
Cork Airport
Telephone (010) 35321 888440
Fax (010) 35321 888327

European College of Aeronautics
Cork Airport
Telephone (010) 35321 31490
Fax (010) 35321 314384

Hibernian Flying Club
Cork Airport
Telephone (010) 35321 88834
Fax (010) 35321 392365

Sligo Aero Club
Sligo Airport
Telephone (010) 353 71 68280
Fax (010) 353 71 68396

Skyfare Services
Sligo Airport
Telephone (010) 353 71 61342
Fax (010) 353 71 68352

Limerick Flying Club
Coonagh Airfield
Telephone (010) 353 61 326600

Kerry Aero Club
Kerry Airport
Telephone (010) 353 66 64786
Fax (010) 353 66 64134

Galway Flying Club
Galway Airport
Telephone (010) 353 91 55477

Waterford Aero Club
Waterford Airport
Telephone (010) 353 51 73133

Kilkenny Aero Club
Kilkenny Airport
Telephone (010) 353 56 21483
Fax (010) 353 56 21483

Westair Aviation
Shannon Airport
Telephone (010) 353 61 363166
Fax (010) 353 61 360544

Trim Flying Club
Trim Co Meath
Telephone (010) 353 46 31514
Fax (010) 353 46 23473

Weston Aero Club
Weston Aerodrome
Telephone (010) 1 6280435
Fax (010) 1 6283068

France

FTI Aviation
Cannes-Mandelieu Airport
Telephone (UK) 0993 822701
Fax (UK) 0993 823004

Sisteron Valley Flying Club
Sisteron-Theze Airfield
Haute Provence
Telephone (UK) 081 462 8117

La Rochelle Flying Centre
La Rochelle-Laleu Airport
Telephone (UK) 0275 474501

Portugal

MSF Aviation Algarve
Faro Airport Portugal
Telephone (UK) 0860 212121

Canada

Aviation International
Toronto Canada
Telephone (UK) 021 705 7357
Fax (UK) 021 705 7357

Brantford Flying Club
PO Box 903
Brantford Ontario Canada
Telephone (CAN) 519 753 2521

PEM Air
Ontario Canada
Telephone (CAN) 613 687 8139
Fax (CAN) 613 687 8558

PFTC
Vancouver Canada
Telephone (CAN) 604 940 0653
Fax (CAN) 604 940 0864

South Africa

Helicopter Training Services
Grand Central Airport Johannesburg
Telephone (UK) 07048 76553

United States of America

Airwise Aviation
Titusville Florida
Telephone (UK) 0732 354320
Fax (UK) 0732 360178

Florida Flight Training
Rockledge Air Park Florida
Telephone (UK) 0373 830415

Merritt Island Air Service
Merritt Island Florida
Telephone (USA) 407 453 2222

Florida Flyers UK
Fort Pierce Florida
Telephone (USA) 407 466 6990
Fax (USA) 407 466 2594

Ormond Beach Aviation Inc
Ormond Beach Airport Florida
Telephone (USA) 904 673 9862

Pelican Airways
Hollywood Florida
Telephone (USA) 305 966 9750
Fax (USA) 305 985 8271

Roberts Air South
Homestead Airport Florida
Telephone (UK) 0908 677110
Fax (UK) 0908 677110

Flight Safety International
Vero Beach Florida
Telephone (USA) 407 567 5178

Sowell Aviation Co
Panama City Florida
Telephone (UK) 0225 873067
Fax (UK) 0225 874231

Naples Air Centre
Naples Florida
Telephone (UK) 0249 815103
Fax (UK) 0249 815103

Tyler International
Panama City Florida
Telephone (UK) 0462 895800
Fax (UK) 0462 895842

Volar Helicopters
Fort Lauderdale Florida
Telephone (UK) 0233 83671

Aviator Incorporated
Dallas Texas
Telephone (UK) 07048 76553

Cam Air
Grand Prairie Texas
Telephone (USA) 214 988 3171
Fax (USA) 214 988 3170

Abilene Aero
Abilene Airport Texas
Telephone (UK) 07048 76553

Pegasus Acme Group
Fort Worth Texas
Telephone (USA) 817 625 7257
Fax (USA) 817 626 3813

Lubbock Aero
Lubbock Texas
Telephone (UK) 07048 76553

Stramel Aviation
Dallas Texas
Telephone (UK) 071 359 8599
Fax (UK) 071 359 8599

Sky Breeze Aviation
Town & Country Airpark Texas
Telephone (UK) 081 893 1221

Wings Aviation
Fullerton California
Telephone (USA) 714 525 7704
Fax (USA) 714 738 5685

Helicopter Adventures
Concord California
Telephone (UK) 081 878 8615
Fax (UK) 081 915 2177

Mazzei Flying Service
Fresno California
Telephone (USA) 209 251 7501
Fax (USA) 209 285 8900

Southeastern Flight Academy
Macon Georgia
Telephone (USA) 912 745 0964
Fax (USA) 912 742 8022

UK/USA Helicopters
Atlanta Georgia
Telephone (USA) 404 936 9291
Fax (USA) 404 936 9294

Silver Hawk Aviation
Rome Georgia
Telephone (USA) 404 235 7357
Fax (USA) 404 290 1410

Northwest Georgia Aviation
Rome Georgia
Telephone (USA) 404 235 7357
Fax (USA) 404 290 1410

Flight International
Newport News Virginia
Telephone (UK) 0233 83671

The Aviatiors
Seattle Washington
Telephone (USA) 206 762 2888

Bolivar Aviation International
Bolivar Tennessee
Telephone (UK) 0638 577260
Fax (UK) 0638 660195

Titan Helicopter Aviation
Academy
New Jersey
Telephone (USA) 609 327 5203
Fax (USA) 609 825 2195

Airgo International
Centralia Airport Illinois
Telephone (UK) 0747 54917

Kanakee School of Aeronautics
Kanakee Airport Illinois
Telephone (USA) 815 939 3553
Fax (USA) 815 939 3212

VIP Flyers
Montrose Colorado
Telephone (UK) 07048 76553

High Country Helicopters
Montrose Colorado
Telephone (UK) 07048 76553

McClure Aviation
North Carolina
Telephone (USA) 704 735 5200

SC Helicopters
South Carolina
Telephone (USA) 803 445 2226
Fax (USA) 803 275 4718

Professional Helicopters
North Little Rock Airport
Arkansas
Telephone (USA) 501 834 6009

Wallace Aviation Helicopters
Missouri
Telephone (UK) 091 2579584/
0780 62214
Telephone (USA) 417 889 1324

Appendix 11

Books, Tapes and Videos
for Further Study

Most of these items may be obtained by mail order from pilot shops such as 'Transair' or 'Harry Mendelssohn', and from the 'Aviation Bookshop' or individual sales departments of the various airsport associations (see Appendix 9 'Useful Addresses').

LIGHT AIRCRAFT

Light Aircraft – Books

Ground Studies for Pilots by S.E.T. Taylor
  and H.A. Parmar
Human Factors for Pilots by Green, Muir,
  James, Gradwell & Green
Human Factors for General Aviation by
  S. Trollip & R. Jenson
Flying for Fun by Keith Carey
Aviation Law for Pilots by S.E.T. Taylor &
  H.A. Parmar
Private Pilot Studies by S.E.T. Taylor,
  H.A Parmar & R.B. Underdown
The Private Pilot's Licence by
  David Ogilvy
The Air Pilot's Manual (Vols 1-5) by
  Trevor Thom

Ground Training for the Private Pilot
  (Vols 1-3) by R.D. Campbell
Flying Training for the Private Pilot
  (Vols 1-2) by R.D. Campbell
CAP 53 The Private Pilot's Licence by
  C.A.A. Publications
CAP 85 A Guide to Aviation Law by
  C.A.A. Publications
CAP 413 Radiotelephony Manual by
  C.A.A. Publications
The Air Pilot's Weather Guide by
  Ingrid Holford
The Cessna 150 & 152 by Bill Clarke
Aviation Enthusiasts Reference Book by
  Bruce Robertson

Light Aircraft – Videos

PPL in a Nutshell
Learning To Fly
VFR Pilot Navigation Explained
Airbourne VFR
Aviation Law
Touchdown
Morse Code
Basic Aerodynamics
Basic Aviation Physiology

Light Aircraft – Audio Tapes

The British PPL Syllabus
New PPL Flight Test Explained
Radio-Telephony
Air Law
Meteorology
Navigation
Aircraft Technical
Human Performance & Limitations
Emergency & Survival Procedures
Fuel Economy

Light Aircraft – Magazines

'Pilot Magazine'
The Clock House,
28 Old Town,
Clapham,
London SW4 OLB
Telephone (071) 498 2506
Fax (071) 498 6920

'Popular Flying'
Terminal Building,
Shoreham Airport,
Shoreham,
West Sussex BN43 5FF
Telephone (0273) 461616
Fax (0273) 463390

'Flyer'
Insider Publications Ltd,
43 Queensferry Street Lane,
Edinburgh EH2 4PF
Telephone (031) 459 4646
Fax (031) 220 1203

HELICOPTERS

Helicopter – Books

Basic Helicopter Aerodynamics by
J. Seddon
Helicopter Pilot Manual by Jeppesen/
Sanderson
Basic Helicopter Handbook by U.S.
Department of Transportation
How to Fly Helicopters by Larry Collier &
Kas Thomas
The Helicopter by John Fay
The Helicopter – An Illustrated History by
Keith Carey
Flying for Fun by Keith Carey
Airborne for Pleasure by Albert Morgan
The Air Pilots Manual Vols 1-5 by
Trevor Thom
Aviation Law for Pilots by S.E.T. Taylor &
H.A. Parmar
Private Pilot Studies by S.E.T. Taylor,
H.A. Parmar & R.B. Underdown
CAP 53 The Private Pilots Licence by
C.A.A. Publications

CAP 85 A Guide to Aviation Law by
C.A.A. Publications
CAP 413 Radio Telephony Manual by
C.A.A. Publications
Human Factors for Pilots by Green, Muir,
James, Gradwell & Green
Human Factors for General Aviation by
S. Trollip & R. Jensen
The Air Pilots Weather Guide by
Ingrid Holford
Instant Weather Forecasting by
Alan Watts
Air Traffic Control by Graham Duke
Aviation Enthusiasts Reference Book by
Bruce Robertson

Helicopter – Videos

Fly The Robinson R22 Helicopter
Aviation Law
VFR Pilot Navigation Explained
Weather, Flight Planning & The Pilot
Basic Aviation Aerodynamics
Weather Hazards

209

Helicopter – Audio Tapes

The British PPL Helicopter Syllabus
Robinson R22 Technical Tape
Radio-Telephony
Air Law
Meteorology
Navigation
Aircraft Technical
Human Performance & Limitations

Emergency & Survival Procedures

Helicopter – Magazines

'Helicopter International'
75 Elm Tree Road,
Locking,
Weston Super Mare,
Avon BS24 8EL
Telephone (0934) 822524

MICROLIGHTS

Microlight – Books

The Trike Flyers Manual by Mark Phillips
Microlight Flying Manual by
    Campbell & Jones
The Dalgety Flyer by Brian Milton
The Microlight Pilots Handbook by
    Brian Cosgrove
*Ultralight & Microlight Aircraft of the
    World* by Norman Burr
Flying for Fun by Keith Carey
Airborne for Pleasure by Albert Morgan
*Ground Training for The Private Pilot
    Vols 1-3* by R.D. Campbell
*Flying Training for The Private Pilot
    Vols 1-2* by R.D. Campbell
Aviation Law for Pilots by S.E.T. Taylor &
    H.A. Parmar
Private Pilot Studies by S.E.T. Taylor,
    H.A. Parmar & R.B. Underdown
Human Factors for Pilots by Green, Muir,
    James, Gradwell & Green
Understanding Flying Weather by
    Derek Piggot
The Air Pilots Weather Guide by
    Ingrid Holford
Instant Weather Forecasting by
    Alan Watts
Aviation Enthusiasts Reference Book by
    Bruce Robertson
CAP 85 The Private Pilots Licence by
    C.A.A. Publications

CAP 85 A Guide to Aviation Law by
    C.A.A. Publications
CAP 413 Radio Telephony Manual by
    C.A.A. Publications

Microlight – Videos

The Dream
Learning To Fly *
VFR Navigation Explained *
Aviation Law *
PPL in a Nutshell *
Airbourne VFR *

Microlight – Audio Tapes

The British PPL Syllabus *
Radio-Telephony *
Air Law *
Meteorology *
Navigation *
Aircraft Technical *
Human Performance & Limitations *
Emergency & Survival Procedures *
Fuel Economy *

Microlight – Magazines

'Flightline'
9 Ladies Walk,
Caton Road,
Lancaster,
Lancs LA1 3NX
Telephone (0524) 841010

*These are primarily aimed at light aircraft & helicopter students but will prove informative to microlight pilots.

GLIDING

Gliding – Books

Beginning Gliding by Derek Piggot
Gliding by Derek Piggot
Going Solo by Derek Piggot
Derek Piggot on Gliding by Derek Piggot
Understanding Gliding by Derek Piggot
The Complete Soaring Guide by
    Ann Welch
The Book of Airsports by Ann Welch
Glider Pilot by Peter Champion
Soaring Across Country by Bill Scull
Gliding & Soaring by Bill Scull
On Being a Bird by Phillip Wills
Flying for Fun by Keith Carey
Airborne for Pleasure by Albert Morgan
Elementary Gliding by Paul Blanchard
The Air Pilots Weather Guide by
    Ingrid Holford
Elementary Meteorology by
    The Met Office
Instant Weather Forecasting by
    Alan Watts

Gliding – Videos

Running On Empty
VFR Pilot Navigation Explained *
Aviation Law *
Basic Aviation Physiology *
Basic Aerodynamics *

Gliding – Audio Tapes

Radio-Telephony *
Air Law *
Meteorology *
Navigation *

Gliding – Magazines

'Sailplane & Gliding'
British Gliding Association,
Kimberley House,
Vaughan Way,
Leicester
Telephone (0533) 531051
Fax (0533) 515939

*These are primarily aimed at light aircraft & helicopter students but will prove informative to glider pilots.

HANG GLIDING

Hang Gliding – Books

Hang Glider Pilot by Ann Welch &
    Gerry Breen
An Introduction to Hang Gliding by
    Bob McKay
Soaring Hang Gliders by Ann Welch &
    Roy Hill
Know The Game Hang Gliding by
    Ann Welch
The Book of Air Sports by Ann Welch
Flying for Fun by Keith Carey
Airborne for Pleasure by Albert Morgan
Hang Gliding Dont's & Dont's by
    Bob McKay
Understanding Flying Weather by
    Derek Piggot
Elementary Meteorology by
    The Met Office
Instant Weather Forecasting by
    Alan Watts

Start Soaring by Noel Whitthall
Hang Gliding Techniques by Dennis Pagen
Hang Gliding Flying Skills by
    Dennis Pagen

Hang Gliding – Videos

Thirmik
The Horizon's Not Level

Hang Gliding – Audio Tapes

None available at present

Hang Gliding – Magazines

'Skywings'
The Old Schoolroom,
Loughborough Road,
Leicester LE4 5PJ
Telephone (0533) 612362
Fax (0533) 611323

PARAGLIDING

Paragliding – Books

Paragliding Flight by Dennis Pagen
Touching Cloudbase by Ian Currer and
    Rob Cruickshank
ABC of Paragliding by Hubert Aupetit
Meteorology & Flight by Tom Bradbury
Understanding Flying Weather by
    Derek Piggot
Flying for Fun by Keith Carey
Airborne for Pleasure by Albert Morgan
The Book of Airsports by Ann Welch
Aviation Law for Pilots by S.E.T. Taylor &
    H.A. Parmar

Paragliding – Videos

Thermik
The Horizon's Not Level

Paragliding – Audio Tapes

None available at present

Paragliding – Magazines

'*Skywings Magazine*'
The Old Schoolroom,
Loughborough Road,
Leicester LE4 5PJ
Telephone (0533) 612362
Fax (0533) 611323

BALLOONING

Ballooning – Books

Hot Air Ballooning by Christine Turnbull
The Balloon Book by Paul Fillingham
Riders of the Winds by Don Dwiggins
Balloons & Airships
Balloons by Charles Dollfus
The Book of Balloons by Erik Norgaard
Flying for Fun by Keith Carey
Airborne for Pleasure by Albert Morgan
The Book of Air Sports by Ann Welch
Understanding Flying Weather by
    Derek Piggot
Instant Weather Forecasting by
    Alan Watts
The Air Pilots Weather Guide by
    Ingrid Holford
Elementary Meteorology by
    The Met Office
Aviation Law for Pilots by S.E.T. Taylor &
    H.A. Parmar
CAP 53 The Private Pilots Licence by
    C.A.A. Publications
CAP 85 A Guide to Aviation Law by
    C.A.A. Pulblications
CAP 413 Radio Telephony Manual by
    C.A.A. Publications

Throw Out Two Hands by Anthony Smith
The Flight of the Small World by Arnold
    Eiloart & Peter Elstob

Ballooning – Videos

VFR Pilot Navigation Explained *
Aviation Law *

Ballooning – Audio Tapes

Air Law *
Meteorology *
Navigation *
Radio-Telephony *

Ballooning – Magazines

'*Aerostat*'
Walnut House,
Old Rectory Road,
Kingswood,
Wotton,
Gloucestershire GL12 8RE
Telephone (0453) 843985
Fax (0453) 843985

'Balloons & Airships'
Kelsey Publishing Ltd,
Kelsey House,
High Street,
Beckenham,
Kent BR3 1AN
Telephone (081) 658 3531
Fax (081) 650 8035

*These are primarily aimed at light aircraft & helicopter students but will prove informative to balloon pilots.

PARACHUTING

Parachuting – Books

The Complete Sport Parachuting Guide by
   Charles Shea Simonds
Parachutist by Peter Hearn
The Sky People by Peter Hearn
Skies Call by Andy Keech
The Parachute Manual by Dan Poynter
Parachuting by Dan Poynter
The Space Age Sport by Ray Derby
Flying for Fun by Keith Carey
Airborne for Pleasure by Albert Morgan
Parachuting for Sport by Jim Greenwood
Falling Free by Cathy Williamson
Sport Parachuting by Russ Gunby
The Falcons Disciples by Howard Gregory
The Book of Air Sports by Ann Welch
Instant Weather Forecasting by
   Alan Watts

Parachuting – Videos

Relative Work 'The Basics'
The World Skydiving Championships
World CRW Championships
Anything is Possible
Flight of the Dream Team
From Wings Came Flight
Travelling 1
Travelling 2
Norman Kent Compilation
Kinesthesia
Visions 1
Visions 2
1991 Bali Boogie Video
Spanish Boogie 1991

Parachuting – Audio Tapes

None available at present

Parachuting – Magazines

'Sport Parachutist'
British Parachute Association,
5 Wharf Way,
Glen Parva,
Leicester LE2 9TF
Telephone (0533) 785271
Fax (0533) 477662

Appendix 12

Key to Abbreviations and Terms

The following abbreviations do not necessarily pertain to the chapters in this book but may be useful to the reader.

AD Airworthiness directive. Issued by the authorities to correct a defect found in an aircraft type after certification.

ADF Automatic direction finder. A radio compass which gives a relative bearing to the radio station to which it is tuned.

ADIZ Air defence identification zone. A block of airspace extending upwards from the surface of the ground or sea within which ready identification, location and the control of aircraft are required in the interests of national security.

Advancing blade That half of the rotor disc in which the rotation of the blade is moving in the same direction of the helicopter. If the helicopter is moving forwards the advancing blade will be in the right half of the rotor disc; if moving backwards it will be in the left half. If the helicopter is moving to the left side it will be in the forward half, and if moving to the right it will be in the rear half.

AFI Assistant flying instructor.

AGL Above ground level.

AIB Accident Investigation Branch of the Department of Trade.

AIC Aeronautical information circular.

Ailerons Moveable control surfaces at the trailing edges of the wings. Primary effect is roll about the longitudinal axis of the aircraft.

Airfoil Any surface designed to obtain a useful reaction from the air through which it moves in the form of lift.

Airspeed Speed of an aircraft in relation to the relative airflow.

Airspeed indicator Instrument which shows the airspeed.

Alternate An airfield detailed in the flight plan to which the aeroplane will proceed if a landing at the intended destination is not possible.

Altimeter Pressure-operated instrument recording height above sea-level or above ground according to its setting.

Altitude Height above sea-level.

AMSL Above mean sea-level.

Angle of attack The angle between the cord line of the wing and the airflow. The angle at which the air flow strikes the wing.

ANO Air navigation order, the legal instrument defining air law, navigation and licence issue in the United Kingdom.

AOA Aerodrome Owners' Association.

AOC Air operators' certificate. Issued by the Civil Aviation Authority and required by aircraft operators' flying charter or scheduled public service flights.

AOG Aircraft on ground. A term used to denote urgency when requesting aircraft spare parts from the maunfacturers or suppliers, meaning that the aircraft cannot fly until the replacement parts have been delivered.

AOPA Aircraft Owners' and Pilots' Association.

APU Auxiliary power unit. Jet aircraft have auxiliary power units to provide power for engine starting and for running the aircraft's systems when on the ground.

ARB Airworthiness requirements board for the CAA which issues airworthiness certificates for aircraft.

Articulated rotor A rotor system in which the blades are free to flap, drag and feather.

Aspect ratio The ratio of wingspan to width of the wing.

ATC Air traffic control.

ATCO Air traffic control officer.

ATIS Automatic terminal information service. A continuous recorded broadcast of routine airport information.

ATOA Air Taxi Operators' Association.

ATPL Airline transport pilot's licence.

ATZ Aerodrome traffic zone. A region of protected airspace surrounding an airfield which has a horizontal radius of 1.5 nautical miles from the airfield boundary extending up to 600 metres (2,000 ft) above the airfield elevation.

AUW All-up weight, a term for the total loaded weight of an aircraft. Maximum AUW is the maximum allowable weight, including payload and fuel specified in the aircraft's certificate of airworthiness.

Azimuth Horizontal angle, or direction; point of the compass.

Back course Some of the localiser transmitters used in instrument landing systems radiate a back beam in the opposite direction to the approach for which the aid is intended.

BAeA British Aerobatic Association.

BALPA British Airline Pilots' Asssociation.

BAUA Business Aircraft Users' Association.

BCPL Basic Commercial Pilot's Licence.

BGA British Gliding Association.

BHGA British Hang Gliding Association.

BHAB British Helicopter Advisory Board.

Billow The fullness of each half of a Rogallo sail when inflated in flight.

Blade damper A spring, friction or hydraulic device installed on the vertical hinge to diminish or dampen blade oscillation hunting around this hinge.

Blade loading The loads placed on the rotor blades of a helicopter, determined by dividing the gross weight of the helicopter by the combined area of all the rotor blades.

BMAA British Microlight Aircraft Association.

BRA British Rotorcraft Association.

CAP Civil air publications, information issued by the CAA (i.e. CAP 53 The Private Pilot's Licence).

CAT Clean air turbulence.

CAVOK Pronounced 'CAV-OK'. Used in weather conditions of at least 10 km (6 miles) visibility with no cloud below 1,525 metres (5,000 ft).

CAVU Ceiling and visibility unlimited. Cloudless conditions with visibility in excess of 10 km (6 miles).

CDI Course deviation indicator, the verticle needle of a VOR which shows the aircraft's position relative to the selected VOR radial.

Ceiling The height above ground or water of the base of the lowest layer of cloud.

Centre of gravity Point about which an aircraft would balance exactly.

Centre of pressure The imaginary point on the chord line where the resultant of all aerodynamic forces of an airfoil section may be considered to be concentrated.

Centrifugal force The force created by the tendency of a body to follow a straight line path against the force which causes it to move in a curve, resulting in a force which tends to pull away from the axis of rotation.

CFI Chief flying instructor.

Chord The width of the wing measured from the leading edge to the trailing edge.

Circuit An imaginary pattern flown around an aerodrome.

Collective pitch control The method of control by which the pitch of all rotor blades is varied equally and simultaneously.

Coriolis effect The tendency of a mass to increase or decrease its angular velocity when its radius of rotation is increased or decreased respectively.

Course The intended direction of flight.

CPL Commercial Pilot's Licence.

CRT Cathode ray tube used on the flight deck of newer large commercial aircraft and business jets in place of conventional instruments.

CS Constant speed, a controllable pitch propeller which maintains constant rpm by altering the angle of the propeller blades automatically in relation to the power setting of the engine.

CVR Cockpit voice recorder.

Cyclic pitch control The control which changes the pitch of the rotor blades individually during a cycle of revolution to control the tilt of the rotor disc and therefore the direction and velocity of horizontal flight.

D & D Distress and diversion cell at the London air traffic control centre. Provides 24-hour watch on emergency radio frequencies; locates and helps pilots who are lost or have some other in-flight emergency.

Delta hinge The hinge with its axis parallel to the rotor plane of rotation. Permits the rotor blades to flap to equalise lift between the advancing half and the retreating half of the rotor disc.

Delta sailwing Any flexible wing hang glider of delta or triangular shape.

Density altitude Pressure altitude corrected for temperature and humidity.

DF Direction finding. A DF steer can be provided by aerodromes with direction finding equipment which locates an aircraft and gives it a vector to steer to the aerodrome.

DH Decision height. The altitude at which a pilot making an ILS approach decides to continue with the approach or go around.

Direction indicator Gyroscopic instrument which, when set to the compass, will show the direction in which the aircraft is heading.

Disc area The area swept by the blades of the rotor. This is a circle with its centre at the hub axis and a radius of one blade length.

Disc loading The ratio of the helicopter gross weight to rotor disc area (total helicopter weight divided by the rotor disc area).

Dissymmetry of lift The unequal lift across the rotor disc resulting from the difference in the velocity of air over the advancing blade half and the retreating blade half of the rotor disc area.

DME Distance measuring equipment. A combination of ground and airborne equipment which gives a continuous distance from station read-out by measuring the time lapse of a signal from the aircraft to the ground station and back.

Doppler Doppler effect is the change in frequency in light, sound or radio waves when source and receiver are in relative motion. Doppler radar systems use this effect for navigation.

Drift Deviation from intended track.

EAA Experimental Aircraft Association.

EAT Estimated approach time.

EGT Exhaust gas temperature. A cockpit device which gives the pilot a read-out of the exhaust gas temperature of an aero engine.

ELT Emergency locator transmitter. An ELT transmitter is a small radio beacon fixed to the aircraft, which is automatically activated by impact or immersion in water and transmits a continuous tone on emergency radio frequencies helping rescue helicopters or search parties locate the crash site.

ETA Estimated time of arrival.

ETD Estimated time of departure.

ETE Estimated time *en route*.

FAA Federal Aviation Adminstration.

FAF Final approach fix. The point at which an instrument approach begins.

FAI *Federation Aeronautique Internationale*. The international body for the verification of aeronautical records and regulations.

FBO Fixed base operator.

Feathering action The action which changes the pitch angle of the rotor blades periodically by rotating them around their axis.

Feathering axis The axis about which the pitch angle of a rotor blade is varied. Sometimes referred to as the *spanwise* axis.

FIN Vertical section of an aircraft tail unit.

Finals The part of a landing sequence or circuit procedure in which the aircraft has made its final turn and is inbound to the duty runway.

FIR Flight information region. United Kingdom airspace is divided into two regions, London and Scottish, throughout which pilots can get a number of services and information from the appropriate air traffic control centre.

FL Flight level. A level of constant atmospheric pressure at which an aircraft with its altimeter set to a standard pressure of 1013,2 milibars will fly. Expressed in 'round metres' (hundreds of feet).

Flapping The vertical movement of a rotor blade about a delta (flapping) hinge.

Flaps Moveable sections at the trailing edges of wings which can be lowered to increase lift.

Flare out or **flare** The change from a steady descent to level flight just above the ground prior to landing.

FOB Fuel on board.

FPM Feet per minute.

Freewheeling unit A component part of the transmission or power train which automatically disconnects the main rotor from the engine when the engine stops or slows below the equivalent of rotor rpm.

Fuselage Section of an aircraft excluding wings and tail unit, housing the pilot, passengers, controls and engine.

G The acceleration force of gravity.
GA General aviation. All flying not covered by military or airline operations.
GADO General Aviation District Office.
GAMA General Aviation Manufacturers' Association.
GAMTA General Aviation Manufacturers' and Traders' Association.
GCA Ground controlled approach. A ground controller gives verbal descent guidance to the pilot using a precision radar to monitor his approach path.
GFT General flying test. The flying test taken by all student pilots before qualifying for their Private Pilot's Licence.
Glide Ratio The ratio between the distance flown and the height lost of a glider in flight. For example, a glide ratio of 5:1 means that from an altitude of 100 metres a glider will travel a theoretical distance of 500 metres.
GMT Greenwich mean time.
GANV Graphic area navigation. A system of direct point-to-point navigation using a VOR/DME and special printed charts.
GPS Global positioning system. A small, hand-portable electronic device which can be carried in an aircraft cockpit and gives latitude, longitude and altitude information accurate to within a few metres anywhere in the world.
GPWS Ground proximity warning system. A radar-based device which gives pilots an audible warning of terrain close to an aeroplane's flight path.
Ground effect The cushion of denser air confined beneath the rotor system of a hovering helicopter; gives additional lift and thus decreases the power required to hover.
Groundspeed Actual speed of an aircraft relative to the ground beneath it.
GS Glide slope. The vertical part of a guidance instrument landing system which gives a safe glide path to the runway.
Gyroscopic precession A characteristic of all rotating bodies. When a force is applied to the periphery of a rotating body, parallel to its axis of rotation, the body will tilt in the direction of the applied force 90° later in the plane of rotation.

HAI Helicopter Association International.
Heading Direction in which an aircraft is travelling.
HF High frequency radio band for long-range communications in the 3.30 Mhz range.
Holding Pattern A racetrack manoeuvre to keep an aircraft within specified airspace while awaiting further instructions from air traffic control.
Hovering in ground effect Maintaining a fixed position over a spot on the ground or water which compresses a cushion of high density air between the main rotor and the ground or water surface and thus increases the lift produced by the main rotor. Normally the main rotor must be within one half rotor diameter to the ground or water surface in order to produce an efficient ground effect.
Hovering out of ground effect Maintaining a fixed position over a spot on the ground or water at some altitude above the ground at which no additional lift is obtained from the ground effect.
HSI Horizontal situation indicator. A cockpit navigation display, often part of a flight director system.
HUD Head-up display. A system of projecting information visually on to the windscreen of a military fighter aircraft.

Hunting The tendency of a rotor blade (due to Coriolis effect) to seek a position ahead of or behind that which would be determined by centrifugal force alone.

IAS Indicated air speed.
IATA International Air Transport Association.
ICAO International Civil Aviation Organisation.
IF Instrument flying.
IFR Instrument flight rules.
ILS Instrument landing system. The standard bad weather landing aid which uses radio beams to provide the pilot with vertical and horizontal guidance during the approach to land. The localiser gives azimuth guidance, while the glide slope defines the correct descent profile. Marker beacons and high-intensity runway lights are also part of the ILS system. Indicators in the cockpit take the form of needles, bars or LEDs.
IMC Instrument meteorological conditions. Conditions below the VMC minimums.
INS Inertial navigation system. A gyroscopic-based instrument which senses acceleration, deceleration and directional change, thus computing the position of an aircraft with great accuracy. Mostly used in airliners and larger business aircraft.
ISA International standard atmosphere. A set of standard conditions of temperature and pressure which serves as a basis for comparing actual conditions.
Isobars Lines drawn on weather maps joining points of equal pressure.

KHz Kilohertz. The frequency of a radio wave. Measured in thousands of cycles per second.
Knot One nautical mile per hour. The standard unit of speed measurement in aviation.

LATCC London Air Traffic Control Centre.
LF Low frequency.
Locator A low- to medium-frequency, non-directional beacon used as an aid during an aircraft's final approach.
Loran A low-frequency, over-ocean radio navigation system.
LTA Lighter than air.

Mach The ratio of true airspeed to the speed of sound (Mach 1 is the speed of sound).
MATZ Military air traffic zone. An area of protected airspace around certain military airfields normally extending for an 8 km (5 mile) radius around the airfield and from ground level to 915 metres (3,000 ft) above aerodrome level.
Mayday International radio distress call.
MEA Minimum *en route* altitude.
MHz Megahertz. The frequency of radio waves. Measured in millions of cycles per second.
Minimums Weather condition requirements for particular mode of flight.
Mixture control Enables the pilot to vary the mixture of petrol and air going to the engine.
MLS Microwave landing system. A microwave-based instrument landing and approach system which is intended to replace the ILS system.

NATS National Air Traffic Services. A part of the CAA which provides air traffic control in the UK.
NBAA National Business Aircraft Association.

NDB Non-directional beacon. A medium frequency aid which transmits with a morse code identifier superimposed on the signal. Signals are received by the aircraft's ADF.

NOTAM Notices to airmen issued by the CAA to notify pilots of new or changed aeronautical facilities or hazards.

NTSB National Transportation Safety Board.

OASC Officer and Aircrew Selection Centre. The facility at RAF Cranwell in Lincolnshire where aircrew candidates for the Army Air Corps, Marines, Fleet Air Arm and Royal Air Force are selected.

OAT Outside air temperature.

OATS Oxford Air Training School.

OBS Omni-bearing selector is part of a VOR indicator and is the knob used to select a radial from a VOR.

Overshoot To climb away from a runway after making an approach to land.

PAN International radio call signifying urgency.

PAPI Precision approach path indicator.

PAR Precision approach radar providing an air traffic controller with information on range, altitude and heading of an aircraft on final approach. Enables him to talk down a pilot in instrument conditions.

PFA Popular Flying Association.

Phonetic A Alpha B Bravo C Charlie D Delta E Echo F Foxtrot G Golf H Hotel I India J Juliet K Kilo L Lima M Mike N November O Oscar P Papa Q Quebec R Romeo S Sierra T Tango U Uniform V Victor W Whiskey X X-ray Y Yankee Z Zulu.

Pitch Movement about the transverse axis – nose up or nose down.

Pitch angle The angle between the chord line of the rotor blade and the reference plane of the main rotor hub or the rotor plane of rotation.

Polar A diagrammatic presentation of performance giving rate of sink against airspeed.

PPL Private Pilot's Licence.

PPO Prior permission only.

Procedure turn A manoeuvre which reverses the direction of an aircraft's flight in order to establish it on the intermediate or final approach course. The outbound course and distance in which the turn must be completed are specified in the published approach procedure.

PSI Pounds per square inch. A measure of pressure.

Q-code A code system developed in the days when air to ground communication was by morse transmission. Many routine phrases and questions were reduced to three letters.

QDM The magnetic bearing of the direction-finding station giving the bearing.

QFE Atmospheric pressure at aerodrome elevation. With its sub-scale set to the aerodrome QFE an altimeter will indicate height above that aerodrome.

QFI Qualified flying instructor.

RAS Rectified airspeed indicated. Airspeed corrected for instrument position error.

Reflex A reflex aerofoil is one in which the section curves slightly upwards towards the trailing edge. This improves the longitudinal (pitch) stability.

Required track Line drawn on a map joining point of departure and destination.

Rigid rotor A rotor system with blades fixed to the hub in such a way that they can feather but cannot flap or drag.

RMI Radio magnetic indicator. A navigation aid consisiting of a combined gyro compass VOR and/or ADF display which will indicate an aircraft's heading, position relative to a selected VOR radial or bearing and with ADF the position of the aircraft's nose relative to the selected station.

RNAV Area navigation. A system of radio navigation which gives point-to-point off-airways navigation by displacement of VORs to any desired position via an on-board computer.

Rogallo Generic name for the delta-shaped hang glider originated by Dr Francis Rogallo.

Roll Movement about longitudinal axis of an aircraft.

RT Radio telephony.

Rudder Moveable section of trailing edge of fin used to help in steering.

RVR Runway visual range. Horizontal meaurement of visibility along a runway.

SAR Search and rescue.

SAS Stability augmentation system. An automatic helicopter flight control system used to enhance handling qualities.

SATCO Senior air traffic control officer.

SBAC Society of British Aerospace Companies.

Semirigid rotor A rotor system in which the blades are fixed to the hub but are free to flap and feather.

SID Standard instrument departure. A standard IFR departure route which enables air traffic controllers to issue abbreviated clearances and thus speed the flow of IFR traffic.

SIGMET A warning of severe weather issued by meteorological offices.

Sink rate The rate of descent of a glider. For example, a sink speed of 3 m/sec means that (theoretically) it will descend to earth at this rate.

Slip The controlled flight of an aircraft in a direction not in line with its fore and aft axis.

SOB Souls on board.

Socked in Airfield closed to air traffic because of bad weather.

Solidity ratio The ratio of total rotor blade area to total rotor disc area.

SOP Standard operating procedure.

Spin State of autorotation of an aircraft descending steeply nose down.

Spoilers Any external surface which can be deflected into the arflow to create drag.

SSR Secondary surveillance radar.

Stall Breakdown of airflow over the wing of an aircraft.

STOL Short take-off or landing.

TAF Terminal area forecast. A forecast of weather conditions expected at an aerodrome.

Tailplane Horizontal section of a tail unit.

TAS True airspeed. Rectified airspeed corrected for height and outside air temperature.

Taxiing Movement of an aircraft under its own power on the ground.

TBO Time between overhauls. The number of hours of operation that may be expected before an engine needs to be overhauled.

Tip draggers Spoilers (usually vertical at the wingtips) which can be deflected separately to create drag at one wingtip to cause a glider to yaw and turn.

Top path plane The plane in which rotor blade tips travel when rotating.

Tip speed The rotative speed of the rotor at its blade tips.

Tip stall The stall condition on the retreating blade which occurs at high forward speeds.

TMA Terminal control area.

Torque A force or combination of forces that tend to produce a countering rotation motion. In a single rotor helicopter, where the rotor turns counter-clockwise, the fuselage tends to rotate clockwise (when looking down on the helicopter).

Track The flight path of an aircraft over the ground.

Translational lift The additional lift obtained through airspeed because of increased efficiency of the rotor system (whether it be when transitioning from a hover into forward flight or hovering in a wind).

Transponder The airborne receiver/transmitter part of the SSR system.

TSO Technical standard order.

Turnbuckles Another name for bottlescrews. Used to adjust the length of cables.

UAS University air squadron.

UHF Ultra-high-frequency radio frequencies in the 300-3,000 MHz band.

UIR Upper information region.

Undercarriage Wheels or skids and their supporting legs.

U/S Unserviceable.

VASI Visual approach slope indicator. A coloured light system giving visual guidance to the glide path of a runway.

Venturi effect The speeding up of the air as it is drawn through a confined space.

VFR Visual flight rules.

VHF Very-high-frequency radio frequencies in the 30-300 MHz band used for most civil air/ground communications.

VLF/OMEGA Worldwide system of long-range area navigation.

VMC Visual meteorological conditions.

VOLMET Meteorological broadcasts of recorded weather information at a selection of aerodromes.

VOR Very-high-frequency omnidirectional range. A radio navigational aid operating in the 108-118 MHz band. VOR is the most commonly used radio navigation aid in private flying but has a limited range.

VP Variable pitch propeller.

VSI Vertical speed indicator. One of the primary flight instruments showing rate of climb and descent.

Yaw The skidding or sideways movement of an aircraft when it is not flying through the air in the direction it is pointing.

Zulu All times for flight operations anywhere in the world are given in Zulu time – Greenwich mean time.

Index